ETHICS IN MENTAL HEALTH RESEARCH

Principles, Guidance, and Cases

James M. DuBois

UNIVERSITY PRESS

2008

OXFORD
UNIVERSITY PRESS

Oxford University Press, Inc., publishes works that further
Oxford University's objective of excellence
in research, scholarship, and education.

Oxford   New York
Auckland   Cape Town   Dar es Salaam   Hong Kong   Karachi
Kuala Lumpur   Madrid   Melbourne   Mexico City   Nairobi
New Delhi   Shanghai   Taipei   Toronto

With offices in
Argentina   Austria   Brazil   Chile   Czech Republic   France   Greece
Guatemala   Hungary   Italy   Japan   Poland   Portugal   Singapore
South Korea   Switzerland   Thailand   Turkey   Ukraine   Vietnam

Published by Oxford University Press, Inc.
198 Madison Avenue, New York, New York 10016

www.oup.com

Oxford is a registered trademark of Oxford University Press

This publication is designed to provide accurate and trustworthy information regarding its subject
matter. However, it is sold with the understanding that neither the publisher nor the author is engaged
in rendering legal or other professional services. If legal advice or other expert assistance is needed,
the services of a competent professional should be sought.

Library of Congress Cataloging-in-Publication Data

DuBois, James M.
    Ethics in mental health research: principles, guidance, and cases /
James M. DuBois.
        p. ; cm.
    Includes bibliographical references.
    ISBN: 978-0-19-517993-4
    1. Psychiatry—Research—Moral and ethical aspects—United States.   2. Psychiatry—Research—
Moral and ethical aspects—United States—Case studies. 3.   Psychiatry—Research—Law and
legislation—United States. I. Title. [DNLM: 1. Ethics, Research—United States.   2. Mental
Disorders—United States.   3. Case Reports—United States.   4. Research—legislation &
jurisprudence—United States.   5. Research Design—United States. WM 20 D815e 2008]
    RC337.D73   2008
    174.2'9689 — dc22   2007009644

Ethics in Mental Health Research

To Drs. Jean Campbell and Joan Sieber

Acknowledgments

I would like to acknowledge a great many people who helped to realize this book. I thank Dr. Lawrence Friedman of the National Heart, Lung, and Blood Institute, and the National Institutes of Health, for a T15 training grant (1T15HL072453). Funding from that grant supported some of the time dedicated to writing the first draft of this manuscript. I thank Dr. Danny Wedding for inviting me to collaborate with the Missouri Institute of Mental Health in developing the training program. I thank Jesse Goldner and Michelle Langowski for legal research provided as part of the training grant, some of which was incorporated into this book. I thank several research assistants who contributed to literature reviews, proofreading, and/or coauthoring case narratives that appeared first on www.emhr.net: Emily Anderson, Jeff Dueker, Angela Dunn, Sarah Hill, and Karen O'Koniewski. The following people provided critical comments on portions of this book: Judith Burgan, Amy Campbell, Dr. Ron Claus, and Dr. Gerry Koocher. I thank them all. For comments on the entire manuscript, I am deeply grateful to Dr. Ana Iltis. I thank Joan Bossert, my editor at Oxford University Press, their peer reviewers, and assistant editors for supporting this manuscript. As always, I thank my wife Susan for her support and patience. I thank Dr. Jean Campbell of the Missouri Institute of Mental Health for her collaboration on the NIH training program and for sharing her experiences and thoughts, which have deeply shaped my own. From her I have learned a deeper meaning of the term "participant" in research and the importance of listening to mental health consumers and all those we seek to serve. Perhaps no other scholar has shaped my thinking on matters of research ethics so deeply as Dr. Joan Sieber, who contributed to the training program and with whom I have had the privilege of collaborating on other publication projects. I thank my mentor, Professor Giselher Guttmann, for encouraging me to integrate my interest in ethics with my interest in psychology. As always, I thank my parents—Thomas, Jeanne, and Terry DuBois—and my wife, Susan, for their enduring support.

Contents

Ethics in Mental Health Research

Introduction

Why Focus on Mental Health Research?

Mental disorders are common in the United States and internationally. An esti-
mated 26.2 percent of Americans ages 18 and older—about 1 in 4 adults—suffer
from a diagnosable mental disorder in a given year. . . . In addition, mental disor-
ders are the leading cause of disability in the U.S. and Canada for ages 15–44. . . .
In 2004, 32,439 (approximately 11 per 100,000) people died by suicide in the U.S.
More than 90 percent of people who kill themselves have a diagnosable mental
disorder, most commonly a depressive disorder or a substance abuse disorder.
—National Institute of Mental Health, *The Numbers*
Count: Mental Disorders in America

Mental health research broadly understood refers to research on the state of mental
health and the epidemiology, prevention, etiology, or treatment of mental disorders
(including substance abuse and developmental disorders).[1] Mental health research may include minimal risk procedures with so-called "normal" populations
(e.g., observation of college students or telephone surveys of the general public).
But mental health research is also conducted with participants who are labeled
in a variety of ways, including "addicted," "ADHD," "demented," "depressed,"
"mentally retarded," "schizophrenic," and "seriously emotionally disturbed."
These labels can be stigmatizing and take the focus off of the person, yet research
frequently targets people precisely insofar as they suffer from one or more mental
disorders.

Two high-level government advisory bodies have considered whether special
research protections should be provided to people with mental health disorders who
participate in research. In 1978, as United States research regulations were being
developed, the National Commission (discussed in detail in chapter 1) produced
a report and recommendations on Research Involving Those Institutionalized as
Mentally Infirm (National Commission for the Protection of Human Subjects
of Biomedical and Behavioral Research, 1978). While the National Commission believed that research should sometimes be conducted with people with
mental disorders even when they are unable to give consent themselves, it

---

1. Alternatively, one might speak of "behavioral health" research. While this term can be taken in a
very inclusive fashion, too often it is confused either with behavioral and social science research or
with research in health psychology; thus, the term "mental health" is used throughout.

3

recommended that a series of special protections be incorporated into regulatory law. Two decades later, President Clinton's National Bioethics Advisory Commission (NBAC) revisited the subject in a report entitled Research Involving Persons with Mental Disorders That May Affect Decisionmaking Capacity (National Bioethics Advisory Commission, 1999). NBAC also recommended the development of regulations that would offer special protections to people with mental disorders. However, in neither case were regulations implemented, despite the fact that nearly all of the National Commission's reports generated regulatory law (Jonsen, 1998).

In chapter 6, "Thinking About Harms and Benefits," we will see that there may be good reasons for developing regulatory protections that correspond to specific kinds of vulnerabilities rather than to vulnerable groups. However, even if special regulatory protections in mental health research are not prudent, special ethics education is.

THE NEED FOR MENTAL HEALTH RESEARCH ETHICS

History teaches us that there are special challenges in mental health research. First, successful treatments for mental health disorders have been particularly difficult to find (Torry et al., 1999). When combined with the fact that care for seriously impaired persons has often been viewed as a burden, the lack of successful treatments has led to research or experimental therapies that were often bizarre and harmful. Toward the end of his book, *Mad in America*, Whitaker writes:

> Rarely has psychiatry been totally without a remedy advertised as effective. Whether it be whipping the mentally ill, bleeding them, making them vomit, feeding them sheep thyroids, putting them in continuous baths, stunning them with shock therapies, or severing their frontal lobes—all such therapies "worked" at one time, and then, when a new therapy came along they were suddenly seen in a new light, and their shortcomings revealed. (Whitaker, 2002, p. 253)

While the days of such extreme measures may be past, questions of research benefits and risks remain, as do memories of past abuses.

The benefits of research to mental health consumers are frequently mixed and fall short of expectations. Mental health consumers often have different research priorities, for example, research on recovery or support systems that assist consumers in living with mental illnesses, but these are not always the most attractive to scientists or pharmaceutical companies (Scott, 1993; Whitaker, 2002). Consumers often do not consider an "effective" drug to be a tremendous benefit when its side effects are debilitating (including, for some patients, hypotension, insomnia, sedation, and sexual dysfunction). Moreover, while the U.S. government is investing large amounts of money into research that is independent of the interests of for-profit companies,[2] a 1999 review of NIMH-funded studies found that only 12% of

2. NIMH alone currently spends $1.4 billion per year on mental health research (National Institute of Mental Health, 2006).

NIMH research funds were directed to clinical and treatment-related research on severe mental illnesses (Torry et al., 1999).

While much of mental health research is minimal risk, some of it can be harmful. For example, the use of placebos presents a risk of relapse, heightened probability of suicide, and an inability to reestablish response to formerly effective medications (Shamoo, 1997). There is also general agreement among advocates and researchers that gene therapy may hold the greatest promise in fundamentally addressing severe mental illnesses (National Alliance for the Mentally Ill, 2004; National Institute of Mental Health, 2003); yet such research has been significantly slowed by a high-profile death of a participant and fears that current techniques are not safe (Sapolsky, 2003). Additionally, the stigma that has often been attached to mental disorders such as schizophrenia or drug addiction affects the research enterprise. For example, greater harms to patients can ensue if confidentiality is breached and others learn about participation in a study of substance abuse than, say, participation in a study of coronary stents.

Finally, respecting the self-determination of participants with mental health disorders can be tricky. Some cognitive disorders may interfere with a person's ability to grant informed consent (Appelbaum, 1996). Their capacity to make decisions may wax and wane, yet they may want to retain a voice. Their family members may have strong feelings about being included in the informed consent process, yet they may lack legal guardianship. Other factors, for example, the absence of universal health care coverage and the poverty that commonly attends mental illness (Wilton, 2004), make the use of financial and health care incentives in research potentially unduly influential (Lind, 1996; Westhoff, 2004). Yet, despite obstacles, many consumers want to be able to participate in potentially beneficial research (Campbell, 1996; Hall & Flynn, 1999).

This last point suggests the need for a balanced approach to research ethics. It is widely acknowledged that research holds an important key to improving the lives of people who suffer from mental disorders. This is asserted not only by researchers and research agencies (Michels, 1999; National Institute of Mental Health, 2003), but also by mental health advocacy and consumer groups (Hall & Flynn, 1999; National Alliance for the Mentally Ill, 2004). One recent survey found that 27% of mental health consumers had participated in a research study, and 82% expressed a willingness to participate (Hall, 2001).

Research has already provided some significant benefits to mental health consumers. Rates of recovery or successful treatment of acute phases of major depression can be as high as 80%, especially when medications and cognitive therapy are combined (Keller et al., 2000; Michels & Marzuk, 1993b), which is significantly higher than response rates to placebo (12%) during similar periods of time (Keller et al., 2000). Similar treatments have also been successful in significantly reducing relapse rates (Paykel et al., 2000). Moreover, tremendous progress has been made in the development of reliable diagnoses, mental health epidemiology, and the basic science needed for future clinical treatments (Michels & Marzuk, 1993a, 1993b).

Because research can significantly benefit the general public and mental health consumers, it is genuinely unfortunate when efforts by well-meaning regulators and IRBs slow the progress of research without actually increasing protections to participants. Yet, some researchers and professional bodies have alleged that precisely this is happening (American Psychological Association, 2001; Azar, 2002; Michels, 1999). (Chapter 1 explores the tension and overlap between ethical and regulatory oversight approaches to human subjects protection.)

This book seeks to remind everyone involved in the research enterprise that the main ethical conflict in human research is not typically between good and evil, but between competing goods—such as the good of safe research and the good of knowledge gained from research. Balancing competing goods can be extremely difficult in a world characterized by uncertainty, a world with a history of surprising harms and serendipitous discoveries. One of the main purposes of *Ethics in Mental Health Research* is to explore ethical criteria and social processes for balancing competing goods in research.

THE GOALS OF PROFESSIONAL ETHICS TRAINING

This book was developed as part of an ethics course funded by the National Institutes of Health for people who conduct and review mental health research. Over the past decade, the United States government has significantly increased funding for programs that promote education and research in the areas of research ethics, research integrity, and the responsible conduct of research.

Has it helped? Is there evidence that such programs significantly improve behavior? It is difficult to say. There is some reason to infer that they contribute to relatively modest changes in behavior (Rest & Narvaez, 1994; Rest et al., 1999). However, there is little evidence that research ethics education directly reduces scientific misconduct or human subjects abuses (Committee on Assessing Integrity in Research Environments, 2002; Steneck, 2000).

Why is this the case? Two kinds of answers can be given. First, it is hard to gather such data in an ethical and scientifically trustworthy manner. Self-reports of misbehavior may not be accurate, obtaining trustworthy data for pre-intervention behavior is rarely possible, and obtaining trustworthy data post-intervention would be highly intrusive.

Second, depending on one's view of human motivation and action, there may be no reason to assume that we can create an "ethical vaccine" or a prevention program that will eliminate unethical behavior. If we adopt a view of human beings as causal agents who freely generate their own behavior (Taylor, 1983), then we will be utterly disinclined to believe that education can cause good behavior. But even if we adopt a pan-deterministic view of human action and reject human freedom and accountability, surely the factors that cause behavior—genetics, upbringing, environmental reinforcers, and social models (De Palma & Foley, 1975)—are so complex that it remains naïve to believe that reading one book or attending a class can cause (in the strict sense of effective causation) good behavior.

However, there are empirical and a priori reasons for believing that we can facilitate ethical behavior. We can assist people in knowing what society expects of them. And it seems ethically imperative to do so when stiff penalties exist for failing to meet regulatory or institutional expectations. Data also exist suggesting that we can assist people in learning about the consequences of certain actions (Gibbs, 2003); we can heighten sensitivity to ethical issues (Bebeau et al., 1985); we can foster empathy and understanding of others (Endicott, 2001; Gibbs, 2003); and we can improve principled ethical reasoning (Rest et al., 1999) and moral problem solving (Bebeau, 1995). So even if ethics education cannot cause ethical action, it can give researchers a better opportunity to do what is right and puts society in a better position to hold individuals and institutions accountable for bad behavior.

This book can be used alone as a form of professional research ethics education. However, it was designed to be used in group settings where case discussion is possible, and together with the DVD *Dialogues on Ethical Research in Behavioral Health*. The latter contains interviews with experts in research ethics as well as discussion groups with mental health consumers who relate their experiences participating in mental health research. This books is also supported by a Web site, www.emhr.net, which contains bibliographies, links to federal research regulations, additional cases for group discussion, and assessment tools. These various educational tools were designed to work together to facilitate moral development and responsible research habits.

The facilitative approach adopted in this project assumes good will and good intentions. It assumes that research holds a key (not the key, but an important key) to improving the lives of people with mental health disorders and to reducing the prevalence of mental disorders in the general population. It further assumes that researchers—even if they have other motives such as earning a living or prestige—do want to improve the lives of people and to treat participants with respect. This book explores how researchers of good will can pursue these noble goals. And indeed, it is an exploration, for answers to ethical questions in research are not always obvious and are rarely known at the outset. However, reducing "unwarranted certainty" and provoking critical thinking is typically better than providing an oversimplistic answer (Sieber, 2004).

THE STRUCTURE OF THIS BOOK

This book focuses on research conducted with participants who have mental health disorders, including developmental and substance abuse disorders. Nevertheless, because mental health research ethics introduces discussions of so many ethical issues, it is a useful lens for approaching the broader subject of human subjects protections, including minimal risk behavioral and social science research. While most case studies addressed in this book discuss research conducted with people with mental health disorders, the studies range from high-risk clinical trials to minimal risk reviews of existing data and surveys.

The first three chapters of this book develop theoretical foundations. Chapter 1 explores the current situation in research ethics with the heavy emphasis many institutions place on regulatory compliance. It explores relationships between compliance and ethics and insists that genuine ethical analysis of research ethics questions is what is most urgently needed. Chapter 2 presents a framework for research ethics based on three pillars: ethical principles, virtues or moral character, and ethical procedures (including IRB review and community consultation). Chapter 3 provides a framework for addressing ethical dilemmas and balancing competing goods and principles. This framework can also be used to guide group discussion of ethics cases.

The remaining chapters are dedicated to applied topics: informed consent, decision-making capacity, risk-benefit analysis, participant recruitment, privacy and confidentiality, and conflicts of interest. As the subtitle suggests, each chapter includes: reflections on how ethical principles relate to a cluster of fundamental problems in research; an overview of the major issues, a review of the literature, and references to regulatory guidance; and an analysis of one or more challenging ethical cases from mental health research. Tables are used throughout to summarize major regulatory and ethical factors that researchers need to consider as they design and conduct research.

THE QUESTION OF LANGUAGE

We cannot speak without language, yet sometimes the language we use is controversial, and conveying respect while using words can be challenging. Language changes, and terms that were once "politically correct" or acceptable are no longer so. For example, W. E. B. DuBois and Martin Luther King spoke of "Negroes," but most African American leaders would discourage use of the term. People belonging to groups frequently disagree on what they want to be called— for example, "people with mental disorders," "mental health survivors," "consumers," or "clients." Words in themselves are neutral, yet any term can be used pejoratively. Perhaps the most important thing is that we try to express to others an interest in speaking respectfully.

When referring to people who would meet the diagnostic criteria for a specific mental health disorder, this book will typically use "people first" language, that is, it will speak of people with schizophrenia, people with depression, and so forth. However, when speaking of people with mental health disorders as a group, the terms "people with mental disorders," "mental health consumers," and "patients" will be used in different contexts. None of these is a perfect term. Not all people like the term "disorder" because it can carry negative connotations. Yet not everyone with a diagnosis seeks treatment and becomes a consumer or a patient. Moreover, the term "consumer" can imply that mental health care providers sell a product, and that their relationship to clients or patients is above all a business relationship rather than a professional healing relationship. For this reason, I believe use of the term "patient" by mental health care providers is often not only appropriate but highly preferable insofar as it reminds us of imbalances in power and of fiduciary obligations borne by clinicians. Nevertheless, the term "mental health consumer" has been adopted as a way of acknowledging the mental health consumer movement that seeks to use a language of empowerment and to emphasize freedom of choice over dependency (Campbell & Schraiber, 1989; Kaufmann, 1999). Moreover, in the context of research, it is useful to acknowledge that regardless of diagnosis, participants may or may not also be in the role of client or patient; and this can have implications for the professional obligations of the research.

Similarly, debate exists over the term "human subjects." The term "participants" is generally preferable to the term "subjects," as it reminds us that everyone involved in a study should participate knowingly and willingly, rather than be "subjected" to experimentation. However, for precision's sake, I generally use the term "subjects" when citing regulations that refer to subjects or when referring to people whose inclusion in a study was not genuinely informed or voluntary (e.g., the subjects in the Tuskegee syphilis trial discussed in the next chapter), thus precluding genuine participation.

REFERENCES

American Psychological Association. (2001). Research ethics: Comments submitted by APA on the draft of the NBAC report on ethical and policy issues in research involving human participants. Retrieved January 8, 2007, from www.apa.org/science/comment_nbac-01.html.

Appelbaum, P. S. (1996). Patients' competence to consent to neurobiological research. *Accountability in Research*, *4*(3–4), 241–251.

Azar, B. (2002). Ethics at the cost of research? *Monitor on Psychology*, *33*(2), 42.

Bebeau, M. J. (1995). Moral reasoning in scientific research: Cases for teaching and assessment. Bloomington, IN: Indiana University. Available online at: www.indiana.edu/~poynter/mr-main.html. Retrieved January 6, 2004.

Bebeau, M. J., Rest, J. R., & Yamoor, C. (1985). Measuring dental students' ethical sensitivity. *Journal of Dental Education*, *49*, 225–235.

Campbell, J. (1996). Toward collaborative mental health outcomes systems. In D. Steinwachs, L. Flynn, N. Grayson, & E. Skinner (Eds.), *Using client outcomes information to improve mental health and substance abuse treatment* (pp. 68–78). San Francisco: Jossey-Bass.

Campbell, J., & Schraiber, R. (1989). The well-being project: Mental health clients speak for themselves (a report of a survey conducted for the California Department of Mental Health, Office of Prevention). Sacramento: California Network of Mental Health Clients.

Committee on Assessing Integrity in Research Environments, Institute of Medicine, National Research Council of the National Academies. (2002). *Integrity in scientific research: Creating an environment that promotes responsible conduct.* Washington, DC: National Academic Press.

De Palma, D. J., & Foley, J. M. (Eds.). (1975). Moral development: Current theory and research. Mahwah, NJ: Lawrence Erlbaum Associates.

Endicott, L. (2001). Ethical sensitivity: Nurturing character in the middle school classroom. Minneapolis, MN: Community Voices and Character Education Partnership Project.

Gibbs, J. C. (2003). Moral development and reality: Beyond the theories of Kohlberg and Hoffman. Thousand Oaks, CA: Sage.

Hall, L. L. (2001). NAMI consumer views of research. Retrieved January 8, 2007, from http://www.nami.org/Content/NavigationMenu/Inform_Yourself/About_Research/NAMI_Consumer_Views_of_Research.htm.

Hall, L. L., & Flynn, L. (1999). Consumer and family concerns about research involving human subjects. In H. A. Pincus, J. A. Lieberman, & S. Ferris (Eds.), *Ethics in psychiatric research* (pp. 219–235). Washington, DC: American Psychiatric Association.

Jonsen, A. R. (1998). The birth of bioethics. New York: Oxford University Press.

Kaufmann, C. L. (1999). An introduction to the mental health consumer movement. In A. V. Horwitz & T. L. Scheid (Eds.), *A handbook for the study of mental health*. New York: Cambridge University Press.

Keller, M. B., McCullough, J. P., Klein, D. N., Arnow, B., Dunner, D. L., Gelenberg, A. J., et al. (2000). A comparison of nefazodone, the cognitive behavioral-analysis system of psychotherapy, and their combination for the treatment of chronic depression. *New England Journal of Medicine*, *342*(20), 1462–1470.

Lind, S. E. (1996). Financial issues and incentives related to clinical research and innovative therapies. In H. Y. Vanderpool (Ed.), *The ethics of research involving human subjects: Facing the 21st century* (pp. 185–202). Frederick, MD: University Publishing Group, Inc.

Michels, R. (1999). Editorial: Are research ethics bad for our mental health? *New England Journal of Medicine*, *340*(18), 1427–1430.

Michels, R., & Marzuk, P. M. (1993a). Progress in psychiatry: First of two parts. *New England Journal of Medicine*, *329*(8), 552–560.

Michels, R., & Marzuk, P. M. (1993b). Progress in psychiatry: Second of two parts. *New England Journal of Medicine, 329*(9), 628–638.

National Alliance for the Mentally Ill. (2004). Roadmap to recovery and cure: Final report of the NAMI policy research institute task force on serious mental illness research. Retrieved January 8, 2007, from http://www.nami.org/Content/NavigationMenu/Inform_Yourself/About_Public_Policy/Policy_Research_Institute/NAMI_Research_Task_Force_Report-03–2004.pdf

National Bioethics Advisory Commission. (1999). Research involving persons with mental disorders that may affect decisionmaking capacity: Vol. 2. Commission papers. Bethesda, MD: National Bioethics Advisory Commission.

National Commission for the Protection of Human Subjects of Biomedical and Behavioral Research. (1978). Research involving those institutionalized as mentally infirm: Report and recommendations. Washington, DC: Department of Health, Education, and Welfare.

National Institute of Mental Health. (2003). Breaking ground, breaking through: The strategic plan for mood disorders research. Retrieved January 8, 2007, from http://www.nimh.nih.gov/strategic/mooddisorders.pdf.

National Institute of Mental Health. (2006a). The numbers count: Mental disorders in America. Bethesda, MD: National Institute of Mental Health.

National Institute of Mental Health. (2006b). Setting priorities at NIMH. Retrieved January 8, 2007, from http://www.nimh.nih.gov/strategic/strategicplanmenu.cfm#SettingPriorities.

Paykel, E. S., Scott, J., & Teasdale, J. D. (2000). Antidepressants plus cognitive therapy reduced relapse in residual depression. *Evidence-Based Mental Health, 3*(May), 48.

Rest, J. R., & Narvaez, D. (Eds.). (1994). Moral development in the professions: Psychology and applied ethics. Hillsdale, NJ: Lawrence Erlbaum Associates.

Rest, J. R., Narvaez, D., Bebeau, M. J., & Thoma, S. J. (1999). Post-conventional moral thinking: A neo-Kohlbergian approach. Mahwah, NJ: Lawrence Erlbaum Associates, Inc.

Sapolsky, R. M. (2003). Gene therapy for psychiatric disorders. *American Journal of Psychiatry, 160*(2), 208–220.

Scott, A. (1993). Challenging assumptions: Consumers/survivors reform the system, bringing a "human face" to research. *Resources, 5*(1), 3–6.

Shamoo, A. E. (Ed.). (1997). Ethics in neurobiological research with human subjects: The Baltimore conference on ethics. Amsterdam: Gordon and Breach.

Sieber, J. E. (2004). Using our best judgment in conducting human research. *Ethics and Behavior, 14*(4), 297–304.

Steneck, N. (2000). Assessing the integrity of publicly funded research. In N. Steneck & M. Sheetz (Eds.), *Investigating research integrity: Proceedings of the first ORI research conference on research integrity* (pp. 1–16). Bethesda, MD: Office of Research Integrity.

Taylor, R. (1983). Metaphysics (3rd ed.). Englewood Cliffs, NJ: Prentice-Hall.

Torry, E. F., Knable, M. B., Davis, J. M., Gottesman, I. I., & Flynn, L. M. (1999). A mission forgotten: The failure of the National Institute of Mental Health to do sufficient research on severe mental illnesses. Retrieved January 8, 2007, from http://www.psychlaws.org/nimhreport/AMissionForgotten.pdf.

Westhoff, B. (2004, May 12–18). Get poked, get paid. *Riverfront Times*, pp. 18–27.

Whitaker, R. (2002). *Mad in America*. Cambridge, MA: Perseus.

Wilton, R. (2004). Putting policy into practice. Poverty and people with serious mental illness. *Social Science and Medicine, 58*(1), 25–39.

1

Research Ethics and Regulatory Compliance

Competing or Complementary Approaches?

*In truth, investigators are much better positioned during the course of their stud-
ies to protect the interests of individual research subjects than are the IRBs.
Paradoxically, the person most likely to do something to harm a subject, the
investigator, is also the person most capable of preventing such harm. And so,
as Beecher (1966) concluded many years ago, the only true protection afforded
research subjects comes from a well-trained, well-meaning investigator.*
— Greg Koski (former director of the Office for Human Research
Protections), "Beyond Compliance . . . Is It Too Much to Ask?"

Clinical bioethics has succeeded in capturing the imagination of the American
public. It engages topics of obvious importance—topics such as the removal of
life support, prenatal genetic screening, and organ transplantation. Frequently
clinical issues involve interesting intellectual puzzles such as the justification for
procuring organs from patients who are pronounced dead using neurological criteria. How do we know whether such patients are dead or alive? On the one hand,
so-called "brain death" is like a guillotine: it indicates the end of communication
between the brain and the body because the brain has irreversibly lost all functions. On the other hand, brain-dead patients can maintain spontaneous circulation
with ventilator support, and some brain-dead women have sustained a pregnancy
for months. Should we remove organs from patients declared dead using neurological criteria? If so, may we do this because they are dead or because we have
their permission? Is organ donation a duty? Do people have a right to donate organs? Is it ethical to offer payment to people to encourage donation? Once donation has occurred, how do we ensure fair distribution of procured organs?

Despite the more dramatic nature of some clinical decision making, very similar questions exist in the realm of *research ethics*. How do we know whether
an experimental treatment shows sufficient promise to justify withholding an
effective treatment from someone with a serious health disorder? Do we allow
people to participate in research primarily because we believe in the safety of the
study or because we have the participants' permission? Do people have a duty
to participate in research given that most of us will benefit significantly from the
fruits of the work? Do people have a right to choose to participate in a research

study—even when others have reservations about its safety? Once research has produced benefits, how do we ensure the fair distribution of these benefits, especially among populations that participated in the development of the products? Like questions about brain death and organ donation, these questions are interesting, complex, and challenging. Engaging such questions is not only intellectually rewarding but may improve the ethical quality of the research we conduct with human participants.

Research ethics need not be boring or superficial. Nevertheless, we sometimes find that research ethics training fails to critically engage ethical questions and focuses instead on compliance with research regulations and institutional rules. We find people asking questions such as: Do the regulations require a signature on this consent form, or why take falsifying data so seriously? The first question addresses a matter of legal compliance; the second addresses a behavior so obviously wrong it does not merit discussion. Exactly how did research ethics develop a culture that differs significantly from clinical bioethics?

THE CURRENT CONTEXT OF RESEARCH ETHICS

Brief reflection on recent events will illustrate the unfortunate tendency to focus on regulatory compliance when faced with matters of research ethics.

First, during the past decade, several large research universities that receive millions of dollars in federal research grants have had their human research programs frozen.[1] Several deaths have resulted from research studies, and these have brought tremendous negative publicity to research institutions and funding agencies. These events have led to a "risk management" mentality at many research institutions. Institutional Review Board (IRB) members are examining not only risks to participants, but also risks to their institutions and to themselves as IRB members (Koski, 2003).

Second, when federal intervention has led to shutting down programs, remediation efforts have focused primarily on the operation of IRBs, which are charged with implementing federal regulations governing research with human participants (Borror, Carome, McNeilly, & Weil, 2003). Box 1.1 presents information on when studies require IRB review.

Third, this approach to research oversight has given rise to a whole industry of professionals who specialize in regulatory compliance. Examples include for-profit IRBs (see chapter 10) and IRB staff members who are licensed as Certified IRB Professionals (CIPs).[2]

Fourth, governmental agencies have mandated training in so-called "human subjects protections" (Cooper & Turner, 2002).[3] However, such training seldom includes ethics education as traditionally understood. Such programs generally do

1. The Office for Human Research Protections (OHRP) posts a list of all the "determination letters" it has produced following its formal compliance oversight evaluations of various research institutions at http://ohrp.osophs.dhhs.gov/compovr.htm.
2. Information on Certification as an IRB Professional is at http://www.primr.org/certification.html.
3. This term is unfortunate not only for its use of the term "subjects" but because it refers only to duties to protect, ignoring duties to treat people respectfully and justly.

Box 1.1 When Does a Study Require Review by an IRB?

- Regulations state that all federally funded research falls under the purview of an IRB; but most IRBs insist on at least a preliminary review of *all* human subjects research
- Research means a "systematic investigation, including research development, testing, and evaluation, designed to develop or contribute to generalizable knowledge. Activities that meet this definition constitute research for purposes of federal policy, whether or not they are conducted or supported under a program that is considered research for other purposes. For example, some demonstration and service programs may include research activities." (U.S. Department of Health and Human Services, regulation 45CFR46.102d; hereafter cited only by regulation number)
- IRBs may decide to "exempt" research in six categories. Exempt research may receive no review or review by office personnel or the chair, depending on IRB policies. The six categories are:
  (1) Research conducted in established or commonly accepted educational settings, involving normal educational practices such as research on regular and special education instructional strategies …
  (2) Research involving the use of educational tests (cognitive, diagnostic, aptitude, achievement), survey procedures, interview procedures, or observation of public behavior, unless data obtained is identifiable and could place subjects are risk …
  (3) Research involving the use of educational tests (cognitive, diagnostic, aptitude, achievement), survey procedures, interview procedures, or observation of public behavior that is not exempt under paragraph (b)(2) of this section under special conditions …
  (4) Research involving the collection or study of existing data, documents, records, pathological specimens, or diagnostic specimens, if these sources are publicly available or if the information recorded is unidentifiable …
  (5) Research and demonstration projects conducted by or subject to the approval of Department or Agency heads that study, evaluate, or otherwise examine public benefit or service programs …
  (6) Taste and food quality evaluation and consumer acceptance studies (see 45CFR46.101b for more details)
- Other forms of research may receive either full board review or "expedited" review. Expedited studies must be reviewed, but they may be reviewed more quickly by just one member of the IRB (e.g., the IRB chair). (45CFR46.110 and 45CFR46.111)

not inquire into whether and why certain actions are right or wrong; rather, they simply present regulatory expectations, frequently accompanied by a canonical explanation of how government-sanctioned ethical principles justify these expectations.[4]

Finally, research with human participants is one of the only ethical domains in which a federally sanctioned ethical framework exists. "The Belmont Report: Ethical Principles and Guidelines for the Protection of Human Subjects of Research (Belmont Report)" constitutes a systematic presentation of three ethical principles—respect for persons, beneficence, and justice—apart from any regulatory rules (National Commission, 1979). However, while the Belmont Report aimed to provide people with overarching principles to guide ethical reflection where rules and regulations fail to provide specific guidance, one might argue that it has discouraged rather than facilitated ethical reflection. Its three principles, adopted largely uncritically, rarely find application beyond what the report itself spells out (Jonsen, 1998).

These accounts of recent events beg the question: How did we find ourselves in a situation in which failures to treat participants ethically are interpreted as *compliance* failures with remedies that focus on increasing compliance through education and oversight?

IF YOU WANT TO UNDERSTAND THE PRESENT . . .

. . . you must understand the past. Two research studies loom large in history as failures to adequately protect human research participants in the United States: the Willowbrook hepatitis studies and the Tuskegee syphilis study.

The Willowbrook hepatitis studies took place at the Willowbrook State School in New York for "mentally defective persons" from 1956 to 1971 (R. J. Levine, 1988). Researchers fed different strains of live hepatitis viruses to children to study the disease and to attempt to develop a vaccine against it. By almost any standard, the experiments involved good science and significant knowledge, and strides toward a hepatitis vaccine followed from the studies (Rothman & Rothman, 1984). Dr. Saul Krugman, the principal investigator, defended the studies by insisting that the only solution to the problem of hepatitis at Willowbrook required gaining new knowledge that might lead to the development of a vaccine. But, in reply to critics in the journal *Lancet* (Goldby, 1971/1972), he also enumerated several other less utilitarian considerations to justify the experiments:

> Our proposal to expose a small number of newly admitted children to the Willowbrook strains of hepatitis virus was justified in our opinion for the following reasons: 1) they were bound to be exposed to the same strains under the natural conditions existing in the institution; 2) they would be

---

4. A common way of satisfying this requirement is to complete the online training NIH offers at: http://www.cancer.gov/clinicaltrials/learning/page3. It takes approximately 2 hours to complete and requires only rote knowledge of regulatory expectations. Although such education may serve a purpose, it is not ethics education in the sense espoused by either philosophers or developmental psychologists.

admitted to a special, well-equipped and well-staffed unit where they would be isolated from exposure to other infectious diseases which were prevalent in the institution; . . . 3) they were likely to have a subclinical infection followed by immunity to the particular hepatitis virus; and 4) only children with parents who gave informed consent would be included. (Krugman, 1971/1972, p. 1008)

A number of commentators in the medical literature agreed with Krugman, including the editors of the *Journal of the American Medical Association* (Edsall, 1969; Katz, 1972; Lasagna, 1969). However, critics noted other ethical concerns. First, the use of this particular population raised concerns insofar as they had three inherent vulnerabilities: all had mental retardation, they were children, and they lived in an institution (Goldby, 1971/1972). Second, inadequate consent practices sometimes unduly influenced enrollment decisions (e.g., a somewhat misleading recruitment letter was sent by the director of the school prior to placement), and at times, due to overcrowding, Dr. Krugman's experimental wing had the only available openings (Rothman & Rothman, 1984). Moreover, even if the children might have naturally suffered exposure to hepatitis, the study's design clearly did not qualify as naturalistic observation or a "study in nature." The investigators deliberately fed children a live virus (Rothman, 1982). Finally, instead of working to achieve more sanitary living quarters, which would have helped to prevent the spread of hepatitis, researchers preyed upon the substandard living conditions (Goldby, 1971/1972; Rothman & Rothman, 1984). While most textbooks in research ethics today greatly oversimplify the ethics of the study, it has become one of the classic examples of risky clinical research conducted with inadequate consent on a vulnerable and captive population.

The "Tuskegee Study of Untreated Syphilis in the Negro Male" originated at an agency of the U.S. Public Health Service (PHS). It began in 1932 with what might have seemed reasonable motives. Treatments for syphilis in the early twentieth century—primarily administering toxic mercury and arsenic compounds—often produced consequences worse than the natural course of the disease. The purpose of the syphilis study was to observe the natural course of untreated syphilis among black men. At the time, some assumed that syphilis ran a different course among different races of people. Moreover, a recent study of whites with untreated syphilis conducted in Oslo claimed that in two out of three cases no adverse health consequences resulted from untreated syphilis (Edgar, 1992). Dunn and Chadwick (1999) claim that PHS had become a major force in promoting rural medical care, and they further state that the study began from a genuine concern for minority health problems. Others do not view the origins of the study so charitably but rather see evidence of racism and disrespect from the beginning (Brandt, 1978). For example, while available treatments were far from ideal, a documentary film, *Deadly Deception*, shows public health ads that promoted the use of current treatments as effective, and they were widely used by those who could afford them ("The deadly deception: The Tuskegee study of untreated syphilis in the Negro male," 1993).

The study eventually enrolled 399 black men with syphilis and another 200 black men as a control group. Subjects were not told the true purpose of the study; consent coordinators described a study of "bad blood" (Jones, 1993) and promised that subjects would get free medical care. This "care" involved physical exams, a detailed medical history, a spinal tap without anesthesia, and regular visits throughout the study to establish the sequela of syphilis. Eventually, it included autopsy. It did not include treatment either for syphilis or secondary problems, including heart disease (Edgar, 1992).

By today's standards, the study fell short from the very beginning insofar as recruitment was deceptive and manipulative: trustworthy people from the community recruited subjects, undue influence was exerted by offering significant incentives, and subjects were deceived about the actual purpose of the study. However, the most flagrant violations—those that put it on a par with other infamous instances of human rights abuses—occurred in the 1940s when penicillin was developed and eventually became the accepted treatment for syphilis. Not only did investigators fail to provide penicillin to the men, but they also secretly made great efforts to ensure the men would not receive penicillin from other sources (Jones, 1993).

The study continued until 1972 when Peter Buxton, a public health official working for PHS, went to the press after complaining to officials at PHS with no effect. In July of 1972, the *Washington Star* and the *New York Times* ran front-page stories on the study. While the Tuskegee syphilis study may have provoked initial outrage among the larger U.S. community, it did far more than that within the African American community. It reinforced suspicions of the medical community and triggered a persistent legacy of mistrust and reduced willingness to participate in medical research (Gamble, 1993; Jones, 1992).

The Willowbrook and Tuskegee studies did not occur in a historical vacuum. In one sense, they are made worse by the fact that the international community, largely under the leadership of the United States, had already painfully witnessed the need for human research ethics.[5] Following Nazi experiments on Jews, the mentally infirm, and other people labeled as "defective," the allied powers convened the Nuremberg trials. The second set of trials—the Nazi doctors trial—resulted in the Nuremberg Code (1947), which listed ten principles to guide the conduct of human experimentation, the first of these being a requirement for the voluntary informed consent of participants (Annas & Grodin, 1992). (The Nuremberg Code is published in box 1.2.) The United States led these trials and the development of the Code. Simultaneous with the Nuremberg trials, the American Medical Association (AMA) developed its first code of research ethics (1946). In 1964, the World Medical Association developed the first Declaration of Helsinki, which included 32 guidelines for the conduct of medical research. (These codes of ethics are published at www.emhr.net.) Thus, the Willowbrook and Tuskegee studies were not simply violations of the research ethical principles of today, but also of widely promulgated codes in effect during the time the studies were conducted.

---

5. The Willowbrook and Tuskegee studies were by no means the only studies of that era that raised serious ethical concerns. For more on the history of research from World War II through the 1960s, see Beecher (1966) and Katz (1972).

Box 1.2 The Nuremberg Code (1948)

1. The voluntary consent of the human subject is absolutely essential. This means that the person involved should have legal capacity to give consent; should be so situated as to be able to exercise free power of choice, without the intervention of any element of force, fraud, deceit, duress, over-reaching, or other ulterior form of constraint or coercion; and should have sufficient knowledge and comprehension of the elements of the subject matter involved as to enable him to make an understanding and enlightened decision. This latter element requires that before the acceptance of an affirmative decision by the experimental subject there should be made known to him the nature, duration, and purpose of the experiment; the method and means by which it is to be conducted; all inconveniences and hazards reasonable to be expected; and the effects upon his health or person which may possibly come from his participation in the experiment.
The duty and responsibility for ascertaining the quality of the consent rests upon each individual who initiates, directs or engages in the experiment. It is a personal duty and responsibility, which may not be delegated to another with impunity.

2. The experiment should be such as to yield fruitful results for the good of society, unprocurable by other methods or means of study, and not random and unnecessary in nature.

3. The experiment should be so designed and based on the results of animal experimentation and a knowledge of the natural history of the disease or other problem under study that the anticipated results will justify the performance of the experiment.

4. The experiment should be so conducted as to avoid all unnecessary physical and mental suffering and injury.

5. No experiment should be conducted where there is an a priori reason to believe that death or disabling injury will occur; except, perhaps, in those experiments where the experimental physicians also serve as subjects.

6. The degree of risk to be taken should never exceed that determined by the humanitarian importance of the problem to be solved by the experiment.

7. Proper preparations should be made and adequate facilities provided to protect the experimental subject against even remote possibilities of injury, disability, or death.

8. The experiment should be conducted only by scientifically qualified persons. The highest degree of skill and care should be required through all stages of the experiment of those who conduct or engage in the experiment. *(continued)*

9. During the course of the experiment the human subject should be at liberty to bring the experiment to an end if he has reached the physical or mental state where continuation of the experiment seems to him to be impossible.

10. During the course of the experiment the scientist in charge must be prepared to terminate the experiment at any stage, if he has probable cause to believe, in the exercise of the good faith, superior skill and careful judgment required of him that a continuation of the experiment is likely to result in injury, disability, or death to the experimental subject.

Reprinted from *Trials of War Criminals Before the Nuremberg Military Tribunals Under Control Council Law No. 10, Vol. 2* (Washington, D.C.: U.S. Government Printing Office, 1949), 181–182; available online at http://206.102.88.10/nihtraining/ohsrsite/guidelines/nuremberg.html (accessed May 4, 2007).

REACTIVE REGULATIONS

In the 1960s and 1970s, among people who took a keen interest in the ethical treatment of human participants in research, significant disagreement existed over just how to provide research protections. Beecher (1966), whose writings first brought to light the Willowbrook study and other ethically questionable studies published in medical journals, argued for professional self-regulation and education. In response to Beecher's article of 1966, Wolfensberger argued for self-regulation and recommended protections through the use of scientific codes of conduct (Wolfensberger, 1967). Shortly thereafter, Louis Jaffe argued for a common law, rather than regulatory or statutory approach (Jaffe, 1969). While the National Commission worked to develop recommendations for Congress, Eisenberg argued for education as the proper route to providing protections. In fact, he claimed that doing nothing would be better than overly restricting research, for it is morally imperative to conduct medical research that improves people's lives (Eisenberg, 1977).

But none of these positions carried the day following the shock that ensued from the exposé of the Tuskegee study in 1972. In response to the exposé, a Department of Health, Education, and Welfare (DHEW) advisory panel was created to investigate the Tuskegee study and to make recommendations (Katz, 1987). In 1973, congressional hearings chaired by Senator Edward Kennedy were held (Caplan, 1992). As a result of these events, in 1974 DHEW promulgated regulations that raised the National Institutes of Health's 1966 *Policies for the Protection of Human Subjects* to the status of regulatory law, and Congress passed the National Research Act (Penslar, 1993). This act created the National Commission for the Protection of Human Subjects of Biomedical and Behavioral Research (National Commission), which issued 17 reports during its work from 1974 to 1978, many of which provided a foundation for new regulations. As a result of the DHEW regulations, IRBs became the dominant mechanism for human research oversight and protection.

This regulatory approach to human subjects protection has not only continued but significantly developed, including very recent developments such as the privacy rule of the Health Insurance Portability and Accountability Act (HIPAA) of 2001. The history of the development of the U.S. regulatory system is detailed in an article suggestively titled "Goodbye to all that: The end of moderate protectionism in human subject research" (Moreno, 2001).

A legal approach admittedly has a number of strengths. Laws are one way for a nation to demonstrate publicly its commitment to protect all people who participate in research. Laws additionally influence behavior both through sanctions and through the role they play in shaping and communicating social norms (Geisinger, 2002). Evidence exists that researchers, institutions, and industry sponsors do change at least some behavior in response to regulations. For example, following implementation of the HIPAA privacy rule, an unprecedented wave of notices of privacy practices were distributed to patients and participants in health research.

However, the strengths that a legal approach brings are accompanied by significant weaknesses, some of which are discussed below. In large part, these arise from the fact that regulations are reactive. For example, in the wake of Tuskegee, the Belmont Report's principle of justice was understandably interpreted primarily as forbidding the exploitative inclusion of vulnerable populations. In effect, this meant that researchers were discouraged from including minorities, the mentally disabled, women, prisoners, and children from studies. An unspoken assumption behind this policy was that participation in research brings risks and that the benefits of participation rarely outweigh these risks. However, this assumption is not shared by potential participants who believe that research studies offer their last chance of hope; nor by those who realize it is too late for them to benefit but strongly wish to help others to avoid their suffering; nor by people who take medications that have not been tested for safety or efficacy among populations to which they belong (e.g., children or women) (Getz & Borfitz, 2002). Many participants who once would have been systematically excluded find research highly desirable. Consider, for example, that today, about 95% of children with leukemia are enrolled in clinical trials (Getz & Borfitz, 2002). Whereas only 4% of people with acute lymphoblastic leukemia survived in 1964, in 2006, 94% of patients treated at St. Jude Children's Research Hospital survived (http://www.stjude.org, retrieved on January 10, 2007).

In fact, the activities of people with cancer and HIV eventually led to a new understanding of what justice might entail and to revised regulations governing the inclusion of vulnerable populations (Dresser, 2001; C. Levine, 1988, 1996).

REGULATIONS CANNOT REPLACE ETHICS

To answer the question whether ethics and regulatory compliance are competing or complementary approaches, we first need to ask what are the goals of each. As we just saw, many U.S. research regulations were reactive; specifically, they were reactions to abuses of human subjects. Accordingly, our current research oversight system focuses on the protection of human subjects from harm (and secondarily, the protection of their rights—though these rights remain unenumerated and seldom play a significant role in IRB discussions).

Certainly, the broader field of human research ethics needs to be concerned with protecting participants. But, even as the Belmont Report suggests, there are other values at stake. An ethical approach to research should seek to actively foster research that is potentially beneficial, should explore whether there is a right to participate in research or even a duty, and should take the question of just compensation for participant time as seriously as the question of undue influence. Insofar as some of these aims diverge from the narrow aim of protection, research ethics may compete with certain regulatory trends and a dominant understanding of what the task of IRBs is. Reflecting an emphasis on nonmaleficence or protection from harm, the so-called Common Rule's title is "Protection of Human Subjects"—not "Ethics in Human Research" (Department of Health and Human Services, 2001).[6] The fact that research regulations tend to focus on one good—protection of research participants—already points to one insufficiency of a strictly regulatory approach to research ethics. But several others are worth mentioning

First, regulations are slow in responding to the needs of people. As the activity of HIV and cancer research advocates in the 1990s showed, excessive protectionism may not be desirable, yet changes in established policies may lag years behind the recognition of a need for change (Dresser, 2001; C. Levine, 1996).

Second, the regulations were never meant to resolve every issue. They were meant to provide minimum standards that institutions are expected to meet in protecting human participants in research. In fact, the regulations cannot be adequately implemented without engaging in ethical analysis. For example, determining where justifiable persuasion ends and undue influence begins ultimately requires ethical judgment (Vanderpool, 2002).

Third, neither local IRBs nor governmental oversight bodies can monitor all behavior; and attempting to do so would be not only futile but invasive and wasteful of resources. This helps explain why Beecher referred to the "more reliable safeguard provided by the presence of an intelligent, informed, conscientious, compassionate, responsible investigator" (Beecher, 1966). Professional ethics aims to fill the oversight gap by forming character and training people to identify ethical issues and providing them with resources (knowledge, references, and problem-solving skills).

Fourth, researchers in partnership with participants are typically in a better position to determine what is genuinely respectful, beneficial, or harmful to participants and their communities than IRBs and other oversight bodies (Koski, 1999).

Fifth, an excessive focus on regulations risks shifting researchers' focus away from the well-being of participants and the scientific endeavor onto "doing whatever it takes to expedite the oversight process" (Kahn & Mastroianni, 2001). This shift in focus is also contrary to the developmental aims that ethics education often has, insofar as it encourages moral reasoning that is less mature and developmentally desirable than principled ethical reasoning (DuBois, 2004; Rest, Narvaez, Bebeau, & Thoma, 1999).

Finally, one reason that we typically view principled ethical reasoning as developmentally and ethically superior to reasoning that focuses on following the law

6. The "Common Rule" and other federal research regulations can be found at www.emhr.net.

is that individual laws can be bad. For example, in 1907, Indiana became the first state to pass a compulsory sterilization law. It did so in the name of science. The bill stated that heredity had been shown to play a dominant role in the "transmission of crime, idiocy, and imbecility." Over the next two decades, thirty state legislatures approved sterilization bills, and repeatedly they did so based on an argument that science had proven that "defectives breed defectives" (Whitaker, 2002).[7]

The idea that regulations are a poor substitute for research ethics is not a radical idea of a few elite ethicists: a recent director of the Office of Human Research Protections published an article, "Beyond Compliance . . . Is It Too Much to Ask?" (Koski, 2003), which was consistent with earlier calls for a move beyond the culture of compliance to a "culture of conscience and responsibility" (Kahn & Mastroianni, 2001).

REGULATIONS AND ETHICS: POINTS OF INTERSECTION

Do these facts suggest that we should not have policies and regulations regarding issues such as the inclusion of vulnerable participants? No. Egregious abuses of human subjects continued long after the Nuremberg Code and the Declaration of Helsinki were adopted. As noted above, various forms of law influence behavior both through sanctions and through the role they play in shaping and communicating social norms (Geisinger, 2002). However, the six concerns identified above do suggest at least three things.

First, researchers, IRB members, and others involved in the conduct and oversight of research ought to learn to deliberate ethically within the space that regulations provide. The regulations that govern research often do leave researchers and IRBs a certain amount of discretion in finding ethical solutions to many challenges, even if IRBs too often seek to follow them "in rote fashion with little attention to ethics" (Vanderpool, 2002).[8]

Second, ethics should lead the way. Ethical reflection should provoke discussions aimed at regularly refining policies and regulations. And it should inspire us to go beyond the regulations in seeking to respect and benefit people in just ways.

Third, many of our regulations can be defended on ethical grounds (e.g., the requirement that informed consent ordinarily be given or that risks be minimized to what is reasonable and necessary). We need to explain the ethical foundations of our rules in order to foster voluntary and reasonable compliance with regulations.

While the primary purpose of this book is to present a framework for *ethical* deliberation in human subjects research and to examine some of the most pressing ethical issues in mental health research, it also summarizes the most important

7. Whitaker expounds on these bills: "Their lists of degenerate hereditary types were often long. In its 1913 bill, Iowa said that those in need of sterilization included 'criminals, rapists, idiots, feeble-minded, imbeciles, lunatics, drunkards, drug fiends, epileptics, syphilitics, moral and sexual perverts, and diseased and degenerate persons'—a catch-all description, in essence, for people viewed as social 'scum' by the legislature" (2002, p. 58).

8. For example, the application of the regulations to social and behavioral research often requires ethical creativity, but the regulations provide more leeway than is commonly acknowledged (Citro, Ilgen, & Marrett, 2003).

behavioral expectations that the regulations set out. Moreover, it assumes that there is a prima facie (or presumptive) duty to follow regulations and policies aimed to protect participants in research (DuBois, 2004).

Further EMHR Resources

- See www.emhr.net for links to current research regulations
- Unit one of the *Dialogues* DVDs contains interviews with James Korn, Jean Campbell, and mental health consumers that further address ethical concerns in the history of mental health research and the development of current research protections

REFERENCES

Annas, G. J., & Grodin, M. A. (Eds.). (1992). *The Nazi doctors and the Nuremberg Code: Human rights in human experimentation.* New York: Oxford University Press.

Beecher, H. K. (1966). Ethics and clinical research. *New England Journal of Medicine, 274,* 1354–1360.

Borror, K., Carome, M., McNeilly, P., & Weil, C. (2003). A review of OHRP compliance oversight letters. *IRB: Ethics & Human Research, 25*(5), 1–4.

Brandt, A. M. (1978). Racism and research: The case of the Tuskegee Syphilis Study. *Hastings Center Report, 8*(6), 21–29.

Caplan, A. L. (1992). When evil intrudes. *Hastings Center Report, 22*(6), 29–32.

Citro, C. F., Ilgen, D. R., & Marrett, C. B. (2003). *Protecting participants and facilitating social and behavioral sciences research.* Washington, DC: National Academies Press.

Cooper, J. A., & Turner, P. (2002). Investigator training. In R. J. Amdur & E. A. Bankert (Eds.), *Institutional review board: Management and function* (pp. 349–352). Boston: Jones & Bartlett.

The deadly deception: The Tuskegee study of untreated syphilis in the Negro male. (1993). In WGBH (Producer), *Films for the Humanities and Sciences.* Boston: WGBH.

Department of Health and Human Services. (2001). Code of federal regulations. Protection of human subjects. Title 45 public welfare, part 46. Washington, DC: Government Printing Office.

Dresser, R. (2001). *When science offers salvation. Patient advocacy and research ethics.* New York: Oxford University Press.

DuBois, J. M. (2004). Is compliance a professional virtue of researchers? Reflections on promoting the responsible conduct of research. *Ethics & Behavior, 14*(4), 383–395.

Dunn, C. M., & Chadwick, G. (1999). *Protecting study volunteers in research: A manual for investigative sites.* Boston: CenterWatch.

Edgar, H. (1992). Outside the community. *Hastings Center Report, 22*(6), 32–36.

Edsall, G. (1969). A positive approach to the problem of human experimentation. In P. A. Freund (Ed.), *Experimentation with human subjects* (pp. 276–292). New York: George Braziller.

Eisenberg, L. (1977). The social imperatives of medical research. *Science, 198,* 1105–1110.

Gamble, V. N. (1993). A legacy of distrust: African Americans and medical research. *American Journal of Preventive Medicine, 9,* 35–38.

Geisinger, A. (2002). A belief change theory of expressive law. *Iowa Law Review, 88,* 38–73.

Getz, K., & Borfitz, D. (2002). *Informed consent: A guide to the risks and benefits of volunteering for clinical trials*. Boston: CenterWatch.

Goldby, S. (1971/1972). Experiments at the Willowbrook State School. In J. Katz (Ed.), *Experimentation with human beings* (p. 1007). New York: Russell Sage Foundation.

Jaffe, L. L. (1969). Law as a system of control. In P. A. Freund (Ed.), *Experimentation with human subjects* (pp. 197–217). New York: George Braziller.

Jones, J. H. (1992). The Tuskegee legacy: AIDS and the black community. *Hastings Center Report, 22*(6), 38–40.

Jones, J. H. (1993). *Bad blood: The Tuskegee syphilis experiment* (2nd revised ed.). New York: Free Press.

Jonsen, A. R. (1998). *The birth of the Belmont Report*. Retrieved January 10, 2006, from www.georgetown.edu/research/nrcbl/nbac/transcripts.

Kahn, J. P., & Mastroianni, A. C. (2001). Moving from compliance to conscience. *Archives of Internal Medicine, 161*, 925–928.

Katz, J. (1972). *Experimentation with human beings*. New York: Russell Sage Foundation.

Katz, J. (1987). The regulation of human experimentation in the United States—A personal odyssey. *IRB: A Review of Human Subjects Research, 9*(1), 1–6.

Koski, G. (1999). Resolving Beecher's paradox: Getting beyond IRB reform. *Accountability in Research, 7*(2), 213–225.

Koski, G. (2003). Beyond compliance . . . Is it too much to ask? *IRB: A Review of Human Subjects Research, 25*(5), 5–6.

Krugman, S. (1971/1972). Experiments at the Willowbrook State School. In J. Katz (Ed.), *Experimentation with human beings* (p. 1008). New York: Russell Sage Foundation.

Lasagna, L. (1969). Special subjects in human experimentation. In P. A. Freund (Ed.), *Experimentation with human subjects* (pp. 262–275). New York: George Braziller.

Levine, C. (1988). Has AIDS changed the ethics of human subjects research? *Law, Medicine & Health Care, 16*(3–4), 167–173.

Levine, C. (1996). Changing views of justice after Belmont: AIDS and the inclusion of "vulnerable" subjects. In H. Y. Vanderpool (Ed.), *The ethics of research involving human subjects* (pp. 105–126). Frederick, MD: University Publishing Group.

Levine, R. J. (1988). *Ethics and regulation of clinical research* (2nd ed.). New Haven, CT: Yale University Press.

Moreno, J. D. (2001). Goodbye to all that: The end of moderate protectionism in human subjects research. *Hastings Center Report, 31*(3), 9–17.

National Commission. (1979). *The Belmont report: Ethical principles and guidelines for the protection of human subjects of research*. Washington, DC: Department of Health, Education, and Welfare.

The Nuremberg Code. (1948). Retrieved January 11, 2007, from http://www.emhr.net/ethics.htm.

Penslar, R. L. (1993). *Institutional review board guidebook*. Washington, DC: Office for Human Research Protections, Department of Health and Human Services. Retrieved January 11, 2007, from http://www.hhs.gov/ohrp/irb/irb_guidebook.htm.

Rest, J. R., Narvaez, D., Bebeau, M. J., & Thoma, S. J. (1999). *Postconventional moral thinking: A neo-Kohlbergian approach*. Mahwah, NJ: Lawrence Erlbaum Associates.

Rothman, D. J. (1982). Were Tuskegee and Willowbrook "studies in nature"? *Hastings Center Report, 12*(2), 5–7.

Rothman, D. J., & Rothman, S. M. (1984). *The Willowbrook wars*. New York: Harper & Row.

Vanderpool, H. Y. (2002). An ethics primer for IRBs. In R. J. Amdur & E. A. Bankert (Eds.), *Institutional review board: Management and function* (pp. 3–8). Boston: Jones & Bartlett.

Whitaker, R. (2002). *Mad in America*. Cambridge, MA: Perseus.

Wolfensberger, W. (1967). Ethical issues in research with human subjects. *Science, 155*, 47–51.

2

An Ethical Framework for Research

Once the leap is made to human experimentation, subject and object merge. It is this merger of the subject and object of human experimentation that makes it problematic; the researcher uses the human "object" as her model for nature. Nonetheless, the human subject retains humanity, and the experimenter is also obligated to respect the rights and welfare of this subject-object.

The Nazi concentration camp experiments demonstrate that once the subject is converted into a pure object, anything is possible, including experimentation without limitation.

—George Annas and Michael Grodin, *The Nazi Doctors and the Nuremberg Code: Human Rights in Human Experimentation*

What actions are right and should be done? What character traits will help us to know and do what is right? What processes should be followed in determining what is right in social contexts? These three questions form the heart of ethical inquiry.

Inquiry into which actions are right and which are wrong constitutes the narrow field of ethics. This is the domain of ethical *principles*, very general guidelines for evaluating actions. Examples of general principles include respect for autonomy or justice. It is also the domain of more specific norms or rules, for example, rules requiring us to obtain informed consent or to distribute the benefits and burdens of research as equally as possible.

Inquiry into which character traits help us to know and do what is right introduces us to the domain of *virtue ethics*, which might be considered a subspecialty of psychology in the broadest sense. For example, intellectual humility may help researchers to know and do what is right (as opposed to intellectual arrogance, which may thwart open inquiry or prevent one from admitting and fixing errors).

Inquiry into the processes that should be used to determine what actions should or should not be done introduces us to the domain of *procedural ethics*, a subspecialty of social ethics and politics. For example, subjecting research protocols to review by IRBs or soliciting input from participant communities lends a moral authority to a protocol that would be lacking if it were developed by just one individual, who may not adequately know or consider the best interests of prospective participants.

In what follows, it will be assumed that the first domain—the domain of principles that guide us in determining what is right or wrong—is epistemologically the most basic. This means that we judge whether or not a trait is in fact virtuous in terms of whether it assists us in knowing and doing actions that are deemed right according to ethical principles and norms. Similarly, we judge which procedures are ethical in terms of whether a given procedure assists us or thwarts us in performing actions that are deemed right according to ethical principles and norms.

Other ways of conceiving the relationship between the three domains of ethics are possible, but counter-intuitive. We could judge actions to be ethically right if performed by a virtuous person; but this seems to confuse morally good character and motives with morally right actions. Even a saint or a moral hero can err in judgment—with the purest motives—and perform an action that is not morally right. We might say that the individual is not subjectively guilty or blameworthy; nevertheless, the action considered in and of itself was wrong.

Similarly, one could say that any policy that is issued using just procedures is right. But again, unless we are thoroughgoing positivists who deny that an action can be right or wrong considered on its own merits in a specific context, it is naïve to believe that a good committee who follows sensible procedures cannot issue decisions that are ethically flawed. Later in the chapter, we will discuss the difference between decisions that are substantively right versus procedurally right. The key point here is that the concept of what is substantively right is more basic; procedures are deemed right when they generally contribute to substantively right decisions.

For this reason, more time will be spent on the nature of ethical principles than on virtues and procedures. It is not that virtues and procedures are unimportant—they often critically determine whether right judgments are actually made and acted upon—but that the concept of principles is more basic. It is also at this level that the Belmont Report and most major codes of ethics operate.

ETHICAL PRINCIPLES: DETERMINING RIGHT ACTION

No institutional review board (IRB) today would approve either the Tuskegee syphilis study or the Willowbrook hepatitis trials. But the Tuskegee study continued for 40 years until a whistle was finally blown in 1972. Clearly some people at PHS considered the studies unobjectionable. And even after the Willowbrook trials were exposed and criticized, Saul Krugman, the principal investigator, continued to defend the ethical legitimacy of the trials (Katz, 1972; Rothman & Rothman, 1984). Dr. Krugman was not a renegade physician but someone who received highest honors from the New York State Department of Health and the American Pediatric Society, someone who had the reputation of being caring and generous.[1] Similarly, Michael Davidson, the principal investigator of Bronx Veterans Administration L-dopa studies, which intentionally provoked "toxic psychosis" in many participants without informing participants of this and other risks, wrote:

> It would not be advisable to talk to the patients about psychosis or relapse . . . .
> [Doing so] might cause unnecessary anxiety, and therefore, would not be in the

---

1. New York University's School of Medicine has a Web site honoring Dr. Krugman: http://library. med.nyu.edu/library/eresources/featuredcollections/krugman/.

best interest of the patient. Although this approach might appear paternalistic by 1994 standards, protecting patients, psychiatric and medical, from "bad news" were [sic] accepted standards in 1979. (Whitaker, 2002, p. 244)

Dr. Davidson's explanation seeks to provide a beneficent reason for an action that he concedes falls short of what today's IRBs would expect. His rationale plainly appeals to an evolution in ethical thinking.

These facts lead us to ask: is ethics entirely relative, or are there transhistorical and transcultural principles that can help us to explain just why and to what extent a given experiment is unethical?

The United States Congress assumed that there are. In 1974, following the Tuskegee study exposé, Congress established the National Commission for the Protection of Human Subjects of Biomedical and Behavioral Research (National Commission). Among other things, it requested that the National Commission "identify the basic ethical principles that should underlie the conduct of biomedical and behavioral research involving human subjects" (National Commission, 1979). The result of the National Commission's efforts to identify such principles is the Belmont Report.

THE BELMONT REPORT

The Belmont Report was the result of numerous commission meetings from February 1976 to June 1978. The initial process included not only debate among commissioners, but input from six consultants, five of whom—Kurt Baier, Alasdair MacIntyre, James Childress, H. Tristram Engelhardt Jr., and LeRoy Walters—submitted philosophical essays on the nature of moral principles. Stephen Toulmin then developed a meta-analysis of the papers for the National Commission, which was refined and then used by Tom Beauchamp—also a philosophical consultant—to produce a final polished draft of the Belmont Report (Jonsen, 1998a). The Report was published in the Federal Register on April 18, 1979.

While each of the Belmont principles is intentionally abstract (and thus capable of applying to a broad range of situations), the Report also illustrates what the Commission believed to be some of the basic practical requirements of the principles.

Principles and Applications

The first of the three Belmont principles is respect for persons. The Report states that this principle "incorporates at least two ethical convictions: first, that individuals should be treated as autonomous agents, and second, that persons with diminished autonomy are entitled to protection" (National Commission, 1979). What is an autonomous person? An "individual capable of deliberation about personal goals and of acting under the direction of such deliberation" (B.1).[2] According to the commission, respecting autonomy is taking into account the considered

---

2. Because the Belmont Report has been published in so many different print and online formats, I provide references to subsections of the Belmont Report rather than page numbers.

choices people make and refraining from obstructing them unless their choice will clearly harm others.

The application of this aspect of the principle of respect is found in informed consent. The commission identified three aspects to informed consent: information, comprehension, and voluntariness (C.1), and briefly discussed challenges to each of these—for example, research that requires incomplete disclosure, the involvement of proxy decision makers, and risks of coercion and undue influence—all of which are discussed in later chapters.

However, the commission also noted that not every human being is capable of self-determination. "The capacity for self-determination matures during an individual's life, and some individuals lose this capacity wholly or in part because of illness, mental disability, or circumstances that severely restrict liberty" (B.1). The commission stated that the degree of protection that a person needs is to a large extent dependent upon the degree to which they are capable of exercising self-determination.

The second of the principles is beneficence. The report states that beneficence refers to a twofold obligation: "(1) do not harm and (2) maximize possible benefits and minimize possible harms" (B.2). The commission acknowledged that these obligations can be difficult to fulfill, partly due to ignorance (risks and benefits can be hard to calculate), partly because participants are not always the beneficiaries of research, and partly because it is often difficult to weigh benefits against risks, especially when risks are greater than minimal. Thus, the principle of beneficence appears to operate as shorthand for a series of ethical considerations. This means that it is possible not only that the principle of beneficence might conflict with another principle such as respect for persons, but that "the different claims covered by the principle of beneficence may come into conflict and force difficult choices" (B.2).

The application of the principle is rather obvious: we are obliged to minimize risks and to conduct a risk/benefit analysis that examines the ratio of "probabilities and magnitudes of possible harm and anticipated benefits" (C.2). The kinds of harms that should be considered are manifold: "psychological harm, physical harm, legal harm, social harm and economic harm" (C.2). The report notes that risks and benefits may affect the individual participant, families of participants, special groups of participants, and society at large. In general, risks and benefits affecting the individual research subject should carry special weight. However, the Report notes that sometimes benefits to others may be sufficient to justify the risks involved "so long as the subjects' rights have been protected" (C.2). Presumably, subjects' rights include at a minimum the right to grant voluntary informed consent. Interestingly, while our regulations are clearly focused on protecting participants in research, the report states that in addition to protecting participants from risks of harms, beneficence requires "that we be concerned about the potential loss of the substantial benefits that might be gained from research" (C.2). (Chapter 6 examines risk/benefit analysis in detail.)

The third Belmont principle is justice in the sense of "fairness in distribution" or "what is deserved" (B.3). It is concerned with the distribution not only of the benefits of research (e.g., resulting products such as new medications and knowledge), but also the burdens of participation in research. The report notes that one traditional definition of justice is that "equals should be treated equally," but the meaning of this principle has been interpreted differently. The commission offers five formulations of how distribution might be considered equal: "(1) to each person an equal share, (2) to each person according to individual need, (3) to each person according to individual effort, (4) to each person according to societal contribution, (5) to each person according to merit" (B.3). Rather than settling on one formulation, the report suggests that each can have merit in certain contexts, and that it is necessary in a given situation to specify in what regard people ought to be treated equally.

While justice can be relevant to a number of issues related to research, the report applies the principle primarily to the selection of subjects. This requires consideration of fair treatment not only among individuals but groups of individuals. The commission focused above all on the fair treatment of people who belong to vulnerable groups, including children, prisoners, the institutionalized mentally infirm, racial minorities, the economically disadvantaged, and the very sick. Those who are dependent or whose capacity for free consent is compromised "should be protected against the danger of being involved in research solely for administrative convenience, or because they are easy to manipulate as a result of their illness or socioeconomic condition" (C.3). In general, the report urges that when "research is proposed that involves risks and does not include a therapeutic component, other less burdened classes of persons should be called upon first to accept these risks of research, except where the research is directly related to the specific conditions of the class involved" (C.3).

The general approach that the Belmont Report adopts has been labeled a form of principlism—an ethic that is based upon the use of so-called "midlevel" principles. Such principles are less general than a first-level principle such as the principle of utility,[3] which is supposed by utilitarians to guide all actions; but they are less specific than concrete norms such as "do not lie" or "do not kill" (Beauchamp & Childress, 2001). However, while embracing a principled approach, the National Commission notes ways in which each of the principles may be difficult to apply and insists that people must take into account the specific facts of each concrete situation when applying principles. Thus, the application of principles should not be opposed to case-based or casuistic reasoning; rather, the two are complementary (Beauchamp, 1993; Jonsen, 1998b).

The Evolution of Principlism

Tom Beauchamp and Jim Childress, who played key roles in the development of the Belmont Report, went on to develop "principlism" as a method of approaching biomedical and research ethical issues. In a short article on the Belmont Report, Beauchamp suggests that the National Commission fell short in the way that it

3. One version of the principle of utility is the one propounded by John Stuart Mill, urging us to act so as to produce the greatest amount of happiness for the greatest number of people (Mill, 1861/1979).

described and enumerated midlevel moral principles. Referring to Jim Childress, with whom he co-authored *Principles of Biomedical Ethics*, he writes:

> I thought then and still do that the commission was mistaken in the way it delineated the principle of respect for persons. I thought it was mixing together two independent principles: a principle of respect for autonomy and a principle of protection and avoidance of harm to incompetent persons. Jim thought, and argued vigorously, that the principle of beneficence should be distinguished from the principle of non-maleficence. (Beauchamp, 1993, p. S9)

Throughout this book, the Belmont principles will be translated into the more common language of four principles. As Beauchamp suggests, the National Commission clearly had in mind autonomy, beneficence, nonmaleficence, and justice. Yet the extra protections for individuals with diminished autonomy, which they lumped together with the idea of respecting autonomy, are better conceived as duties of nonmaleficence (that is, they are ways of avoiding harm). And there are good reasons to distinguish between the principle of beneficence (or doing good for others) and the principle of nonmaleficence. Within the Belmont Report and within traditional ethics (Gert, Culver, & Clouser, 1997), it is common for duties not to harm—so-called perfect duties—to admit of fewer exceptions than duties to benefit. Thus, for example, regardless of the benefits that might accrue from research, the Belmont Report—consistent with the Nuremberg Code—states that "brutal or inhumane treatment of human subjects is never morally justified" (C.2).

HUMANIZING THE BELMONT PRINCIPLES

What justification did the National Commission offer for the selection of its principles? Very little. The issue of justification is nowhere systematically addressed. The report simply states, "three basic principles, *among those generally accepted in our cultural tradition*, are particularly relevant to the ethics of research involving human subjects" (B, Introduction, emphasis added). But if the justification is only based on general acceptance within a culture, then the principles have very little appeal. We live in a culturally diverse society, and we conduct research with people from other nations and cultures. More important, we know that Nazi culture had its own generally accepted norms, which suggests that general acceptance within a culture does not amount to ethical justification.

Beauchamp and Childress, in their development of principlism, suggest that the principles come from "common morality." They suggest that the common morality consists of a small set of norms that "all morally serious persons share"— even across time and communities (Beauchamp & Childress, 2001). While they recognize a larger subset of specific norms such as "don't lie" or "obtain informed consent" as prima facie (i.e., presumptively valid but capable of being overridden by competing norms or goods), the four principles provide "an analytical framework that expresses the general values underlying rules in the common morality" (Beauchamp & Childress, 2001). But they do not propose that there is an underlying intuition or normative commitment that guides common morality; in fact, they oppose the idea (Beauchamp & Childress, 2001).

What I would like to propose is an overarching principle or commitment that helps us to understand why the four principles are not merely arbitrarily adopted in common morality. In doing so, I hope to provide a foundation that will "humanize" the principles—that is, explain how all ethical principles are expressions of respect for humanity, whether humanity in ourselves or others.

Humanizing ethical principles is important because it seems that many ethical violations stem less from genuine uncertainty about what is right than from a *disregard for humanity*, a tendency to treat human beings as objects. Often this disregard is not for humanity as a whole, but the humanity of a subset of individual human beings. On one end of the spectrum, we find outright denials of the humanity of subjects—as occurred in Nazi research with Jews and mentally disabled people, who were viewed as subhuman. Similarly, the racism that enabled the Tuskegee study to continue for so long rests on a view of human beings of different races as being inferior. At the other end of the spectrum, we find lapses in the application of the Golden Rule, actions such as forgetting to share the results of a study with participants or rushing participants to sign a consent form, rather than taking time to inform them and answer questions.

Thus, humanizing principles is meant to yield a theoretical foundation for principles that both illuminates why they are widely embraced in common morality and reminds researchers of the humanity they share with participants.

The Mother of All Principles

The mother of all ethical principles for human interactions is *respect for human beings*. However, I use this phrase to mean something different from the phrase "respect for persons" found in the Belmont Report. In the Belmont Report, respect for persons was reduced to respecting autonomy or self-determination. However, why should we adopt a view of respect that is reducible to respecting autonomy or self-determination? Respect has been defined in various ways, but none of them seems to justify reducing respect to respect for autonomy alone. For example, Thomas Lickona has defined respect as "showing regard for the worth of someone or something" (Lickona, 1991).[4] This is compatible with the Kantian principle of respect, which suggests that the kind of worth human beings possess is intrinsic: "act in such a way that you treat humanity, whether in your own person or in the person of another, always at the same time as an end and never simply as a means" (Kant, 1785/1993, p. 36).[5] Kant did indeed view human beings as having intrinsic worth because they are rational beings. But showing respect for a human being requires

---

4. This notion of respect is similar to Kant's, only more neutral with regard to its object: "the legislation itself which determines all worth must for that very reason have dignity, i.e., unconditional and incomparable worth; and the word 'respect' alone provides a suitable expression for the esteem which a rational being must have for it" (Kant, 1785/1993, p. 41).
5. For a development of Kant's notion of human beings as "ends in themselves," see Donagan, 1977, at section 7.4.

that we show regard for the human being as a whole, not merely the rational, self-determining part.

I propose that human beings have at least four characteristics that deserve special regard, and each helps us to understand one of the midlevel principles that the National Commission and principlists acknowledge.

The Four Principles Humanized

In what follows, each of the four principles is translated into a form of respect for a specific aspect of human nature.

1. *The Principle of Autonomy.* Human beings are capable of making rational choices that determine their actions and themselves. Accounts of the dignity of persons—and why persons rank higher than plants and nonhuman animals—frequently appeal to this characteristic of persons. *Respect for persons as rational, self-determining beings* can be called autonomy. In the context of research, this will require obtaining informed consent as long as this dimension of the person is actualized (i.e., as long as they are capable of rational self-determination).[6] Interestingly, of the four characteristics of persons, this is the only one that is not always present, even if some of the other characteristics admit of degrees (or exist on a continuum). When this characteristic is not present (say, in a human being who is very young or developmentally disabled), respect for the human being's worth must be expressed in ways other than respecting autonomy, for example, through heightened protections, as the Belmont Report requires.

2. *The Principle of Beneficence.* Human beings are not eternal, perfect, self-sufficient beings. We stand in need of goods. We are born unable to speak a language, to move about, or to meet our basic needs for food and shelter. We depend on others initially to survive and later to flourish. *Respect for persons as finite and in need of goods* is beneficence. Without respecting this dimension of persons, we fail to show proper regard for human beings—we fail in respect. Some have argued that there are no duties of beneficence, but only moral ideals (Gert et al., 1997). However, the fact that we cannot survive, much less flourish, without the beneficent actions of others suggests that it is not an optional form of respect for human beings, that there are some duties of beneficence, even if these are more context-specific than duties of nonmaleficence. Human beings' limited ability to provide basic goods to others helps explain why duties of beneficence are limited duties that often exist only within special relationships (such as a parent-child, teacher-student, or researcher-participant relationship).

3. *The Principle of Nonmaleficence.* While people are vulnerable to different degrees and it makes sense in certain contexts to highlight specific vulnerabilities (such as being institutionalized), all human beings are vulnerable to a variety of physical, psychological, and social harms. We are vulnerable to insult, pain, injury, and death. *Respect for persons as vulnerable to harm* is nonmaleficence.

4. *The Principle of Justice.* Human beings are all of equal worth. *Respect for persons as equal in worth* is justice, broadly understood. There are also specific

---

6. Just what should count as rational will be explored in chapter 5, "Decision-Making Capacity and the Involvement of Surrogates."

forms of justice, different ways of being concerned with equality. Research ethics is often fundamentally concerned with distributive justice or the fair distribution of the risks and benefits of research. While risks and benefits are, as the Belmont Report notes, distributed according to a variety of rules—rules that are sometimes controversial and sometimes conflict—they are all meant to reduce wrongly biased or arbitrary distribution. The fundamental equal worth of all human beings is precisely what provides the rationale for prohibiting arbitrary or wrongly biased distribution.

Are the Four Principles Complete? An Argument for Relationality as a Fifth Principle

Some authors have argued that at least some of the Belmont principles are not universal, but artifacts of American culture. This allegation is most commonly directed toward the principle of autonomy. It is easy to point to cultures where people see themselves as part of a community rather than autonomous individuals. In such cultures, people may feel uncomfortable providing individual informed consent; they may want their community leader to grant permission on behalf of all (Newton, 1990; Porter, 1996). In other cases, people appear far less interested in privacy, understood as a form of controlling the access of others to themselves. They may want "private" health information to be discussed with family and even friends, because they, too, are interested in and affected by the health of the member of their community (Monshi & Zieglmayer, 2004).

The question we need to ask is whether individuals in these cultures lack the particular human dimension that the humanized principle of autonomy aims to respect. That is, are they actually incapable of making rational choices that determine their actions and themselves? In some contexts, that may be the case. If, for example, a culture does not educate women and does not allow them to make decisions concerning their lives, they may lack the experience necessary to develop their rational, self-determining potential to the extent necessary to give informed consent to participate in a clinical trial. The human potential is there, and it deserves regard to whatever extent possible. Just the same, in such cases, the principle of autonomy will take a back seat to other principles—for example, nonmaleficence or heightened protection from harm—given the participants' developmental status.

However, what is perhaps more commonly the case in cross-cultural research is that the principle of autonomy is relevant, but we discover that it inadequately captures the whole truth about human beings. In addition to being capable of making rational choices that determine their actions and themselves, human beings are intrinsically related to others. Other cultures may have a heightened awareness of this dimension of human beings, namely, their relationality. We need others and are needed by others. Our well-being and the well-being of others are bound together.

This truth about human beings is captured in the principle of the common good. However, this principle can be understood in fundamentally different ways, some of which might be harmful in a research context. For example, if the principle of the common good is understood in a crude utilitarian fashion that views the good of "the many" as automatically trumping the good of the individual, then

Table 2.1 Humanized Principles for Research Ethics

Principle	Dimension of the Human Being Respected by Principle
Autonomy	Human being as rational and self-determining
Beneficence	Human being as finite and in need of goods
Nonmaleficence	Human being as vulnerable to harm
Justice	Human being as equal in value to all other persons
Relationality	Human being as intrinsically related to others, a member of communities

we can justify using human subjects in deadly and deceptive research as long as it will yield knowledge that significantly benefits a large number of people. Or, if we conceive of human beings simply as constitutive parts of communities—for example, a nation—and only value the community for its own sake, then similar abuses of individuals might be justified.

What is rather being proposed here is that relationality be recognized as a fifth principle. The *principle of relationality* denotes *respect for human beings insofar as they are essentially related to other human beings*. Whereas the principle of justice reminds us that ethical principles apply to others as much as to the self, the principle of relationality reminds us that in order to flourish, actions must respect the relationships that an individual is in or should be in. Thus, if a woman insists that her husband must also give permission and sign the consent form for intrauterine research conducted on their baby, then respecting her wish is not merely respecting her as rational and self-determining, but as existing in a family relationship.[7] If a member of a tribe insists that he is subordinate to the chief, then respecting his relationality requires that the chief be approached for permission, even if respect for the individual requires that we also have that individual's verbal consent or at least assent.

Table 2.1 summarizes the five ethical principles we have identified in humanized form.

Why "Human Beings" Rather Than "Persons"?

According to Aristotle, we come to know the nature of a being by seeing it actualized, even though a being preserves its nature even when it is not fully actualized (Aristotle, 1941 trans.). Thus, human nature is not best understood by looking at a baby that has a lot of potential but has actualized little; it is best understood by looking at adults "in their prime." This is, for example, how we grasp that human beings are by nature "rational animals" (i.e., living, sensitive beings who can understand

---

7. The Common Rule (45CFR46) at section 204(e), which addresses research on pregnant women and fetuses, states that "if the research holds out the prospect of direct benefit solely to the fetus then the consent of the pregnant woman and the father is obtained in accord with the informed consent provisions of subpart A of this part, except that the father's consent need not be obtained if he is unable to consent because of unavailability, incompetence, or temporary incapacity or the pregnancy resulted from rape or incest." Thus, in some cases, regulations might require such consent, even if the justification for such consent may not be framed in terms of relationality.

reality, make reasoned judgments, and base actions on such judgments). But, and this is crucial for research ethics, a human being does not cease to belong to the species just because it does not actualize all of the potentials that human beings have. Thus, vulnerable people (e.g., very young children or people with severe mental disorders) are not worthy of less respect than others, for they remain human beings.

This view contrasts sharply with the views of those who would restrict respect for human beings to those who fit a narrow understanding of what it is to be a person, that is, to those who preserve rationality and autonomy (Singer, 1993). Yet, the Aristotelian view that human nature is fully present even in people who do not actualize all human potentials is wholly consistent with the Common Rule and the Belmont Report; for these documents generally provide extra rather than fewer protections for vulnerable people who lack specific human capacities, such as the ability to make considered decisions.[8]

Are Principles Sufficient in Discerning Right Action?

A list of principles alone clearly will not suffice to navigate the challenges that research ethics can present. Even within their legitimate sphere—the activity of determining whether actions are right or wrong—principles alone do not suffice. First, principles and the rules that flow from them may conflict. For example, research on promising treatments for mental health disorders may involve testing medications to establish safe dosages or using placebos instead of known effective treatments. Here duties of beneficence and nonmaleficence may appear to collide. Principles provide a language for discussing ethical problems. They remind us of core commitments, of dimensions of human beings that ought to be respected in action. But they do need to be supplemented by practical guidelines for justifying decisions when principles, rules, or commitments appear to collide. Such guidelines are presented in chapter 3, "Solving Ethical Problems."

Second, principles need to be supplemented by metaphysics—a view of human nature and the world—in order to move beyond the level of generalities to concrete plans of action. For example, are individuals parts of communities such that a leader can grant informed consent for all members? Are people ultimately responsible for their actions, and if so, when distributing benefits "equally" (say, free trial medication after a study has ended) should we consider merits (say, whether a participant actually followed the protocol)? Are fetuses human beings with the same rights to protection that born human beings have? Two people might very well embrace all five principles yet arrive at radically different conclusions depending on their view of human nature and the world.

Finally, even when we agree upon a goal such as developing an effective treatment for depression, there are always multiple ways of striving for the goal.

---

8. Some people might wonder whether this framework leaves room for consideration of the ethical treatment of animals. It leaves room for such a considerations, but—like the Belmont Report—it does not aim to provide a framework for them. However, an ethic of respect—an ethic that aims to flesh out what it means to show regard for the worth of someone or something—could be developed in accord with the specific worth of animals.

Some of these will be unethical, but there may not be one right approach: there may be several acceptable approaches, each with pros and cons. Particularly in such cases, processes become important—processes for soliciting the input from stakeholders to achieve a decision that can be supported by those involved, even if it is not their first choice.

EXCURSUS: PRINCIPLES AND RIGHTS TALK

The "Common Rule," regulation 45CFR46, which guides the work of IRBs, repeatedly speaks of the need for IRBs and researchers to "protect the rights and welfare" of participants (Department of Health and Human Services, 2001) (see 103[b.1], 107[a], and 123[b]). What are rights and how are they related to principles and other ethical concepts? Principles are used to determine which actions are right or wrong. We frequently state the rightness or wrongness of an action in terms of obligations or duties: if it is right to get informed consent, then we have a duty or obligation to do so; if it is wrong to breach confidentiality, then we have a duty or obligation to protect confidentiality. The language of rights basically describes the same phenomenon, but rather than describing it from the perspective of the moral agent or acting person, it describes it from the perspective of the recipient of an action (Finnis, 1993). If participants have the right to abstain from participation in research until they have given informed consent, then someone—usually the principal investigator—has an obligation to obtain informed consent. If participants have a right to be asked to participate only in research that has scientific merit, then someone—an investigator, an IRB, or a scientific review committee—has a duty to review research protocols to ensure that they are scientifically sound.

Because obligations stem from a variety of sources—including law, ethics, and institutional policies—we may speak of different kinds of rights, for example, legal and moral rights. As noted already, the Common Rule repeatedly speaks of the need to protect the rights of participants. However, it nowhere clarifies whether it refers to natural human rights, legal rights, institution-granted rights, or whatever people invoke as moral rights. For example, an IRB member might claim that participants have a right to give consent even in exempt survey research or have a right to compensation for injury, even though federal regulations grant neither right.

I would argue that in the process of interpreting regulatory law, reference to rights should be restricted to legal rights. That is not to say that IRBs should be unconcerned with "moral rights"; but to the extent that they show concern for nonlegal rights, they must be aware that they are going beyond compliance and are engaging in ethical deliberation. Accordingly, they should accept a heightened duty to provide ethical arguments on behalf of requirements based on moral rights. Additionally, the concept of moral rights may add confusion to discussions given the loose way that the term is used in some circles (where people are quick to invoke their rights without considering who has the corresponding duty or why they supposedly have the duty). It may be preferable for IRBs to speak of right ways of treating participants or designing and conducting research whenever they refer to rights that do not derive from the law.

On this interpretation of rights, we lose little by doing ethics in the language of principles and obligations rather than the language of rights. Rather than being a competing model of ethical analysis, rights-based reasoning presupposes systems that generate obligations, whether these are systems of laws or of moral principles.

MORAL VIRTUES

In contrast to rights, virtues bring at least two fundamentally new things to ethics. First of all, the idea of "virtuous action" reminds us that intentions matter (Beauchamp & Childress, 2001; Waide, 1988). Obtaining informed consent in order to comply with IRB demands is not the same as obtaining consent out of respect for the participant as a human being. Conducting research to benefit humankind is not the same as conducting research simply to promote one's career or name. Actions are not considered virtuous unless they are done for right reasons. Second, the concept of virtue reminds us that there are character traits that are not immediately related to ethical principles but are needed in order to implement the principles well.

What are moral virtues? Without claiming to offer an authoritative answer, I propose the following conception, which is wholly compatible with an ethical framework based on humanized Belmont principles: virtues are *morally good character traits that help us to respect the goods to which principles commit us*. For example, honesty is a character trait that enables others to be self-determining insofar as it is a condition for accurate information; it helps others to avoid the harm that follows from acting on false information; and it preserves trust in language, a necessary condition for human flourishing. Thus, it helps us to respect persons as rational and self-determining (autonomy), as vulnerable to harm (nonmaleficence), and in need of goods (beneficence). It is a morally good trait when we have the trait of being honest for right reasons, for example, out of respect for others and not merely because we expect we might get caught lying and be punished.

Which specific traits should count as virtues? Lists often appear arbitrary. One recent character education approach lists 42 virtues (Narvaez, 2001); the Christian tradition has recognized four cardinal virtues—prudence, temperance, justice, and courage—and three theological virtues—faith, hope, and charity (Geach, 1977); Beauchamp and Childress focus on just five virtues needed by health care professionals and researchers: compassion, discernment, trustworthiness, integrity, and conscientiousness (Beauchamp & Childress, 2001). While there is a certain amount of arbitrariness to lists of virtues, this simply reflects the facts (a) that some virtues are like general principles—they subsume others; (b) people use different language to get at the same phenomenon—for example, some speak of justice, others of fairness, sometimes referring to the same thing; and (c) the list of traits that can in some fashion aid us in respecting others is long.

Why should we treat ethical principles as more conceptually basic than virtues such as caring and courage? In part this is because many of the traits that we call virtues can be used to support ethical or unethical purposes: care for a person may lead to overprotective treatment of the individual or to unfair treatment of others; or courage may help the criminal to be more effective. Reference to humanized principles helps us to understand why and when a trait is virtuous.

Some philosophers have recognized practical wisdom (Aristotle), prudence (Aquinas), or discernment (Beauchamp & Childress) as a sort of overarching virtue. Beauchamp and Childress write:

> The virtue of discernment thus involves understanding both *that* and *how* principles and rules are relevant in a variety of circumstances. It requires attention and sensitivity attuned to the demands of particular contexts . . . . Discernment is often manifest through a creative response in meeting responsibilities, which principles and rules structure but do not fully determine. (Beauchamp & Childress, 2001)

Even a virtue such as benevolence can be exercised imprudently, for example, by enrolling competent adults in a promising research study without their knowledge because we imagine it will benefit them. Because doing so interferes with participants' ability to protect their own interest and to develop their capacity as self-determining persons, it is not truly beneficent or respectful regardless of the outcomes.

What are the *professional* virtues of researchers? Those traits that will help researchers not only to respect persons, but to respect persons precisely by actualizing the goal of their profession: gaining new knowledge.[9] These will include honesty, intellectual humility, perseverance, generosity, trustworthiness, competence, collegiality, and many others. (In chapter 10, which addresses conflicting interests and roles, we will see that many forms of research, but especially clinical research with patients, involve multiple and sometimes conflicting goals, such as gaining new knowledge and providing treatment to patients.)

Throughout this book, references to virtues will be few and far between. There are two reasons for this. First, modeling virtue is important in the development of moral character (Leone & Graziano, 1992); and classical wisdom maintains that virtues ultimately can only be acquired through virtuous action—that is, by performing right actions with right intentions (Aristotle, 1980). No one to my knowledge has ever claimed that virtues can be learned from a book. Second, as noted above, appeals to virtue do not help us to determine what is right or wrong. Virtues as character traits that support right action done for the right reasons should be identified and fostered. But because we are treating principles as more primary in determining what is right or wrong, our analysis of actions will appeal to the principles that flow from respect for human beings.

ETHICAL PROCESSES: OVERSIGHT, INCLUSION, AND CONSENT

In recent years, increasing attention has been paid not only to substantive justice but to procedural justice. The difference between the two is frequently illustrated

9. The idea of relating professional virtue to the goals of a profession derives from Pellegrino's development of an Aristotelian virtue ethic for health professionals (Pellegrino, 1995).

by the distinction between the decision of a court (substance or content) and the process used to issue the decision, or between the pay raise an employee receives (substance) and the process used to determine pay raises (Greenberg, 1987).

Procedural justice has been defined as "the correct application of a procedure that is likely to increase the chance of the outcome being just" (Tschentscher, 1997, p. 105). *Objective* procedural justice concerns "the capacity of a procedure to conform to normative standards of justice, to make either the decisions them-selves or the decision-making process more fair by, for example, reducing some clearly unacceptable bias or prejudice" (Lind & Tyler, 1988, p. 3). *Subjective* pro-cedural justice concerns "the capacity of each procedure to enhance the fairness judgments of those who encounter procedures" (Lind & Tyler, 1988, pp. 3–4). Whereas philosophers have focused primarily on establishing criteria for evaluat-ing objective procedural justice, social psychologists (especially working in the fields of management and law) have investigated subjective procedural justice.

In the fields of management and business, positive judgments about corporate procedures have been correlated with greater satisfaction with decisions, pay, and employment; greater willingness to cooperate; and stronger levels of trust in, and commitment to, corporations (Lind & Tyler, 1988). In the field of law, positive judgments about court procedures have been correlated with increased support for the legitimacy of courts and willingness to support even unpopular decisions (Tyler, 1988; Tyler & Rasinski, 1991).

Judgments about procedural justice seem natural to human beings and are evi-denced even in small children, who distinguish between blame when reasonable doubt exists or does not exist, and blame when witnesses are consulted or ig-nored (Gold, Darley, Hilton, & Zanna, 1984). However, judgments about what processes are actually deemed relevant or just appear to vary significantly across situations (Tyler, 1988).

Korsgaard, Schweiger, and Sapienza (1995) have noted that procedural justice theorists tend to see fair procedures as serving two main purposes. The first is "to help protect individuals' interests; over the long run, fair procedures should result in individuals' receiving what they are due" (p. 65). The second "is symbolic and helps to strengthen individuals' relationships with a group, leader, and organization. Fair procedures serve as a sign to individuals that they are valued and respected . . . and thus promote harmony and trust in relationships with others" (1995, p. 4).

This last statement opens the doors to a broader notion of procedures in ethics. Theorists are not yet speaking of "procedural respect." Yet, that is precisely what we want in procedures, using the term "respect" in the broad sense developed in this chapter: we want processes that are focused not only on fair outcomes but also on outcomes that make people feel that regard for their worth is shown. And this is done by using processes that will enhance outcomes that are not only fair but in accord with the decisions individuals make and beneficial rather than harmful.

In chapter 3, a framework for decision making is presented that lends structure to ethical deliberation. It focuses on achieving ethically satisfactory outcomes (substance); yet using it may improve processes, and using it well may require additional inclusive processes, for example, the input of oversight bodies and/or stakeholders.

In the past, the process for making decisions regarding research design and implementation rested almost entirely with researchers. But already in 1972, Jay Katz in his groundbreaking book *Experimentation with Human Beings* repeatedly asked the following process questions: How and by whom should research policy be formulated? How and by whom should the research process be administered? How and by whom should the consequences of research be reviewed? (Katz, 1972).

We still await definitive answers to these questions. However, researchers today are asked to engage at least two processes aimed at ensuring and improving the ethics of studies: the informed consent process and the IRB review process. Additionally, many believe that the process of community consultation or partnership building is also an important process in developing respectful research. As we will see, informed consent and community consultation or partnerships are key ways of involving stakeholders, whereas IRB review—guided by specific regulations aimed at protection of human subjects—is more heavily focused on substance.

Informed Consent

The most basic procedural element to human research ethics is informed consent. While informed consent has already been mentioned above as following from the principles of autonomy and beneficence, and later chapters address different dimensions of consent in detail, it is worth noting its procedural aspect. Regardless of whether a study is considered beneficial for a participant, whether an IRB has approved it, or whether a community has provided input, ordinarily a study should not proceed without a consent process occurring between the researcher and each individual participant. Because participants are the most direct stakeholders in a study, and because there is a subjective element to determinations of the relative merits of risks and benefits, only this process can ensure that respect is accorded to participants as human beings when their active participation is required and risks or burdens are assumed.

Again, this procedural element illustrates well the fact that proper procedures should not only aim at just or fair outcomes but should themselves enhance respect (e.g., for persons as rational and self-determining) and the likelihood of outcomes that are beneficent.

IRB Review

While IRBs are supposed to have a diverse membership, they need only have one "community" member, that is, one person not affiliated with the research institution (Department of Health and Human Services, 2001) (see section 107.d), and naturally this community member cannot possibly speak on behalf of all the various communities represented in an institution's research programs. In this sense, the processes IRBs use to offer protections are largely "paternalistic." While they provide oversight, they are not required to, and rarely do, provide oversight by the primary stakeholders. Moreover, there exists the risk that IRBs, as boards of an institution comprised primarily of employees, will go beyond consideration of risks to participants and focus on risks to the institution. At times, these interests may be at odds; for example, an institution may want a signed consent form whereas participants may be reluctant to sign a form (Levine, 1988).

Nevertheless, the IRB process ensures that the research protocol complies with key regulatory (substantive and procedural) requirements: that risks are minimized and reasonable in relation to anticipated benefits, that the selection of participants is equitable, that informed consent will be sought and appropriately documented, and as appropriate, that data will be monitored to ensure safety and that provisions will be made to protect the privacy of subjects and confidentiality of data (Department of Health and Human Services, 2001) (see section 111).

Additionally, the IRB is authorized to play a significant role in oversight: it should provide ongoing review at least on an annual basis; it may observe the informed consent process; it reviews adverse events in drug and medical device research; and it has the authority to suspend or terminate research that does not comply with IRB requirements or that proves unexpectedly harmful.

Many of the requirements of IRBs do not directly enhance protections or respect for participants, but they are necessary to enable oversight (e.g., signed consent forms, annual updates, or adverse event reports when the event is clearly not related to research). This is often called the "administrative burden" of the IRB process, not least of which is the delay caused by review. In the introduction, we examined the history of human subjects abuse that gave rise to the IRB oversight system. However, the reasons for oversight are not merely historical or related to reestablishing trust: many researchers are unaware of how best to protect and respect participants, and conflicts of interest are ubiquitous. Thus, the administrative burden of IRB review may be viewed as a necessary evil.

Nevertheless, the Belmont Report states that we should also be "concerned about the potential loss of the substantial benefits that might be gained from research" (C.2). This means that IRBs have a very difficult job. On the one hand, they have a duty to foster safe and respectful research, which necessarily requires some level of administrative burden; on the other hand, they should be concerned to reduce this burden to the minimum necessary and to issue decisions that do not unnecessarily hinder the progress of research.

Participants and Community Members

In describing the transformation of chlorpromazine (Thorazine) from a drug touted as a "chemical lobotomy, useful for making patients sluggish and emotionally indifferent" to a "safe and effective medication for schizophrenia" (Whitaker, 2002, p. 158), Whitaker writes:

> Unfortunately, it was a good-news tale that was missing one key voice: that of the mentally ill. There had been little mention of how they felt about these wonder drugs. It was a glaring absence, and, as usual, their perceptions were quite at odds with society's belief that a safe "antischizophrenic" treatment had been found. (2002, pp. 158–159)

Increasingly, people are recognizing the need to give a voice to stakeholders, to participants as well as their communities, who are affected when benefits are gained, when trust is undermined, or when results further stigmatize a community (Campbell, 1997; Centers for Disease Control and Prevention et al., 1998).

In an important and timely work, Dresser looks at both the opportunities and challenges that research advocacy—whether by patients, families, or community members—brings to the research enterprise.[10] She notes that community members are playing a wide variety of roles, including advocating for policies and funding, setting research agendas, planning studies, examining how results should be disseminated and used, evaluating scientific merit, supplying constituents with information, and expanding access to promising research (Dresser, 2001). She observes that community members have enhanced research quality by providing information and input on the value of study questions; promoted ethical research by assessing what risks are reasonable to the community or what benefits are sought; and brought practical advantages to studies by assisting with recruitment and retention. Additionally, governmental bodies have called for greater use of participatory models of research, which go beyond consulting community members to including them as co-investigators (Centers for Disease Control and Prevention et al., 1998; Ochocka, Janzen, & Nelson, 2002; O'Fallon, Tyson, & Dearry, 2000).

Including community members in research roles beyond that of a subject is an important form of respecting human beings (Campbell, 1997; Hall & Flynn, 1999). First, it is a form of respecting autonomy, or the self-determining and rational dimension of people. Second, it is a form of justice, a way of acknowledging the equal worth of participants by giving them input into how research is conducted. Finally, it is often essential to determining what is truly of benefit to people or what risks are considered to be disproportionate.

Nevertheless, as Dresser notes, researchers sometimes fear that scientific values and study designs may be jeopardized by community members (e.g., when they seek to control the dissemination of results) or that community members sometimes lack the authority to represent diverse communities (e.g., community leaders may have extreme views or conflicts of interest).

Moreover, advocacy often arises because one is passionately committed to a particular good that is not receiving sufficient attention from the public. Advocacy is often a form of reaction, and it aims at a paradigm shift, a new way of looking at things, a new order of priorities. This is not always the best way to achieve a balanced solution to challenging situations. Here it is perhaps helpful to recall the words of a speech that Viktor Frankl delivered to the Fifth International Congress for Psychotherapy in 1961:

> As long as we do not have access to absolute truth, we must be content that our relative truths correct one another, and that we find the courage to be biased. In the many-voiced orchestra of psychotherapy we not only have the right, but the duty to be biased as long as we are conscious of it. (Frankl, 2000, p. 126)

---

10. While the term "community" can refer to a generic segment of society, in this book I generally use it to refer to the subpopulation of people who share traits with the participants in a study—not primarily geographical traits, but traits related to the study's inclusion criteria. Hence, the relevant "community members" for mental health studies are people with mental health disorders.

We might say something analogous about activism and the tensions that can arise between community members and researchers—just as long as we bear in mind that in referring to bias Frankl was not referring to a failure to recognize the value of other people or perspectives, but simply our need to see and articulate things from a definite perspective. In one of his books on metapsychology, Frankl notes that the Latin term *perspectum* means "seen through." Seeing the world through a given lens, or from a given perspective, entails that our knowledge is always limited, like the man who knows an elephant only from holding its trunk. But while it is true that all human knowledge is gained from a subjective perspective, the only thing that is subjective is the perspective through which we approach reality: "this subjectivity does not in the least detract from the objectiveness of reality itself" (Frankl, 1988, p. 59). By humanizing ethical principles, we suggest a specific reality that provides a point of reference, namely, human nature. However, given that human nature is embodied in manifold ways—in people of different sexes, ages, races, and cultures, with different experiences, values, and abilities—any application of ethical principles must take into account these different realities.

Further EMHR Resources

- See www.emhr.net for links to mental health, substance abuse, and public health codes of ethics and regulatory guidance materials

REFERENCES

Annas, G. J., & Grodin, M. A. (Eds.). (1992). *The Nazi doctors and the Nuremberg Code: Human rights in human experimentation.* New York: Oxford University Press.

Aristotle. (1941). Metaphysics. In R. McKeon (Ed.), *The basic works of Aristotle.* New York: Random House.

Aristotle. (1980). *The Nicomachean ethics* (D. Ross, Trans.). Oxford: Oxford University Press.

Beauchamp, T. L. (1993). The principles approach. *Hastings Center Report, 23*(6, Suppl.), S9.

Beauchamp, T. L., & Childress, J. F. (2001). *Principles of biomedical ethics* (5th ed.). New York: Oxford University Press.

Campbell, J. (1997). Reforming the IRB process: Towards new guidelines for quality and accountability in protecting human subjects. In A. Shamoo (Ed.), *Ethics in neurobiological research with human subjects* (pp. 299–304). Amsterdam: Gordon and Breach.

Centers for Disease Control and Prevention, Department of Health and Human Services, National Institutes of Health, Food and Drug Administration, Human Resources and Services Administration, Substance Abuse and Mental Health Services Administration, et al. (1998). *Building community partnerships in research: Recommendations and strategies.* Washington, DC: DHHS.

Department of Health and Human Services. (2001). Code of federal regulations. Protection of human subjects. Title 45 public welfare, part 46. Washington, DC: Government Printing Office.

Donagan, A. (1977). *The theory of morality.* Chicago: University of Chicago Press.

Dresser, R. (2001). *When science offers salvation: Patient advocacy and research ethics.* New York: Oxford University Press.

Finnis, J. (1993). *Natural law and natural rights*. Oxford: Oxford University Press.

Geach, P. T. (1977). *The virtues*. Cambridge, England: Cambridge University Press.

Gert, B., Culver, C. M., & Clouser, K. D. (1997). *Bioethics: A return to fundamentals*. New York: Oxford University Press.

Gold, L. J., Darley, J. M., Hilton, J. L., & Zanna, M. P. (1984). Children's perceptions of procedural justice. *Child Development, 55*, 1752–1759.

Greenberg, J. (1987). A taxonomy of organizational justice theories. *Academy of Management Journal, 12*(1), 9–22.

Hall, L. L., & Flynn, L. (1999). Consumer and family concerns about research involving human subjects. In H. A. Pincus, J. A. Lieberman, & S. Ferris (Eds.), *Ethics in psychiatric research* (pp. 219–235). Washington, DC: American Psychiatric Association.

Jonsen, A. R. (1998a). *The birth of bioethics*. New York: Oxford University Press.

Jonsen, A. R. (1998b). *The birth of the Belmont Report*. Retrieved January 11, 2007, from www.georgetown.edu/research/nrcbl/nbac/transcripts.

Kant, I. (1785/1993). *Grounding for the metaphysics of morals* (J. W. Ellington, Trans. 2nd ed.). Indianapolis: Hackett.

Katz, J. (1972). *Experimentation with human beings*. New York: Russell Sage Foundation.

Korsgaard, M. A., Schweiger, D. M., & Sapienza, H. J. (1995). Building commitment, attachment, and trust in strategic decision-making teams: The role of procedural justice. *Academy of Management Journal, 38*(1), 60–84.

Leone, C., & Graziano, W. G. (1992). Moral character: A social learning perspective. In R. T. Knowles & G. F. McClean (Eds.), *Psychological foundation of moral education and character development: An integrated theory of moral development* (pp. 141–168). Washington, DC: Council for Research in Values and Philosophy.

Levine, R. J. (1988). *Ethics and regulation of clinical research* (2nd ed.). New Haven, CT: Yale University Press.

Lickona, T. (1991). *Educating for character: How our schools can teach respect and responsibility*. New York: Bantam Books.

Lind, E. A., & Tyler, T. R. (1988). *The social psychology of procedural justice*. New York: Plenum Press.

Mill, J. S. (1861/1979). *Utilitarianism*. Indianapolis: Hackett.

Monshi, B., & Zieglmayer, V. (2004). The problem of privacy in trans-cultural research: Reflections on an ethnographic study in Sri Lanka. *Ethics & Behavior, 14*(3).

Narvaez, D. (2001). *Nurturing character in the middle school classroom: Introduction to the project and framework*. Minneapolis: Community Voices and Character Education Partnership Project.

National Commission. (1979). *The Belmont report: Ethical principles and guidelines for the protection of human subjects of research*. Washington, DC: Department of Health, Education, and Welfare.

Newton, L. H. (1990). Ethical imperialism and informed consent. *IRB: A Review of Human Subjects Research, 12*(3), 10–11.

Ochocka, J., Janzen, R., & Nelson, G. (2002). Sharing power and knowledge: Professional and mental health consumer/survivor researchers working together in a participatory action research project. *Psychiatric Rehabilitation Journal, 25*(4), 379–387.

O'Fallon, L. R., Tyson, F. L., & Dearry, A. E. (2000). *Successful models of community-based participatory research: Final report*. Retrieved January 11, 2007, from http://www.niehs.nih.gov/translat/cbr-final.pdf.

Pellegrino, E. D. (1995). Toward a virtue-based normative ethics for the health professions. *Kennedy Institute of Ethics Journal, 5*(3), 253–277.

Porter, J. P. (1996). Informed consent issues in international research concerns. *Cambridge Quarterly of Healthcare Ethics, 5*(2), 237–243.

Rothman, D. J., & Rothman, S. M. (1984). *The Willowbrook wars*. New York: Harper & Row.

Singer, P. (1993). *Practical ethics*. New York: Cambridge University Press.

Tschentscher, A. (1997). The function of procedural justice in theories of justice. In K. F. Röhl & S. Machura (Eds.), *Procedural justice* (pp. 105–120). Brookfield, VT: Ashgate.

Tyler, T. R. (1988). What is procedural justice? Criteria used by citizens to assess the fairness of legal procedures. *Law and Society Review, 22*(1), 103–135.

Tyler, T. R., & Rasinski, K. (1991). Procedural justice, institutional legitimacy, and the acceptance of unpopular U.S. Supreme Court decisions: A reply to Gibson. *Law and Society Review, 25*(3), 621–630.

Waide, J. (1988). Virtues and principles. *Philosophy and Phenomenological Research, 48*, 455–472.

3

Solving Ethical Problems

Analyzing Ethics Cases and Justifying Decisions

Decentration is a shift from judgment [based on] attention to the most salient or interesting aspects of a situation to judgment based on a more extensive, equally distributed, and "balanced" attention to a real or imagined situation. Decentration processes naturally lead to certain outcomes: the reduction of self-centered judgment or egocentrism and the emergence of equality and reciprocity prescriptions in the physical and social realms.
—J. C. Gibbs, K. S. Basinger, and D. Fuller, *Moral Maturity: Measuring the Development of Sociomoral Reflection*

Professional ethics is an applied field. It is not primarily about theory and rote knowledge, but about shaping our character and fostering good ethical decisions using appropriate processes. This chapter attempts to provide a bridge from ethical theory to ethical praxis. In what follows, we will examine how people can go about making good ethical decisions when faced with difficult choices in the conduct of research.

ETHICAL DECISIONS AND ETHICAL PROBLEMS

When does a decision become an ethical decision, as opposed to a purely technical decision (e.g., what statistic to use) or an exercise of personal preference (e.g., what clothing to wear when conducting research)? Decisions fall into the realm of ethics when they pertain to things within our control that will either show respect or fail to show respect to human beings.

Understood in this manner, ethical decisions and actions are performed constantly. When we do the right thing without a second thought, we are no less in the domain of ethics than when we are unsure what is the right thing to do or unsure whether we will do it. Moreover, ethics is not neatly separated from the spheres of technical decisions or exercises of personal preferences. For example, if reporting a specific statistic could reveal the identity of some participants or could mislead readers of published clinical data, then the choice of a statistic is both a technical and an ethical choice. Similarly, if a researcher's decision to wear a suit and tie while surveying intravenous drug users who are living on the streets will instill in them a sense of mistrust or discomfort, then it could be viewed as both an expression of personal preference and an ethical decision. In both cases, we see that proper regard for key aspects of human beings requires that a reasonable decision be made.

The ethical character of decisions and actions is sometimes lost on us because we often do the right thing—or at least an ethically acceptable thing—without problems, and we tend to equate ethical decisions with the resolution of ethical problems. While the sphere of ethics is in fact much broader, ethical problems are rightly seen as invitations to further reflection.

Ethical problems come in at least three flavors: volitional, cognitive, and social. As noted already, we often know the right thing to do. The only dilemma that then exists is *volitional*: will I actually *do* what is right? Such dilemmas can be tough when individuals have competing interests or powerful motives for doing other than what is right. This is why the matter of conflicts of interest has attracted so much attention in recent years (B. A. Brody et al., 2003).

When is an ethical decision *cognitively* problematic? It is problematic when we experience *uncertainty* about what is the right thing to do. We might find ourselves in a situation where no matter what we do someone will be harmed, or we might recognize that we cannot help an individual while respecting that individual's free choice.

Finally, there are times when we feel certain what the right thing to do is (considered in itself), and we are willing to do it, but the decision is *socially* problematic because there is *disagreement* among stakeholders (that is, among people who have something at stake in the decision).

In this chapter, we will examine various sources of cognitive uncertainty and social disagreement. We will treat cognitive and social problems side-by-side because in the field of research ethics, decisions typically have both cognitive and social components, and the same factors often contribute to both sources of decision-making difficulty.

CASE STUDIES AS EXERCISES IN ETHICAL DECISION MAKING

While case studies are put to many different uses in ethics,[1] this book will use cases to foster ethical decision-making skills. Accordingly, the cases used in this book are either real or realistic ethical stories of research projects that conclude by asking readers to make an ethical decision. Each of the remaining chapters concludes with the analysis of a case study.

The hepatitis studies at the Willowbrook state school for children with mental retardation, which was discussed in chapter 1, will be used throughout this chapter to illustrate the process of analyzing an ethical situation and justifying a decision. The case is summarized as follows:

Willowbrook Revisited

Hepatitis studies were conducted at the Willowbrook State School for children with mental retardation from 1956 to 1971. Hepatitis was a major problem at

---

1. See the online article "Facilitating Ethics Case Discussions" published in the Case Compendium section of www.emhr.net for a discussion of four different ways that ethics cases are commonly used in professional education and the corresponding aims of each. Throughout this book, the primary use of cases will be to foster ethical decision-making skills.

Willowbrook. Given the unsanitary conditions that the children lived in, it was virtually inevitable that the children would contract hepatitis. This further added to stigmatization of the children, a good number of whom became carriers (and later were reintegrated into public schools). Dr. Saul Krugman, the principal investigator, proposed research that appeared promising in distinguishing between strains of hepatitis and in developing a vaccine. However, his study design involved feeding children local strains of live hepatitis—that is, deliberately infecting them.

Krugman argued that the development of a vaccine would outweigh the anticipated minor harms to these children. He also argued that they were bound to be exposed to the same strains under the natural conditions; they would be admitted to a special well-staffed unit where they would be isolated from exposure to other infectious diseases; they were likely to have only a subclinical infection followed by immunity to the particular hepatitis virus; and only children with parents who gave informed consent would be included.

However, critics of the study thought the parental permission letter downplayed the fact that the children would be intentionally infected with hepatitis. Moreover, due to crowding and long wait lists for admission to the school, at times the only available rooms for children were on the experimental wing, thus influencing the decision of some parents who did not have the resources to care for their children.

Although we will consider the actual course of events, the key question we will ask—albeit with the advantage of hindsight—is whether as IRB members we should approve such a study if it were proposed today under similar conditions.

THE "SO FAR NO OBJECTIONS" (SFNO) APPROACH TO CASE ANALYSIS

Any analytic framework is a conceptual construct, one possible way of comprehending a complex yet unified reality. Thus, many frameworks will be possible, and any framework should be judged in terms of its usefulness in addressing a complex reality. Some frameworks are specific to a profession and the population it serves (Jonsen, Siegler, & Winslade, 2002; Perlin, 1992; Ross, 1986); others are more generic (Jennings, Kahn, Mastroianni, & Parker, 2003; Thomasma, Marshall, & Kondratowicz, 1995). Some of these frameworks are simple, others complex. Simple frameworks may be easy to use but less helpful than highly detailed frameworks. Highly detailed frameworks may be cumbersome, overly pedantic, and force one to waste time addressing issues that are of peripheral importance.

The SFNO approach presented here is a simple *common denominator* approach: it identifies four components that all cases share.[2] While other case analysis frameworks often contain more elements, typically these extra elements:

2. While the SFNO framework was developed independently, it resembles other frameworks that take a common denominator approach, such as Thomasma et al. (1995) and Jennings et al. (2003).

(a) fall within one of the four components (e.g., Jonsen, Siegler and Winslade's [2002] popular medical-ethical framework inquires into specific facts such as the patient's quality of life or medical indications); (b) constitute tips on addressing one of the four elements (e.g., Haddad and Kapp [1991] recommend speaking with others, including one's supervisor); or (c) they venture into criteria for justifying a decision (e.g., H. Brody's [1981] framework moves from analysis to application of the golden rule as options are weighed).

The SFNO approach involves a *root cause analysis* insofar as it examines the three major sources of uncertainty or disagreements regarding decisions:

1. Different people are involved who have competing interests (e.g., a participant may seek therapeutic benefits in research, whereas a researcher may seek new knowledge)
2. Uncertainty or disagreement exists about relevant facts (e.g., about the probabilities and magnitude of harms resulting from an intervention)
3. Uncertainty, conflict, or disagreement exists regarding ethical norms (e.g., a beneficial action will violate the principle of autonomy)[3]

Using the first letter of each element, the following framework can be remembered as the "*So Far No Objections*" framework—an apt name given that it merely lays out elements of an ethical situation but does not yet venture a solution. It simply involves enumerating the following four items:

1. *Stakeholders*: *Who has a stake in the decision being made, that is, who will be significantly affected by the decision made?* In the Willowbrook studies, stakeholders included the children who were subjects (their health was at stake), their families (because they were interested in the well-being of the children and securing their placement in the school), the researchers (they were interested in new knowledge and curing hepatitis), the institution (they bore some level of liability and had a duty to foster the well-being of the children), and society (public health could be protected through the development of a vaccine for hepatitis).

Tip: As illustrated here, in the process of identifying stakeholders, it is always good to state briefly why people are stakeholders or how they are affected.

2. *Facts*: *What factual issues might generate disagreement? What facts are relevant to a solution?* In the case of the Willowbrook studies, factual disagreements surrounded the likelihood that the research would result in a new vaccine, the magnitude of harms the children would experience, and the quality of parental permission. Facts relevant to solving the case include that the children were vulnerable—unable to give consent or understand the risks involved; that efforts were made to minimize possible harms to participants through monitoring and sanitary conditions; that hepatitis was widespread

---

3. As noted above, capturing the complex reality of a moral situation in a framework is always somewhat artificial. The distinction between these three sources of uncertainty is often gray; and interrelationships between them are important to notice. Identifying stakeholders inevitably means identifying those who will be affected by the action in a variety of ways and thus identifying competing interests and values. Likewise, *morally relevant* facts are seen as value-laden or related to the respect we accord to persons, for example, the fact that a law exists requiring informed consent, the fact that a population has been exploited in the past, or the fact that a group of potential participants cannot grant consent.

within the school and under current conditions most children were likely to become infected; and that most cases of infection resulted in no symptoms or only mild symptoms.

Tip: In examining facts, it can be helpful to consult experts and scientific literature. The Web site, www.emhr.net, contains bibliographies for each of the major areas of mental health research ethics and links to guidance documents that often include facts relevant to decision making.

3. *Norms: What ethical principals, norms, or values are at stake? Which do you think are relevant, and which might appear to conflict or generate disagreement?* In the Willowbrook studies, most intermediate ethical principles are relevant: beneficence insofar as the ultimate aim of the study was to enhance public health through vaccine development; nonmaleficence because the study involved infecting children with the hepatitis virus; justice because institutionalized and vulnerable populations often bore the burdens of research without enjoying the benefits; and autonomy because the children could not give consent and their parents' permission may have been unduly influenced. Clearly, some of these principles—for example, beneficence and nonmaleficence—are in conflict. Moreover, the interpretation of what these principles imply is controversial; for example, does nonmaleficence prohibit intentionally infecting someone or merely require extraordinarily good reasons for doing so and a minimization of harms?

Tip: www.emhr.net provides online access to research ethics codes (such as the Belmont Report), specific professional ethics codes, and regulations, all of which inform researchers of norms that society finds relevant to the conduct of research.[4]

4. *Options: What actions or policies deserve serious consideration? If the ethical ideal is not possible, what compromise solutions are most attractive?* Options in the Willowbrook study included conducting it as implemented; seeking alternative populations; changing the parental permission procedures; using smaller experimental populations; and improving sanitation for all children prior to recruitment.

Tip: Options frequently emerge through brainstorming activities with others. Consulting with IRB members, funding agencies, participant communities, and other researchers can be invaluable. Searching the literature for similar projects is often a good starting point in this creative process.

By analyzing the Willowbrook study, we see that ethical decisions can be very complex. While some ethical problems hinge on just one element (say a factual disagreement), others involve disagreements about stakeholders, facts, norms, and a perceived lack of ethically attractive alternatives.

JUSTIFYING ETHICAL DECISIONS

Case analysis breaks down an ethical problem into basic components in order to ensure that no key aspects are ignored. This analytic task is analogous to laying

---

4. Should regulations and other laws be treated as norms or facts? I typically treat the fact that a law exists and its specific content and penalties as facts. However, I list a prima facie duty "to obey the law" as an ethical norm. Once one recognizes this norm, all legitimate laws take on at least a prima facie moral force.

out all of the pieces of a puzzle, right side up, with the four corner pieces in place, before trying to solve it. But once we have identified the sources of uncertainty or disagreement and identified options, we need to decide upon a course of action. How do we know which course of action is ethically best, all things considered? Are there criteria for ethically justifying a decision?

How we ought to justify decisions depends upon the source of the disagreement. The following reflections provide guidelines on resolving different kinds of disagreements. No set of guidelines will provide a magic algorithm for generating one right answer. Prudence is always needed to take into account the specific details of a case. Moreover, answers can only be generated from a specific perspective. This specific perspective involves a view of human nature (e.g., of what it means to flourish as a human being), of one's profession (e.g., of whether the people one serves are best understood as free-market consumers of products or as people to whom special fiduciary obligations exist), and of the hierarchy of values (e.g., of whether protecting health is more important than respecting autonomy or vice versa). Nevertheless, guidelines can provide time-tested means of *ruling out bad decisions* even while leaving room for disagreements across worldviews. (For example, no decision is good if it is known at the outset that it will trample on other values even while failing to achieve the good it is intended to achieve.) Moreover, a framework can structure public deliberations and ensure that important considerations are not ignored. Again, we will continue with discussion of the Willowbrook studies in illustrating a process of justifying decisions.

Disagreements Involving Competing Stakeholders

When disagreements revolve around the fact that different people have competing interests, we have to ask two questions:

1. Do reasons exist for giving priority to the interests of one party over another? For example, in the research context, the safety of individual participants is generally put above the interest society has in gaining new knowledge.
2. Who is invested with decision-making authority? For example, the legal and ethical doctrine of informed consent gives participants the right to make the decision whether or not to participate in research. Institutional Review Boards have decision-making authority to prevent or stop a research study that appears overly risky. And researchers have the authority to determine whether potential participants meet inclusion criteria.

Dilemmas arise when each party has legitimate claims to competing goods or when decision-making authority is unclear in a specific realm. Resolving such dilemmas will typically involve examining laws (statutes, regulations, and cases) and professional codes for guidance; considering whether mediation would be helpful; and asking whether some parties should recuse themselves.

Simply becoming aware of the various stakeholders in a given situation may raise awareness of competing but legitimate goods that should be considered. Perhaps above all, it reminds one of the need for ethical processes such as community consultation and IRB review, processes that frequently force one to clarify goals and to compromise so as to balance competing interests.

As we have seen, the Willowbrook study involved several key stakeholder groups: the children, their parents, the researchers, and society. But as a matter of historical fact, various stakeholders did not generate much disagreement. The authority of parents to decide whether their children should participate in the hepatitis studies was uncontested. The fact that the interests of parents—for example, in placing a mentally retarded child who needs tremendous time and energy from caregivers—did not always coincide with the interests of the children was not considered. Here we see that IRB review using publicly developed guidelines might have introduced a "disinterested" third party that could assess whether or not the study was safe enough (or at least that the risks really were similar to those encountered in daily living at Willowbrook) to justify even approaching parents for permission.

Disagreements Involving Facts

The term "facts" is being used in a very broad sense here to include mundane facts (e.g., the dose of an investigational drug), as well as probabilities (e.g., of benefits or harms resulting from participation), and controversial worldview beliefs (e.g., that society will only be improved by regularly subjecting humans to harms in research).

Disagreements over mundane facts are perhaps the easiest to resolve, as long as people are committed to empirical methods and data exist.

Disagreements over probabilities are far more difficult. The reason that research is proposed is precisely because we do not have complete knowledge of the topics under investigation prior to conducting a study. Moreover, the significance of a probability (which may be very low) increases as the magnitude of a benefit or harm increases, and this is often a determination that depends on individual values (e.g., how highly one values privacy). Committees that review research should have members with expertise in the areas of research they review and should consult scientific literature as necessary.

Disagreements over worldview beliefs are often the most difficult to resolve. Again, this points to the need to have ethical processes in place to ensure that such differences are aired and solutions are negotiated.

The Willowbrook studies definitely involved significant disagreements over facts. Saul Krugman, the principal investigator, firmly believed that the probability of harms for the children in his study were lower than the probability of harms for children outside of the study because the unsanitary living conditions at Willowbrook meant that nearly all children would become infected with hepatitis, and those in the study were at least monitored and in a sanitary environment. More controversially, he believed that his research would eventually lead to a vaccine that would directly benefit the population to which the participants belonged and society at large. While he was in fact right, most clinical research never yields such major breakthroughs—so detractors were not without factual arguments of their own. Moreover, other methods for providing more sanitary living conditions (and thereby reducing the risk of contracting hepatitis and other diseases) clearly existed.

Disagreements Involving Clashing Ethical Norms and Values

The last observation—namely, that there were other ways to benefit the children at Willowbrook—allows us to recognize an important point as we turn to disagreements that revolve around values. A decision cannot be justified without first clarifying what are our goals. Clearly, as a medical researcher rather than a personal physician, Dr. Krugman's primary goal was not care of the children, but rather gaining new knowledge that would serve science and the public's health through the development of vaccines. This led him to seek to justify decisions that others—for example, child advocates—did not seek to justify.[5]

In stating that we first have to know what our goals are, we are not embracing a crude utilitarian philosophy of "the end justifies the means." Such a philosophy sanctions ignoring other values and ethical norms in the pursuit of worthy goals. Yet there are at least two kinds of ethical norms, and neither should be ignored even when they conflict with worthy goals.

Moral absolutes constitute the first kind of norm. Examples of such norms are "it is wrong to coerce sexual relations" or "it is wrong to kill a human for personal gain." Some people deny that there are any moral norms that apply everywhere, at all times, under all conditions. Nevertheless, professional codes and laws often treat certain behaviors as prohibited under all conditions. Thus, when a worthy goal conflicts with a moral absolute, the absolute trumps the goal. In the Willowbrook study, some have argued that the infections were not in fact part of a "natural experiment"; rather, they were knowingly caused by the researchers (Rothman, 1982). If "thou shall never knowingly infect another with a disease" were a moral absolute, then our deliberations might end here.[6]

Prima facie norms are the second kind of moral norm we encounter. These are norms that express commitment to a value that deserves respect and should always be taken into account. Ordinarily, prima facie norms should be followed. An example might be "protect the confidentiality of data" or "obtain informed consent." The values that underlie these norms are important and always deserve regard. However, sometimes a breach of confidentiality is appropriate (e.g., to prevent a suicide due to depression) and sometimes informed consent should be waived (e.g., in directly beneficial research with young children—here parental permission might suffice). One might argue that the prohibition against knowingly infecting someone is similarly prima facie; for we knowingly infect people whenever we use a live virus in a vaccine. That being the case, we need to explore whether a decision to conduct research that involves knowingly infecting participants with hepatitis can ever be ethically justified. Similarly, we need to explore whether conducting research with mentally retarded children who cannot grant consent could be justified.

5. In chapter 10, "Identifying and Managing Conflicts of Interest," we will consider conflicting roles such as the roles of physician and investigator and the conflicting obligations that these may generate.
6. Whether we are ever obliged by one moral absolute to violate another is debated; but most traditional ethicists who accept the existence of moral absolutes say "no" because (a) there are extremely few moral absolutes and (b) they are all negative (e.g., prohibitions on actions, not positive duties) (Finnis, 1980). However, were the law or a professional code to treat certain positive duties as moral absolutes (e.g., save a life when possible), it would inevitably set up irresolvable moral dilemmas.

In an article, "Public Health Ethics: Mapping the Terrain" (Childress et al., 2002), a group of ethicists, scientists, and policymakers presents a framework for justifying ethical decisions that is attractive for two reasons: first, there is precedence for using each of its conditions in the long history of applied ethics (e.g., in natural law and casuistry); and second, observation of applied ethics committees (such as IRBs) and policy groups reveals that these are intuitive criteria that are commonly used by people as they debate moral issues (albeit sometimes tacitly and frequently unsystematically). What follows is a framework largely based on the one presented in Childress et al. (2002).

When a proposed action conflicts with certain legitimate values or prima facie norms, it may nevertheless be justified if it meets the following criteria:

1. Necessity: *Is it necessary to infringe on the values or norms under consideration in order to achieve the intended goal?* Or would an alternative action achieve the same good aim without infringing on those or other equally weighty values? For example, in the Willowbrook study, one might argue that more research could have been conducted with animals or that adult volunteers could have served as participants. However, Dr. Krugman countered that research with animals could not replace research with humans. Moreover, adult volunteers were likely to become more seriously ill than children; and it was far from inevitable that they would become infected. Thus, adults would clearly be taking on a risk of harm that was well outside those encountered in daily living.

2. Effectiveness: *Will the action be effective in achieving the desired goal?* This question forces us into the realm of prediction, which can range from near certitude (e.g., that something won't work based on past models) to tremendous uncertainty. Krugman argued that his design was rigorous enough to yield knowledge of the different strains of hepatitis and to contribute to the development of a vaccine. Based on the successes in vaccine development witnessed in the 1960s, many were highly optimistic that his goals would be met.

3. Proportionality: *Is the desired goal important enough to justify overriding another principle or value?* Clearly, if the only outcome of the Willowbrook study were to generate data needed for a dissertation, the risks would not be justified. However, given that the risks were lower than might initially be imagined (vis-à-vis normal living conditions at Willowbrook) and that the potential benefits would be tremendous (and in fact were), it is easy to see why some believed the Willowbrook studies passed this test. However, we will revisit this criterion below.

4. Least infringement: *Is the policy or action designed to minimize the infringement of the principle or value that conflicts with it?* As we saw, Dr. Krugman made efforts to address the absence of informed consent and to minimize the risks to his participants. He sought parental permission (though critics noted that there were flaws in the process); he only exposed children to strains of hepatitis that were present in Willowbrook; and he provided monitoring and a sanitary environment. Additionally, nature provided that children typically experience far fewer symptoms than adults.

5. Proper process. *Has the decision been made using proper processes?*[7] Sometimes this involves nothing more than being transparent, that is, not covering

---

7. This last criterion is a development of the "transparency" criterion presented in Childress et al. (2002).

up decisions so as to allow public scrutiny. Sometimes it involves submitting a study to IRB review or obtaining community input. Most frequently, proper process in research minimally involves obtaining informed consent from participants. In the case of the Willowbrook study, it is reasonable to assume that the review processes used were less structured than those that would be used today given that research regulations were nearly nonexistent, IRBs were not widely used or mandated, and community consultation was not common. However, Krugman's studies were reviewed by the Armed Forces Epidemiological Board, which approved and funded the research (Advisory Committee on Human Radiation Experiment, 1995).

This analysis illustrates several things. First, it illustrates that the Willowbrook studies were ethically far more complex than suggested by the cursory presentation they typically receive in ethics texts that use it as a landmark case of research misbehavior (Shamoo & Khin-Maung-Gyi, 2002). This is often the case when researchers are motivated by noble aims and not merely personal gain. Nevertheless, these noble aims do not cause ethical issues to disappear. Second, it shows that clear criteria can be used to explain why such studies are or are not acceptable. Third, it shows that even with clear criteria, disagreement is possible. People will disagree about whether alternatives or options are really viable; whether success should really be expected; whether the anticipated benefits are proportionate to the risks; whether harms have been minimized as far as possible; and whether the processes used to arrive at the decision were adequate.

Perhaps the most common source of disagreement is over the proportionality test. Our analysis of the Willowbrook studies illustrates why this is the case. The proportionality test reintroduces the issue of stakeholders: can anticipated benefits to society be measured against harms to participants? (In the Willowbrook studies, the participants themselves were not expected to benefit from vaccines.) Moreover, comparing values is often like comparing apples and oranges; the value of liberty and the value of health are quite different and cannot be added or subtracted from each other to come up with a value sum. Finally, determining the significance of specific risks and anticipated benefits requires us to consider both their probability and expected magnitude, thus thrusting us into the realm of speculation (National Commission, 1979). Dr. Krugman did not know his research would be successful in contributing to the development of a vaccine; he simply had good reasons to believe it.

Despite the ethical plausibility of the Willowbrook studies, it is highly unlikely that any IRB would permit such research to be conducted today. The reasons concern primarily proportionality and process. Given a history of exploitation of vulnerable populations and the ongoing risk that history could repeat itself, our current regulations require that additional protections be afforded to vulnerable populations (Department of Health and Human Services, 2001) (see section 111[b] and Subparts B-D). The participants in the Willowbrook studies were triply vulnerable: they were children, with mental retardation, living in an institution. Part of what it currently means to offer enhanced protections is that IRB members and researchers are not ordinarily allowed to consider benefits to society in an attempt to justify exposing vulnerable participants to greater than minimal risks. Such research could only be justified if the Willowbrook participants were expected to receive direct, significant benefits. The only benefits that were directly offered to participants involved basic care that should have been a standard part of care at the school (e.g., basic hygiene).

Moreover, the permission of parents was unduly influenced by a variety of factors that interfered with the proper process that was meant to replace the informed consent of subjects. In order to enable truly voluntary permission, parents should not have been asked to enroll children in the study until after they were admitted to the school, and basic benefits such as adequate hygiene should not have been held hostage to participation.

BEYOND ETHICAL UNCERTAINTY

The process of analyzing cases and justifying decisions is clearly a highly reflective exercise undertaken in response to cognitive uncertainty or social disagreement. The frameworks that were illustrated can be helpful in navigating these waters. There is some evidence that the social process of debating and analyzing cases can also have a positive effect on ethical sensitivity, moral reasoning, and even professionalism (Bebeau, 1995; Rest & Narvaez, 1994; Rest, Narvaez, Bebeau, & Thoma, 1999). This is consistent with evidence that the process of adult learning is correlated with the readiness to challenge assumptions and a growing tolerance for ambiguity (Brookfield, 1998).

However, studies of moral exemplars—of people who were selected because they were identified by others as highly moral, self-sacrificing people—indicate that they frequently act out of a sense of moral certainty and view their actions as fulfilling; that is, they do not experience a lot of cognitive or volitional dissonance (Colby & Damon, 1994). How can we reconcile these two competing images of the moral life?

Perhaps an analogy is helpful. Frankl (1997) discusses a psychological case in which a violinist became obsessive about consciously analyzing the most trivial detail of technique, which eventually led to a complete artistic breakdown. Frankl acknowledged that consciously analyzing technique has its place, especially in addressing problems. However, the ultimate goal of musical education is to allow the artist to use his or her technique spontaneously, creatively, and unreflectively. Something similar could be said of ethics education. Its ultimate aim should be the development of moral character that enables persons to do what is right habitually, creatively, and with a sense of integration.

Further EMHR Resources

• Additional decision-making cases on each of the applied topics covered in this book are published in the Online Case Compendium at www.emhr.net. They are published without commentaries to foster group discussions of the cases.

REFERENCES

Advisory Committee on Human Radiation Experiment. (1995). *Final report*. Retrieved January 11, 2007, from http://www.gwu.edu/~nsarchiv/radiation/.

Bebeau, M. J. (1995). *Moral reasoning in scientific research: Cases for teaching and assessment*. Bloomington, IN: Indiana University. Retrieved January 11, 2007, from http://poynter.indiana.edu/mr/mr.pdf.

Brody, B. A., Anderson, C., McCrary, S. V., McCullough, L., Morgan, R., & Wray, N. (2003). Expanding disclosure of conflicts of interest: The views of stakeholders. *IRB: Ethics & Human Research, 25*(1), 1–8.

Brody, H. (1981). *Ethical decisions in medicine* (2nd ed.). Boston: Little, Brown.

Brookfield, S. (1998). Understanding and facilitating moral learning in adults. *Journal of Moral Education, 27*(3), 283–300.

Childress, J. F., Faden, R. R., Gaare, R. D., Gostin, L. O., Kahn, J., Bonnie, R. J., et al. (2002). Public health ethics: Mapping the terrain. *Journal of Law, Medicine and Ethics, 30*(2), 170–178.

Colby, A., & Damon, W. (1994). *Some do care: Contemporary lives of moral commitment*. New York: Free Press.

Department of Health and Human Services. (2001). Code of federal regulations. Protection of human subjects. Title 45 public welfare, part 46. Washington, DC: Government Printing Office.

Finnis, J. (1980). *Natural law and natural rights*. Oxford, England: Clarendon Press.

Frankl, V. E. (1997). *Man's search for ultimate meaning*. New York: Insight Books.

Gibbs, J. C., Basinger, K. S., & Fuller, D. (1992). *Moral maturity: Measuring the development of sociomoral reflection*. Hillsdale, NJ: Lawrence Erlbaum Associates.

Haddad, A. M., & Kapp, M. B. (1991). *Ethical and legal issues in home health care: Case studies and analyses*. Norwalk, CT: Appleton & Lange.

Jennings, B., Kahn, J., Mastroianni, A., & Parker, L. S. (2003). *Ethics and public health: Model curriculum*. Retrieved January 11, 2007, from http://www.asph.org/document. cfm?page = 782.

Jonsen, A. R., Siegler, M., & Winslade, W. J. (2002). *Clinical ethics: A practical approach to ethical decisions in clinical medicine* (5th ed.). New York: McGraw Hill.

National Commission. (1979). *The Belmont report: Ethical principles and guidelines for the protection of human subjects of research*. Washington, DC: Department of Health, Education, and Welfare.

Perlin, T. M. (1992). *Clinical medical ethics: Cases in practice* (1st ed.). Boston: Little, Brown.

Rest, J. R., & Narvaez, D. (Eds.). (1994). *Moral development in the professions: Psychology and applied ethics*. Hillsdale, NJ: Lawrence Erlbaum Associates.

Rest, J. R., Narvaez, D., Bebeau, M. J., & Thoma, S. J. (1999). *Postconventional moral thinking : A neo-Kohlbergian approach*. Mahwah, NJ: Lawrence Erlbaum Associates.

Ross, J. W. (1986). A process for resolving bioethical dilemmas. In J. W. Ross (Ed.), *Handbook for hospital ethics committees* (pp. 25–27). Chicago: American Hospital Association.

Rothman, D. J. (1982). Were Tuskegee and Willowbrook "studies in nature"? *Hastings Center Report, 12*(2), 5–7.

Shamoo, A. E., & Khin-Maung-Gyi, F. A. (2002). *Ethics of the use of human subjects in research*. New York: Garland Science.

4

Informed Consent

It would be interesting to discover the effect upon clinic attendance were the terminology of "bad blood" replaced by a term which would identify this disease with the bad disease which the patients know under a variety of local names. The large Negro attendance is due in part to the fact that in the minds of these people there is nothing to suggest that syphilis is not entirely respectable.
>   —Dr. Harris, cited in James Jones, *Bad Blood: The Tuskegee Syphilis Experiment*

Philosophers have found it remarkable—even "magical"—that we have the ability, merely by intoning the proper words under the right circumstances, to alter the systems of obligations and permissions that envelope us.
>   —K. Kipnis, "Vulnerability in Research Subjects: A Bioethical Taxonomy"

Consider the following scenarios:

> Dr. Wilmont makes an incision in Mr. Navarro and removes one of his kidneys. His kidney will be transplanted into a complete stranger who would die without it.
> Robert takes a yellow pill that looks just like the antidepressant medication he took for the past two years, but in fact it has no active ingredients.
> Shortly after seeing a film together, Jack engages in sexual intercourse with Barbara in the back of his camper van.

Given the lack of details provided in these scenarios, we have no idea whether the actions described are good or evil. Mr. Navarro might be an altruistic living organ donor; Robert might have consented to participate in a placebo-controlled trial of a promising new drug; and Jack and Barbara could be amorous newlyweds. However, one variable could change everything: permission. Without giving their explicit or implicit permission, Mr. Navarro is the victim of organ theft, Robert is the victim of medical or pharmaceutical fraud, and Barbara is the victim of rape.

THE ETHICAL JUSTIFICATION FOR INFORMED CONSENT

As the above examples illustrate, consent or permission has the power to radically transform our ethical evaluation of actions. Failure to obtain adequate informed consent is a hallmark of all classic cases of human subjects abuse, including Nazi research, the Tuskegee syphilis study, secret US radiation experiments, and many questionable cases of mental health research (Keay, 1997).

The very first principle of the Nuremberg Code, which was developed within the trial of Nazi doctors, asserts that "The voluntary consent of the human subject is absolutely essential" (*The Nuremberg Code*, 1948). If taken at face value, the Nuremberg Code would automatically exclude the participation of many people in research. We could never involve people who lack decision-making capacity—for example, small children or people suffering from debilitating delusions. Below, in the section "Deviating from Standard Informed Consent," we will examine whether the duty to obtain informed consent is absolute or allows for exceptions. However, even if the Nuremberg Code's rule is not strictly followed in all contexts, the duty to obtain informed consent is now so widely acknowledged that no major professional code of ethics that addresses research fails to mention it.

In the Belmont Report, we find that informed consent is justified under the principle of respect for persons. This means primarily that "individuals should be treated as autonomous agents" (B1), which implies that "subjects, to the degree that they are capable, be given the opportunity to choose what shall or shall not happen to them" (National Commission, 1979, C.1).

Within a humanized framework of principles, obtaining informed consent is indeed one way of respecting the rational and self-determining dimension of human beings. But it is also a key way of respecting the fact that human beings are in need of a wide variety of goods and are vulnerable to a similar variety of harms. That is, the doctrine of informed consent assumes that, as a general rule, "each person is best able to determine which choices maximally advance his or her own welfare" (Grisso & Appelbaum, 1998, p. 12).

In the past, this assumption was not widely shared among researchers or physicians. It was assumed that the researcher or physician knew what was best (Faden & Beauchamp, 1986). However, professionals tend to be focused on just one aspect of another person's well-being. For example, a physician may be focused primarily on the patient's health (or, in the case of specialists, the proper functioning of just one part of the patient); and researchers may be more concerned with gaining new knowledge than with any aspect of the participant's integrated well-being. In contrast, the participant may be in the best position to know and evaluate the many ways a study might affect him or her. In the case of children or of individuals in cultures that place a high premium on family relationships, it may not be the individual participant alone who plays this role of safeguarding interests; nevertheless, it is questionable whether the researcher is ever competent to play this role.

Although our legal and dominant ethical traditions now emphasize autonomy over paternalism (Faden & Beauchamp, 1986), some reviews of informed consent research call into question whether patients really want to make their own health care decisions.[1] Several large studies found that patients want to be informed, but not with the purpose of exercising autonomy; they would prefer that their

---

1. Although research on the consent process in therapeutic and research settings has been conducted for several decades, the literature remains sparse, and findings are often inconsistent. In part, this is due to

physicians make medical decisions with their best interests in mind (Schneider, 1998; Stanley & Guido, 1996).

Other studies have found that many patients do not even want to be informed (Schneider, 1998). This seems particularly true of people who are so ill or debilitated that they lack the energy or desire to process information. Others believe that negative information—information about risks and burdens—may interfere with positive thinking (Jonsen, Siegler, & Winslade, 2002). Even apart from such unusual circumstances, several studies have found that most potential research participants make decisions whether to participate in a study prior to the informed consent process, that is, prior to any systematic disclosure of risks and benefits (Stanley & Guido, 1996; Weiss Roberts, Warner, Anderson, Smithpeter, & Rogers, 2004).

Patients should have the right to defer to the therapeutic judgment of a health care provider. The patient-provider relationship is a fiduciary relationship, and it is assumed that the provider will put the patient's best interests first (Pellegrino & Thomasma, 1988). Thus, in therapy, informed consent should not be forced upon a patient; if a competent patient chooses to let others make health care decisions, providers should honor and document this wish (Jonsen et al., 2002). However, in the research setting, the assumptions that guide this practice do not hold true. The researcher cannot tailor treatment to the best interests of a participant; the researcher may even be blind to the treatment a patient receives. Therefore, someone must take responsibility for providing informed consent in research, whether the patient or a legally recognized surrogate.

WHAT COUNTS AS INFORMED CONSENT?

Informed consent is one of the most heavily regulated aspects of the research enterprise. The Belmont Report provides three general requirements of informed consent: presenting all information that a "reasonable volunteer" would consider relevant to deciding whether or not to participate in a study; presenting this information in a way that is understandable and ascertaining that the potential participant has comprehended the information; and providing conditions for consent that are free of coercion or undue influence (National Commission, 1979, C.1).[2]

Box 4.1 presents the specific kinds of information that federal regulations require investigators to present during the informed consent process.

Federal regulations further stipulate that additional information should be provided to participants if applicable (e.g., that unforeseen risks might exist for a fetus). The Common Rule also requires that consent be documented in writing, except in extraordinary circumstances.

---

the difficulty of obtaining data. Consent process research requires "piggybacking" on other studies. Yet, investigators may not be comfortable being studied themselves; participants may be reluctant to participate in two studies rather than one; and timing the consent research activities with the primary study may be difficult (Agre, Rapkin, Dougherty, & Wilson, 2002). Inconsistencies in findings may be due to variations in participants' age, subculture, educational level, and degree of illness (Schneider, 1998).
2. Chapter 5 examines the issue of decision-making capacity and chapter 7 examines voluntariness and coercion in the context of participant recruitment. This chapter therefore focuses on providing participants with adequate information and other matters that are basic to the informed consent process.

Box 4.1 Information Investigators Must Present During the Informed
Consent Process

1. A statement that the study involves research, an explanation
   of the purposes of the research and the expected duration of
   the subject's participation, a description of the procedures to
   be followed, and identification of any procedures which are
   experimental.
2. A description of any reasonably foreseeable risks or discomforts
   to the subject.
3. A description of any benefits to the subject or to others which
   may reasonably be expected from the research.
4. A disclosure of appropriate alternative procedures or courses of
   treatment, if any, that might be advantageous to the subject.
5. A statement describing the extent, if any, to which confidentiality of records identifying the subject will be maintained.
6. For research involving more than minimal risk, an explanation as to whether any compensation and an explanation as to
   whether any medical treatments are available if injury occurs
   and, if so, what they consist of, or where further information
   may be obtained.
7. An explanation of whom to contact for answers to pertinent questions about the research and research subjects' rights, and whom
   to contact in the event of a research-related injury to the subject.
8. A statement that participation is voluntary, refusal to participate
   will involve no penalty or loss of benefits to which the subject is
   otherwise entitled, and the subject may discontinue participation
   at any time without penalty or loss of benefits to which the subject is otherwise entitled.

Reprinted from U.S. Department of Health and Human Services, regulation 45CFR46.116.a

These requirements illustrate the fact that the federal research regulations were
written with a special focus on so-called biomedical research with patients. For example, in the vast majority of cases of behavioral and social science (BSS) research,
treatment options and injury compensation guidelines are moot. However, research
that falls into one or more exempt category—as does much BSS research—need
not follow the regulatory requirements regarding informed consent. Information
and consent may still be appropriate, but the specific form that permission takes
should be negotiated with local IRBs using ethical rather than regulatory criteria.
    For several reasons, informed consent is best understood as an ongoing pro-
cess, not as a one-time performance or as a signature on a piece of paper. As a
study progresses, new information may become available that might influence
a person's willingness to remain in a study; an individual may lose the ability
to grant consent; an individual's values or wishes may change; and individuals

always reserve the right to withdraw from a study. Ordinarily, consent to continue in a study is implied by an individual's ongoing participation, but under special conditions—for instance, when important new information becomes available regarding treatment options or study risks—formally "re-consenting" participants may be necessary (Wendler & Rackoff, 2002).

As Sieber (1992) notes, informed consent is an interpersonal process that includes both verbal and nonverbal forms of communication. Mannerisms, eye contact, listening skills, and time spent with a potential participant may communicate whether or not the researcher cares for the individual's well-being and seeks to enable a voluntary informed choice.

THREE LEVELS OF PERMISSION

Permission to participate in research may take many different forms depending on levels of risk, the cognitive or maturational capacities of potential participants, the feasibility of contacting potential participants, and the resources of researchers. This section examines different "levels" of permission that may be granted. The next section examines different parties that may grant permission.

Identification

"Identification" is the highest form of permission for including someone in a research project. Hans Jonas used this term to describe the ideal form of participation, one in which the participant identifies with or completely shares the goals of the researcher. Insofar as the research goal is also the participant's goal, the participant is protected from being "reified" or treated like a mere thing that is experimented upon.

> The ruling principle in our consideration is that the "wrong" of reification can only be made "right" by such authentic identification with the cause that it is the subject's as well as the researcher's cause—whereby his role in its service is not just permitted by him, but *willed*. That sovereign will of his which embraces the end as his own restores his personhood to the otherwise depersonalizing context. To be valid it must be autonomous and informed. (Jonas, 1969, p. 19)

In this passage, we see a very early articulation of the ideal of participatory research, if not in terms of shared tasks (participants as co-investigators) at least in terms of shared goals. Jonas's strong insistence on not treating participants as things is consistent with a humanized approach to the Belmont principles, which seeks to remind researchers at every turn that participants are human beings like themselves.

Explicit Agreement

Explicit agreement implies that an individual understands what participation involves, has considered risks and benefits, and freely agrees to participate. It does not imply that the participant identifies with the goals of research, and it may mean that the participant is more vulnerable to being viewed as a thing rather than a human participant in a project. While Jonas's principle of identification presents an ideal, it also sets a very high bar. It is unattainable by those who are not capable of granting consent for themselves, as well as by those who are willing to participate simply out of generosity or because they seek to gain something from the study that is different from the goals of the research per se.

When risks are reasonable and participants are informed and freely consent, then explicit agreement to participate is adequate. It respects participants as self-determining and capable of guarding their interests. It also satisfies the basic requirements of the Belmont Report and the Common Rule.

Non-Objection

The weakest form of permission is non-objection. This requires only that participants or surrogates are informed and do not object to "participation." For example, a university might inform students that their assessment data might be used for research purposes unless they request that their data be withheld (DuBois, 2002). This form of permission is commonly called "passive consent" (Hoagwood, Jensen, & Fisher, 1996). It is not recognized by research regulations as an adequate form of informed consent. It should not be used as a substitute for informed consent in nonexempt research, nor should it be used merely for administrative ease (Ross, Sundberg, & Flint, 1999).

However, passive consent may be consistent with regulatory requirements when IRBs exempt a study or grant investigators a waiver of informed consent. It may also be ethically appropriate when data are gathered for reasons other than research (e.g., quality improvement) or when risks and burdens are minimal (e.g., observation of behavior in a classroom). While passive consent clearly does not meet the full requirements of informed consent, it does provide a level of transparency through the information process and diminishes risks of coercion by providing an opportunity to opt out.

Researchers and reviewers should determine which level of permission is appropriate on a case-by-case basis by considering questions such as: What level of risk does this study present? Are participants adequately informed? Do they have sufficient opportunity to decline participation? Is the study subject to regulatory guidelines for informed consent, and has it gained IRB approval? Is input needed from community members to clarify the most appropriate form of permission?

THREE LEVELS OF AUTHORITY

Just as we may speak of three levels of permission, we may also speak of three levels of authority to grant permission.

Permission for Oneself

Why is slavery wrong, and why is it socially unacceptable to speak of owning a thing or even an animal but not of owning another person? Some classical and personalist thinkers suggest it is because persons belong to themselves (Crosby, 1996). Human self-belonging is related to the fact that human beings, in contrast to nonpersonal animals or things, are capable of self-determination. The strongest form of permission-granting authority—granting permission for oneself—reflects these two dimensions of self-belonging and self-determination.

As a matter of terminology, while some ethicists and regulations speak of surrogate consent or community consent, others insist that only an individual can grant consent; others may grant permission.

Surrogate Permission

Surrogate permission is permission for a specific other. Typically, surrogates are selected because they know the wishes of the other, or when this is not possible, know the other person and seek to promote his or her best interests. In order to grant permission for another, an individual needs to be recognized as having the authority to do so. Sources of surrogate authority and models for exercising this authority are discussed in the next chapter.

Community Permission

The Public Health Code of Ethics states, "public health institutions should provide communities with the information they have that is needed for decisions on policies or programs and *should obtain the community's consent* for their implementation" (Public Health Leadership Society, 2002, principle 6; emphasis added). While the code speaks of the consent of communities, the idea is problematic. In the strict sense, a community is not a person and is not capable of actions such as giving permission. This makes it difficult to ascertain when permission has been granted in an acceptable manner. Gostin (1991) argues that in population-based research "*consent* is the wrong concept because each of the traditional elements is missing. . . . A better conception is to say that leaders ought to be consulted to obtain a *community consensus*" (p. 194). While some forms of community permission reflect input from members other than leaders, it always involves granting permission for individuals other than oneself for whom one does not have legal guardianship or power of attorney.

Community permission is the weakest level of authority and should not be a substitute for individual informed consent whenever it is feasible. Different community members will have different interests, different levels of trust, different levels of willingness to take risks, and may recognize different people as leaders. Accordingly, those who grant permission on behalf of a community enjoy a limited authority to speak for others. What holds true of leaders also holds true of subgroups of communities who participate in "town hall" or other public meetings. Community permission is much less like giving permission for oneself and much more like granting permission for many others, some of whom may not even be known to community leaders.

Nevertheless, seeking some form of community permission or consensus is important when research will significantly affect a group beyond the immediate participants or when participation will involve groups in a way that prohibits individual consent. It is a way of showing respect and can add an extra layer of protection insofar as people are given information they need to make decisions (Weijer, 1999). Especially when participants are vulnerable, this process can add transparency and enhance trust (Sieber, 1992). (Vulnerability in research is discussed in chapter 6, "Thinking about Harms and Benefits.")

DEVIATING FROM STANDARD INFORMED CONSENT

As already noted, some forms of participation in research do not require formal informed consent, for example, participation in a mail survey. In other instances, the informed consent process may be modified significantly. The following explores some of the more common modifications of informed consent. The regulatory foundation for most modifications of informed consent is contained in the Common Rule's guidelines for modifying or waiving informed consent. See box 4.2 below.

Box 4.2   Regulatory Guidelines for Waiving or Modifying Informed Consent

"An IRB may approve a consent procedure which does not include, or which alters, some or all of the elements of informed consent set forth in this section, or waive the requirements to obtain informed consent provided the IRB finds and documents that:

(1) The research involves no more than minimal risk to the subjects;
(2) The waiver or alteration will not adversely affect the rights and welfare of the subjects;
(3) The research could not practicably be carried out without the waiver or alteration; and
(4) Whenever appropriate, the subjects will be provided with additional pertinent information after participation." (U.S. Department of Health and Human Services, regulation 45CFR46.116d; hereafter cited only by regulation number)

"Except as provided in paragraph (c) of this section, informed consent shall be documented by the use of a written consent form approved by the IRB and signed by the subject or the subject's legally authorized representative. A copy shall be given to the person signing the form." (46.117a)

(c) An IRB may waive the requirement for the investigator to obtain a signed consent form for some or all subjects if it finds either:

(1) That the only record linking the subject and the research would be the consent document and the principal risk would be potential harm resulting from a breach of confidentiality. Each subject will be asked whether the subject wants documentation linking the subject with the research, and the subject's wishes will govern; or
(2) That the research presents no more than minimal risk of harm to subjects and involves no procedures for which written consent is normally required outside of the research context.

In cases in which the documentation requirement is waived, the IRB may require the investigator to provide subjects with a written statement regarding the research." (45CFR46.117.c)

Waiving Signatures

The most common modification of informed consent involves waiving the requirement that the process be documented in writing with a signed consent form. (Box 4.2 presents regulatory requirements for such a waiver.) Researchers may seek a waiver for a variety of reasons. A signed consent form may be the only written record linking a participant to a study and thus present the primary threat to confidentiality (Citro, Ilgen, & Marrett, 2003; Sieber, 2001); participants—for cultural and personal reasons—may be mistrustful of contracts and reluctant to sign forms (Brod & Feinbloom, 1990; Wendler & Rackoff, 2001); and despite being informed that they may discontinue participation at any time, participants may view a signature as binding them to completing a study (Appelbaum, Lidz, & Meisel, 1987).

While the regulations clearly accommodate these concerns in cases of minimal risk research, they are less accommodating of participants' preferences in greater than minimal risk research. Some authors have suggested that this policy actually protects the interest institutions and investigators have in managing legal risk more than participants' interests and have presented alternate forms of documenting consent, for example, by including witnesses to oral consent (Brod & Feinbloom, 1990; Wendler & Rackoff, 2001).

Implied and Passive Consent

Passive consent was discussed above as a form of "non-objection" to participation. It requires that researchers inform individuals and provide an opportunity to opt out of participation or inclusion. It does not require participants to do anything; hence it is called passive.

In contrast, implied consent requires participants to do something that makes reasonable the assumption that they know what participation involves and do not object to participation. For example, a researcher may reasonably assume this when a participant completes a survey and returns it by mail. In other cases, however, the assumption may be questionable. Can we assume that people at a political rally are at least relatively informed and do not object to being observed when a researcher sits and takes notes (Capron, 1982)? Does the performance of any activity in a public space imply consent to being observed by others—even when the behavior may normally be considered private?

Like passive consent, implied consent is not recognized by the regulations as a valid form of providing informed consent, but it may be permitted by IRBs when research qualifies as exempt or qualifies for a waiver of consent. Typically, meeting criteria for these regulatory requirements also involves meeting many of the ethical criteria for the use of implied consent—for example, that risks be minimal.

Deception

While the use of deception is relatively rare in clinical research, it was used in roughly 50% of all studies conducted in social psychology in the 1970s and 1980s (Korn, 1997; Sieber, Iannuzzo, & Rodriguez, 1995). Not surprisingly, many social scientists have strongly defended the use of deception. For example, Humphreys (1975), Milgram (1964), and Douglas (1979) have argued that privacy and autonomy rights must be limited by our need for other goods and that some important knowledge cannot be gained without the use of deceptive or covert techniques. Moreover, some surveys have found that most participants support the use of deceptive methods in research when important knowledge can be gained (Lustig, Coverdale, Bayer, & Chiang, 1993; Milgram, 1974).

The term "deception" has been used to describe deficiencies in the process of informing participants of radically different magnitude, including: outright lying or misinforming, as in the Tuskegee syphilis study; creating illusions, for instance, using so-called confederates to fake behaviors; refraining from disclosing all the information normally disclosed during consent; and disclosing to participants that some aspects of a study will not be disclosed until after the study is complete (Korn, 1997; Sieber, 1982).

Elms (1982) observes that our use of the term "deception" is "so sweeping that it includes Satan's lures for lost souls, the traitor's treachery, the false lover's violation of a pure heart. How could any deception ever be considered ethically justifiable if it keeps such company?" (p. 232). Some researchers clearly share this sentiment. Both principled and utilitarian arguments have been offered against the use of deception: deception may be disrespectful and potentially harmful to subjects, but it may also undermine trust in researchers, encourage insincere forms of participation, and eventually harm science rather than foster its interest (Baumrind, 1964; Sieber, 1982; Warwick, 1982).

Nevertheless, professional ethics codes and regulations have typically adopted a middle course, granting discretion to researchers and IRBs to determine whether the use of deceptive methods is justified in specific cases with special protections in place. For example, the American Psychological Association's (APA) code of ethics states:

(a) Psychologists do not conduct a study involving deception unless they have determined that the use of deceptive techniques is justified by the study's significant prospective scientific, educational, or applied value and that effective nondeceptive alternative procedures are not feasible.

(b) Psychologists do not deceive prospective participants about research that is reasonably expected to cause physical pain or severe emotional distress.

(c) Psychologists explain any deception that is an integral feature of the design and conduct of an experiment to participants as early as is feasible, preferably at the conclusion of their participation, but no later than at the conclusion of the data collection, and permit participants to withdraw their data. (See also Standard 8.08, Debriefing.) (American Psychological Association, 2002, 8.07)

As the code states, the use of deceptive methods is justified—if at all—only after alternative designs have been explored. Sieber (1992) presents alternative designs that may yield trustworthy data in the place of deception designs.

Several authors suggest that obtaining some form of permission for deception—either from participants themselves or community members—may be appropriate particularly when research involves members of vulnerable communities (Pittenger, 2002; Soble, 1978). While this is not always feasible, Elms (1982) argues that simply publishing the results of studies that use deception allows for a level of transparency and oversight that sets researchers apart from (other) "con artists."

As noted above, the APA code generally encourages debriefing participants after deception has been used, but the APA code, U.S. regulations, and many ethicists allow the use of discretion when debriefing is expected to be more harmful than beneficial (Hoagwood et al., 1996; Sieber, 1992).

IS INFORMED CONSENT A FARCE?

Brody (2001) observes that attitudes toward consent vary tremendously:

> At one extreme, some see obtaining informed consent as the realization of one of the most fundamental intrinsic moral values realizable in the research or clinical setting. At the other extreme, some see the whole process as a sham designed primarily for risk management purposes. (p. 1)

While the next chapter explores participant deficits that may affect their ability to grant informed consent, this section explores threats to informed consent that arise with so-called normal populations of participants and then suggests strategies for improving the process.

Shortcomings of the Process

Flaws in the informed consent process are among the most common concerns that IRBs have with researchers and that the Office of Human Research Protections has with IRBs (Borror, Carome, McNeilly, & Weil, 2003).[3] A recent study found that researchers who attempted to simulate an informed consent process for their own studies typically fell far short of regulatory standards (Titus & Keane, 1996). Other studies have demonstrated that some researchers view the informed consent process as an intrusion into their professional relationship with patients, while some fear that informed consent may bias or alter results (Stanley & Guido, 1996)—although evidence of actual consent related bias is mixed (Sigmon et al., 1997; Stanley & Guido, 1996).

However, even when researchers follow standard consent procedures, participants frequently retain little information about study design and risk after granting informed consent (Benson, Roth, Appelbaum, Lidz, & Winslade, 1988; Silva & Sorrell, 1988).

Why do participants comprehend or retain little information about studies they agree to enroll in? While a simple answer does not exist, several variables appear to be at work.

---

3. Also see the monthly journal *Human Research Report*, which reports violations of federal regulations investigated by the Office of Human Research Protections. Violations of informed consent procedures are commonly featured.

At least in medical research, part of the answer may lay in Schneider's thesis that many patients prefer to trust their physicians and some prefer even to remain relatively uninformed about risks and benefits (Schneider, 1998). As argued above, while this may be acceptable within a therapeutic context, it is more problematic in a research setting. Yet some participants suffer from the so-called therapeutic misconception, that is, the misconception that a clinical research study has the primary purpose of providing participants with therapy or medical treatment (Appelbaum, Roth, Lidz, Benson, & Winslade, 1987). When this occurs, trust in a physician may replace interest in study-related information, which in turn diminishes understanding and retention of information. For example, Cassileth and colleagues found that those who lacked a strong opinion about the need for informed consent recalled significantly less information than those who thought informed consent was important (Cassileth, Zupkis, Sutton-Smith, & March, 1980). That many participants find the informed consent process irrelevant is suggested by a recent qualitative study of 28 patients with schizophrenia who enrolled in a trial. Twenty-two of the 28 participants made their decision before reviewing the consent form (Weiss Roberts et al., 2004). Other studies have found similar results (Stanley & Guido, 1996).

How researchers present information also has a direct impact upon participant comprehension. In one of the first published studies of informed consent, Epstein and Lasagna gave consent forms of varying length to participants and found that comprehension was inversely related to the lengths of the form (cited in Stanley & Guido, 1996). Young, Hooker, and Freeberg (1990) found that lowering the reading level of informed consent documents led to significantly improved participant comprehension: 77% of participants who received a low reading level consent form correctly understood the purpose of the study compared to 44% of those who received a high reading level consent form. Nevertheless, multiple studies have found that informed consent forms are consistently written at an unacceptably high level. For example, Ogloff and Otto (1991) found that across all fields, the mean readability scores of consent forms was at the sixteenth-grade level (4 years of postsecondary education). Lawson and Adamson (1995) found that while most participants understood some terms and phrases commonly found in consent forms, such as "efficacy," "ineligibility," and "adverse event," only 13% understood the term "open-label" and less than 5% understood the term "protocol."

Finally, while some studies have found that disclosing detailed risks does not discourage patients from choosing a treatment option (Faden & Beauchamp, 1980), this may be because participants "block" such information. Several studies have found that participants tend to have poor recall of threatening information, and recall of risks is typically worse than recall of other elements of an informed consent form (Silva & Sorrell, 1988).

Improving the Process

In an article on informed consent in mental health research, Keay (1997) repeatedly speaks of "better approximating informed consent"—a phrase that reminds us that informed consent is an ideal that we strive for, although no participant is ever completely informed or completely free of external influences.

Although the informed consent process will always fall short of the ideal, there are ways of significantly improving it. Drawing from their review of empirical studies conducted on informed consent, Silva and Sorrell (1988) suggest several strategies. The following summarizes their recommendations as well as those derived from several more recent studies:

1. Solicit input from participants on the amount of information they desire. Participants tend to recall information best when they perceive it to be neither "too much" nor "too little" (Cassileth et al., 1980).

2. Present information as simply as possible. As noted above, recall is frequently better with concise forms that use modest reading levels. An eighth-grade reading level is commonly cited as ideal (S. J. Philipson, Doyle, Gabram, Nightingale, & Philipson, 1995). Philipson et al. (1999) describe an intervention that successfully assisted researchers in writing consent forms that were significantly more readable.

3. Present any anxiety-inducing information (e.g., about risks and complications) in a nonthreatening manner. While researchers should not "down play" risks, presenting risks in a threatening manner may decrease comprehension and retention of risks.

4. Have a nonclinician investigator present information or follow up on the informed consent process. While Silva and Sorrell advocate for this based on limited empirical evidence, intuitively the therapeutic misconception is likely to be reduced by having a nonclinician obtain informed consent.

5. Provide participants with information (e.g., the consent form) well in advance of requesting a signature to provide adequate time to study and reflect upon information.

6. Explore the use of alternative presentation formats (e.g., video or computer formats). However, this recommendation deserves further research. A large study failed to find significant improvements in tests of participants' knowledge by using video and computer presentation of information versus traditional consent forms. Careful analysis of findings suggested an "all-or-nothing" effect with computer and video methods, that is, participants tended to learn information either extremely well or extremely poorly (Agre & Rapkin, 2003).

7. Actively involve participants in processing information. Several studies have found that "quizzing" participants on consent information can lead to significantly improved recall (Carpenter et al., 2000; Stanley & Guido, 1996; Stiles, Poythress, Hall, Falkenbach, & Williams, 2001; Wirshing, Wirshing, Marder, Liberman, & Mintz, 1998).

While some of these recommendations rest on a fairly solid base of empirical data, the development of best practices will require replication of studies and the use of more sophisticated designs.

Case Study: Withholding Information on Study Purpose

Dr. Jones is a counseling psychologist who has received funding to develop and test an intervention to prevent child abuse among pregnant women in outpatient drug treatment programs. Many current and recovering substance-abusing women are at risk for abusing their children due to difficult life circumstances and a lack of personal and financial resources to cope with the demands of a young child.

Prior research has identified economic and psychosocial factors associated with child maltreatment, including personal childhood experiences of maltreatment, poor mental and physical health, lack of social support, limited education, and limited knowledge of infant development. Yet little research has been done to test intervention programs with mothers who abuse substances to determine whether child abuse rates can be decreased. Dr. Jones plans to use the Parenting Stress Index and a test of knowledge of child development to identify mothers who are at risk of abusing their children. Those who are at risk would then be randomized to receive the experimental intervention, which includes counseling, a brief educational program on child development, and regular social work visits, or to receive social work visits alone. To maximize benefits to all participants, after six months control group participants would receive the full experimental treatment, which is expected to be superior to social work visits alone. The study's dependent variables are (1) predictors of risk (i.e., scores on the Parenting Stress Index and knowledge of child development) and (2) signs of child abuse and neglect. The social work visits would have two purposes: (1) to provide additional resources tailored to the participants' needs, and (2) to look for signs of child abuse and neglect in the home.

Dr. Jones mentions in her proposal to the IRB that participants will be told that the study is a parenting services program but their data might be used in a quality assurance study. She does not want to inform them of the real purpose of the study because she believes some might decline to participate out of fear that their children could be taken away and because labeling them as "at risk of abusing their children" is stigmatizing. She argues that the risks of nondisclosure are far outweighed by the potential benefits to children. She is also adamant that she will protect the confidentiality of the data to protect the women from any potential legal or social harm.[4]

As an IRB member, would you vote to approve the study?

CASE COMMENTARY

The design of the proposed study makes a fair amount of sense from a scientific perspective. As a prospective, randomized controlled study, it has the potential to demonstrate whether or not certain interventions reduce the likelihood of child abuse. Moreover, the proposed study has significant value insofar as it could yield knowledge that will reduce incidence rates of child abuse. Finally, by withholding information on the study's purpose, the investigator will likely get a higher participation rate. Genuine informed consent might produce a skewed population comprised of women who believe themselves highly unlikely ever to abuse their child. Nevertheless, this study presents several ethical problems.

4. This case was coauthored with Emily Anderson.

The potential harms of this study are significant. Women could lose custody of current children that they might have or of their newborns if the study finds that they are negligent or abusive. Moreover, as Dr. Jones herself notes, the study labels women as at risk of abusing their children. Neither of these risks can be ameliorated simply through a promise of confidentiality. Even the use of a Certificate of Confidentiality would be inadequate in this case, because a legal obligation exists to report to authorities suspected abuse of children, an obligation that is in keeping with ethical duties to provide heightened protections to people who are vulnerable and less able to protect themselves.[5] One might argue that this risk is proportionate to the good that might come out of the study. But this overlooks the fact that when we allow participants to undertake greater than minimal risks, we do so on condition that they provide their informed consent.

Therefore, the biggest ethical problem this case presents is the fact that information about the purpose of the study is withheld. As noted above, while it is sometimes permissible to withhold information about a study, research regulations require that at least four conditions be met:

1. The research must involve no more than minimal risk to the subjects
2. The waiver or alteration of the informed consent process must not adversely affect the rights and welfare of the subjects
3. The research could not practicably be carried out without the waiver or alteration, and
4. Whenever appropriate, subjects should be provided with additional pertinent information after participation (45CFR46.116.d)

In this case, the risks are greater than minimal; the rights and welfare of participants could be adversely affected; and debriefing participants on the study's real purpose would almost certainly undermine trust and possibly cause shame and anxiety. As a psychologist, Dr. Jones would have done well to examine the American Psychological Association's Code of Ethics, which reinforces a number of the regulatory requirements (APA Code, 8.07). Finally, because deception may undermine trust in researchers, ethicists and policy makers have generally discouraged its use with vulnerable populations or populations that are likely already to be mistrustful of researchers (Citro et al., 2003).

This case additionally presents a significant problem of timing. Dr. Jones should have approached her IRB prior to obtaining funding, and her funding source should have required this. She now has to convince the funding agency that an alternative design will meet the agency's funding goals or else forfeit the grant.

Is Dr. Jones's study design the only effective way to obtain the data that she seeks? Not necessarily. First, she might consider working with a different population. With the permission of state authorities, she might be able to test the effectiveness of her interventions with a population of women who have a record of abuse but have had custody returned to them. That is, her data might be gathered as part of a genuine public services program, and the purpose could be fully disclosed. (Presumably, this would not pose any new risks to the participants,

---

5. The case study in chapter 9 explores confidentiality and the duty to report in greater detail.

because they would already be monitored with visits from state social workers.) Alternately, she might work with her proposed population but disclose to the women the true purpose of her study. In order to obtain an acceptable rate of participation, she would likely need to obtain input from the women (e.g., through a focus group) on the kinds of protections they would seek. For example, while they might not welcome a social worker into their homes, they might agree to participate in the intervention and assessment if they were assured that low assessment scores would not be viewed as reportable signs of abuse or negligence. They might even agree to complete questionnaires about abusive behavior if the data were both gathered and stored anonymously. Although the reliability of this method might be questioned, Dr. Jones's original design was also imperfect. It was likely to include "observer effects," that is, participants might be expected to change their behavior while observed by a social worker.

In any case, Dr. Jones's proposed study would fail the necessity, proportionality, least infringement, and ethical process tests presented in chapter 3 and an alternative design should be explored.

Further EMHR Resources

- Unit three of the *Dialogues* DVD contains an interview with Gerald Koocher and excerpts of a focus group with mental health consumers on informed consent
- www.emhr.net contains a bibliography and additional case studies on informed consent

REFERENCES

Agre, P., Rapkin, B., Dougherty, J., & Wilson, R. (2002). Barriers encountered conducting informed consent research. *IRB: Ethics & Human Research, 24*(4), 1–5.

Agre, P., & Rapkin, B. (2003). Improving informed consent: A comparison of four consent tools. *IRB: Ethics & Human Research, 25*(6), 1–7.

American Psychological Association. (2002). Ethical principles of psychologists and code of conduct. Retrieved June 2, 2004, from http://www.apa.org/ethics/code2002.pdf

Appelbaum, P. S., Lidz, C. W., & Meisel, A. (1987). *Informed consent: Legal theory and clinical practice.* New York: Oxford University Press.

Appelbaum, P. S., Roth, L. H., Lidz, C. W., Benson, P., & Winslade, W. J. (1987). False hopes and best data: Consent to research and the therapeutic misconception. *Hastings Center Report, 17,* 20–24.

Baumrind, D. (1964). Some thoughts on ethics of research: After reading Milgram's "behavioral study of obedience." *American Psychologist, 19,* 421–423.

Benson, P. R., Roth, L. H., Appelbaum, P. S., Lidz, C. W., & Winslade, W. J. (1988). Information disclosure, subject understanding, and informed consent in psychiatric research. *Law and Human Behavior, 12*(4), 455–475.

Borror, K., Carome, M., McNeilly, P., & Weil, C. (2003). A review of OHRP compliance oversight letters. *IRB: Ethics & Human Research, 25*(5), 1–4.

Brod, M. S., & Feinbloom, R. I. (1990). Feasibility and efficacy of verbal consents. *Research on Aging, 12*(3), 364–372.

Brody, B. A. (2001). Making informed consent meaningful. *IRB: Ethics & Human Research, 23*(5), 1–5.

Capron, A. M. (1982). Is consent always necessary in social science research? In T. L. Beauchamp, R. R. Faden, R. J. J. Wallace, & L. Walters (Eds.), *Ethical issues in social science research* (pp. 215–231). Baltimore: Johns Hopkins University Press.

Carpenter, W. T., Jr., Gold, J. M., Lahti, A. C., Queern, C. A., Conley, R. R., Bartko, J. J., et al. (2000). Decisional capacity for informed consent in schizophrenia research. *Archives General Psychiatry, 57*(6), 533–538.

Cassileth, B. R., Zupkis, R. B., Sutton-Smith, K., & March, V. (1980). Informed consent: Why are its goals imperfectly realized? *New England Journal of Medicine, 302,* 896–900.

Citro, C. F., Ilgen, D. R., & Marrett, C. B. (2003). *Protecting participants and facilitating social and behavioral sciences research.* Washington, DC: National Academies Press.

Crosby, J. F. (1996). *The selfhood of the human person.* Washington, DC: Catholic University of America Press.

Douglas, J. D. (1979). Living morality versus bureaucratic fiat. In C. B. Klockars & F. W. O'Connor (Eds.), *SAGE annual reviews of studies in deviance: Vol. 3. Deviance and decency* (pp. 13–34). Beverly Hills, CA: SAGE Publications.

DuBois, J. M. (2002). When is informed consent appropriate in educational research? *IRB: Ethics & Human Research, 24*(1), 1–8.

Elms, A. C. (1982). Keeping deception honest: Justifying conditions for social scientific research strategems. In T. L. Beauchamp, R. R. Faden, R. J. J. Wallace, & L. Walters (Eds.), *Ethical issues in social science research* (pp. 232–245). Baltimore: Johns Hopkins University Press.

Faden, R. R., & Beauchamp, T. L. (1980). Decision-making and informed consent: A study of the impact of disclosed information. *Social Indicators Research, 7,* 13–36.

Faden, R. R., & Beauchamp, T. L. (1986). *A history and theory of informed consent.* New York: Oxford University Press.

Gostin, L. O. (1991). Ethical principles for the conduct of human subject research: Population-based research and ethics. *Law, Medicine & Health Care, 19,* 191–201.

Grisso, T., & Appelbaum, P. S. (1998). *Assessing competence to consent to treatment: A guide for physicians and other health professionals.* New York: Oxford University Press.

Hoagwood, K., Jensen, P. S., & Fisher, C. B. (1996). *Ethical issues in mental health research with children and adolescents.* Mahwah, N.J.: Lawrence Erlbaum Associates.

Humphreys, L. (1975). *Tearoom trade: Impersonal sex in public places* (Enlarged ed.). New York: Aldine de Gruyter.

Jonas, H. (1969). Philosophical reflections on experimenting with human subjects. In P. A. Freund (Ed.), *Experimentation with human subjects* (pp. 1–31). New York: George Braziller.

Jones, J. H. (1993). *Bad blood: The Tuskegee syphilis experiment* (2nd revised ed.). New York: Free Press.

Jonsen, A. R., Siegler, M., & Winslade, W. J. (2002). *Clinical ethics: A practical approach to ethical decisions in clinical medicine* (5th ed.). New York: McGraw Hill.

Keay, T. J. (1997). Approximating ethical research consent. In A. E. Shamoo (Ed.), *Ethics in neurobiological research with human subjects: The Baltimore conference on ethics* (pp. 149–154). Amsterdam: Gordon and Breach.

Kipnis, K. (2001). Vulnerability in research subjects: A bioethical taxonomy. In National Bioethics Advisory Commission (Ed.), *Ethical and policy issues in research involving human participants: Vol. 2. Commissioned papers and staff analysis* (pp. G1-G13). Bethesda, MD: National Bioethics Advisory Commission.

Korn, J. H. (1997). *Illusions of reality: A history of deception in social psychology.* Albany: State University of New York Press.

Lawson, S. L., & Adamson, H. M. (1995). Informed consent readability: Subject understanding of 15 common consent form phrases. *IRB: A Review of Human Subjects
Research, 17*(5–6), 16–19.

Lustig, B. A., Coverdale, J., Bayer, T., & Chiang, E. (1993). Attitudes toward the use of deception in psychologically induced pain. *IRB: A Review of Human Subjects Research,
15*(6), 6–8.

Milgram, S. (1964). Issues in the study of obedience: A reply to Baumrind. *American Psychologist, 19*, 848–852.

Milgram, S. (1974). *Obedience to authority: An experimental view.* New York: Harper &
Row.

National Commission. (1979). *The Belmont report: Ethical principles and guidelines for
the protection of human subjects of research.* Washington, DC: Department of Health,
Education, and Welfare.

The Nuremberg Code. (1948). Retrieved January 11, 2007, from http://www.emhr.net/
ethics.htm.

Ogloff, J. R. P., & Otto, R. K. (1991). Are research participants truly informed? Readability
of informed consent forms used in research. *Ethics & Behavior, 1*(4), 239–252.

Pellegrino, E. D., & Thomasma, D.C. (1988). *For the patient's good. The restoration of
beneficence in health care.* New York: Oxford University Press.

Philipson, S. J., Doyle, M. A., Gabram, S. G. A., Nightingale, C., & Philipson, E. H. (1995).
Informed consent for research: A study to evaluate readability and processability to
effect change. *Journal of Investigative Medicine, 43*(5), 459–467.

Philipson, S. J., Doyle, M. A., Nightingale, C., Bow, L., Mather, J., & Philipson, E., H.
(1999). Effectiveness of a writing improvement intervention program on the readability of the research informed consent document. *Journal of Investigative Medicine,
47*(9), 468–476.

Pittenger, D. J. (2002). Deception in research: Distinctions and solutions from the perspective of utilitarianism. *Ethics & Behavior, 12*(2), 117–142.

Public Health Leadership Society. (2002). *Principles of the ethical practice of public health,
version 2.2.* Retrieved January 11, 2007, from http://www.apha.org/codeofethics/
ethicsbrochure.pdf.

Ross, J. G., Sundberg, E. C., & Flint, K. H. (1999). Informed consent in school health research: Why, how, and making it easy. *Journal of School Health, 69*(5), 171 176.

Schneider, C. E. (1998). *The practice of autonomy: Patients, doctors, and medical decisions.* New York: Oxford University Press.

Sieber, J. E. (1982). Kinds of deception and the wrongs they may involve. *IRB: A Review
of Human Subjects Research, 4*(9), 1–5.

Sieber, J. E. (1992). *Planning ethically responsible research: A guide for students and
internal review boards* (Vol. 31). Newbury Park, CA: Sage Publications.

Sieber, J. E. (2001). Privacy and confidentiality as related to human research in social and
behavioral science. In National Bioethics Advisory Commission (Ed.), *Ethical and
policy issues in research involving human participants: Vol. 2. Commissioned papers
and staff analysis* (pp. N1-N50). Bethesda, MD: National Bioethics Advisory Committee. Retrieved January 11, 2007, from http://www.georgetown.edu/research/nrcbl/
nbac/human/overvol2.pdf.

Sieber, J. E., Iannuzzo, R., & Rodriguez, B. (1995). Deception methods in psychology:
Have they changed in 23 years? *Ethics & Behavior, 5*(1), 67–85.

Sigmon, S. T., Rohan, K. J., Dorhofer, D., Hotovy, L. A., Trask, P. C., & Boulard, N.
(1997). Effects of consent form information on self-disclosure. *Ethics & Behavior,
7*(4), 299–310.

Silva, M. C., & Sorrell, J. M. (1988). Enhancing comprehension of information for informed consent: A review of empirical research. *IRB: A Review of Human Subjects Research, 10*(1), 1–5.

Soble, A. (1978). *Deception in social science research: Is informed consent possible?* (No. 5): *Hastings Center Report* 8.

Stanley, B. H., & Guido, J. R. (1996). Informed consent: Psychological and empirical issues. In B. H. Stanley, J. E. Sieber, & G. B. Melton, (Eds.), *Research ethics: A psychological approach* (pp. 105–128). Lincoln: University of Nebraska Press.

Stiles, P. G., Poythress, N. G., Hall, A., Falkenbach, D., & Williams, R. (2001). Improving understanding of research concept disclosures among persons with mental illness. *Psychiatric Services, 52*(6), 780–785.

Titus, S. L., & Keane, M. A. (1996). Do you understand?: An ethical assessment of researchers' description of the consenting process. *Journal of Clinical Ethics, 7*(1), 60–68.

Warwick, D. P. (1982). Types of harm in social research. In T. L. Beauchamp, R. R. Faden, R. J. J. Wallace, & L. Walters (Eds.), *Ethical issues in social science research* (pp. 101–124). Baltimore: Johns Hopkins University Press.

Weijer, C. (1999). Protecting communities in research: Philosophical and pragmatic challenges. *Cambridge Quarterly of Healthcare Ethics, 8*, 501–513.

Weiss Roberts, L., Warner, T. D., Anderson, C. T., Smithpeter, M. V., & Rogers, M. K. (2004). Schizophrenia research participants' responses to protocol safeguards: Recruitment, consent, and debriefing. *Schizophrenia Research, 67*, 283–291.

Wendler, D., & Rackoff, J. (2001). Informed consent and respecting autonomy: What's a signature got to do with it? *IRB: Ethics & Human Research, 23*(3), 1–4.

Wendler, D., & Rackoff, J. (2002). Consent for continuing research participation: What is it and when should it be obtained? *IRB: Ethics & Human Research, 24*(3), 1–6.

Wirshing, D. A., Wirshing, W. C., Marder, S. R., Liberman, R. P., & Mintz, J. (1998). Informed consent: Assessment of comprehension. *American Journal of Psychiatry, 155*(11), 1508–1511.

Young, D. R., Hooker, D. T., & Freeberg, F. E. (1990). Informed consent documents: Increasing comprehension by reducing reading level. *IRB: A Review of Human Subjects Research, 12*(3), 1–5.

5

Decision-Making Capacity and the Involvement of Surrogates

Don't know the reason, stayed here all season
With nothing to show but this brand new tattoo.
But it's a real beauty, a Mexican cutie,
How it got here I haven't a clue.

—Jimmy Buffett, *Margaritaville*

In the context of health care and research, decision-making capacity refers to the ability of individuals to provide informed consent for treatment or participation in research. Whereas the last chapter focused on the kinds of information a researcher must provide to enable informed consent, this chapter examines what the participant must bring to the consent dialogue.

The topic of decision-making capacity too often evokes horrifying images. We recall the character of McMurphy in the film *One Flew Over the Cuckoo's Nest*, who possessed decision-making capacity but was treated as incompetent and had a prefrontal lobotomy performed on him without his consent. In the context of research, the opposite scenario more frequently raises concern. The Advisory Committee on Human Radiation Experiments, the Office for Protection from Research Risks, and mental health advocates have all examined cases of research—conducted since the Tuskegee syphilis study and the development of protective regulations—in which participants were recruited into high-risk studies when they lacked adequate decision-making capacity (Dresser, 1999). At the same time, denying competent participants the ability to enroll in a study they wish to enroll in may represent an extreme form of paternalism that stigmatizes individuals, interferes with their ability to foster their well-being, and violates autonomy. These various ethical dimensions of decision-making capacity and informed consent are summarized in table 5.1.

Deviations from the practice of obtaining voluntary informed consent remind us that informed consent is meant to serve a dual purpose. First, it is a form of respecting autonomy, that is, respecting people as rational and self-determining. But when people are not capable of exercising rationality or self-determination, informed consent procedures can become farcical. Second, informed consent is intended to enable individuals to protect their interests, to decide which risks are worth adopting given anticipated benefits in the light of their vision of well-being. But again, when people are not able to protect their interests by exercising informed self-determination, then, as the Belmont Report observes, others have a heightened duty to protect them.

Table 5.1 The Ethical Dimensions of Decision-Making Capacity

	Is Permitted to Make Decision	Is Not Permitted to Make Decision
Has decision-making capacity	Appropriate. Efforts should be made to include others in consent process as the participant wishes, and to ensure that capacity is maintained throughout study.	Violation of autonomy. Stigmatizing. Harms ability to protect self by declining participation; or harms ability to promote self-interests by enrolling.
Lacks decision-making capacity	Mockery of autonomy. Denied heightened protections while unable to protect self.	Appropriate. Alternative forms of permission may be explored, including assent and surrogate permission.

Ethical challenges arise not only because researchers sometimes fail to take an adequate interest in decision-making capacity and informed consent, but perhaps above all because there are many borderline cases and capacity assessment is not entirely objective. Ethical challenges are compounded by the fact that currently regulations and practice guidelines leave many questions unanswered (Moreno, 1999). This chapter is intended to explore what decision-making capacity is, how it is assessed, and how research participation should be approached when individuals lack decision-making capacity. It concludes by analyzing two cases that enter into the gray zone.

WHAT IS DECISION-MAKING CAPACITY?

While the terms "competence" and "decision-making capacity" are sometimes used synonymously, most literature on the subject treats competence as a legal concept and capacity as a clinical concept.

Competence refers to the legal capacity to make decisions in a certain realm, such as financial or health care decisions. Legal competence may be determined by legislation or on a case-by-case basis by the courts. Typically, people under the age of 18 are considered incompetent to make health care decisions, regardless of whether they possess the cognitive capacity to do so.[1] Exceptions to this rule vary from state to state but often include those who are married, pregnant, serving in the military, or living on their own and financially supporting themselves (Menikoff, 2001). Courts typically declare someone incompetent to make decisions only when an important decision needs to be made and there is evidence that the individual lacks the functions necessary to make reasoned decisions (Grisso & Appelbaum, 1998).

Decision-making *capacity* refers to the functional abilities that are needed to make reasoned decisions. As the President's Commission observed, this func-

1. Evidence exists that the cognitive abilities of older teenagers is often indistinguishable from that of adults, and even children from ages 6–9 sometimes make decisions that are similar to those of adults (Koocher & Keith-Spiegel, 1990). At the same time, the ability to appreciate information is often deficient, and children appear more easily influenced by others than are adults (Miller, Drotar, & Kodish, 2004).

Table 5.2 Functional Elements of Decision-Making Capacity

Function	Illustration
Understanding	Understanding of information that is disclosed, e.g., the purpose of the study, risks, benefits, and alternatives
Appreciation	Appreciation of how the information pertains to one's own circumstances, e.g., how a phase I trial is not expected to yield direct benefits to the individual participant and how the risks might affect one's quality of life
Reasoning	Reasoning with the information, e.g., weighing the benefits against the risks both of participating and of alternative courses of action
Expressing a choice	Expressing a decision, e.g., a decision to participate, and signing a consent form

tional approach to determining capacity deviates from an earlier approach that focused on an individual's status or diagnosis, for instance, schizophrenia or depression (President's Commission, 1982). The reasons for the shift in approaches are elucidated below.

The Four Functions Approach to Decision-Making Capacity

The capacity to make decisions to participate in research refers to four general abilities or functions, which are summarized in table 5.2.

Understanding

Capacity requires potential participants to understand information that is disclosed about a study, for example, the purpose of the study, risks, benefits, and alternatives. Saks has called this a "pure understanding" component; it requires only that the participant comprehend what is said, not that the participant believe it. Although this sets a fairly modest bar, the following short thought experiment indicates its significance: Imagine being asked to make any important decision the implications of which are described in a foreign language. One is simply not in a position to decide in that case. Pure understanding, then, is a prerequisite for competency (Saks, 1999, p. 66).

Appreciation

Appreciation of information requires that potential participants not only understand the relevant information but believe it and relate it to their own situation. This standard may be failed, for example, when a participant remains firmly convinced that he or she will receive optimal therapy in a clinical trial even after an investigator has explained that the trial is in phase I and is not expected to yield direct benefits. At the same time, assessment of this capacity requires discretion because "it is—more often than we like to think—an open question what is true; very few beliefs are completely indisputable" (Saks, 1999, p. 69). For example, individuals who lack access to adequate health care may actually be justified in believing that an early clinical trial might provide superior monitoring and basic care versus what they would receive otherwise.

Reasoning

Reasoning refers to the ability to put information together to reach a conclusion, for instance, about how best to achieve a goal. It may involve the ability to weigh the benefits against the risks of participating and of alternative courses of action. This may require fairly sophisticated reasoning skills when a study involves several treatment arms (e.g., placebo + x; placebo + y; y + x), each with different known risks and expected benefits.

At the same time, very basic reasoning may suffice in many cases. Koocher and Keith-Spiegel give an example of a child who objected to participation in a study (with no direct benefit expected) "because he did not want to miss the afternoon cartoon shows on television" (1990, 114). Indeed, this straightforward piece of reasoning puts together information about participation requirements and a sacrifice that the potential participant did not deem proportionate to expected benefits.

Expressing a Choice

The ability to express a decision is clearly not the same as the ability to make a decision. However, because informed consent is best understood as a two-way dialogue that culminates in a decision by the potential participant, it is reasonable that the ability to express a choice be included in the standards for capacity. Of course, here accommodations may be necessary in order to enable an individual to exercise capacity, for example, the choice may need to be expressed in writing or through an interpreter.

Defining Incapacity

The following is a useful definition of incapacity that reflects criteria used in ethics, clinical practice, and law to determine whether an individual should be allowed to provide informed consent:

> [Incapacity] constitutes a status of the individual that is defined by *functional* deficits (due to *mental illness, mental retardation, or other mental conditions*) judged to be sufficiently great that the person *currently* cannot meet the *demands* of a specific decision-making situation, weighed in light of its potential *consequences*. (Grisso & Appelbaum, 1998, p. 27)[2]

Each of the italicized words suggests an important point about incapacity (Grisso & Appelbaum, 1998, pp. 18–27).

---

2. Although Grisso and Appelbaum distinguish between incapacity and legal incompetence, they also use the term "incompetence" in a loose nonlegal sense in this passage. To avoid confusion, I have replaced the term "incompetence" with the term "incapacity," for it is clear that their definition is not restricted to the legal concept.

First, incapacity may be caused by impaired mental states, but they do not automatically imply each other. A young child may lack capacity without mental impairment; and most people with major depression or schizophrenia preserve decision-making capacity (Appelbaum & Grisso, 1995; Appelbaum, Grisso, Frank, O'Donnell, & Kupfer, 1999; Berg & Appelbaum, 1999). Similarly, patients who are involuntarily committed have been found by some courts to retain the right to refuse medications or electroshock therapy and may maintain capacity and accordingly the right to consent to research (Holder, 1983).

Second, incapacity refers to a deficit in one or more of the four functions listed above. This explains why it would be wrong to identify incapacity with a mental disorder, because people with mental disorders may preserve these functions.

Third, incapacity pertains to the demands of a specific task. For example, a person might be unable to manage money well (due to impulsivity or a lack of appreciation of the consequences of using a credit card) but still remain competent to make medical decisions.

Fourth, decision-making capacity may change. Treatments may restore decision-making capacity, whereas a high fever may cause someone temporarily to lose capacity. Some disorders, such as Alzheimer's disease in its early stages, are marked by fluctuations in capacity. Here the distinction between a psychological determination of incapacity and a legal determination of incompetence becomes significant. Once declared legally incompetent, a person remains legally incompetent until a court says otherwise, regardless of whether decision-making capacity returns.

Finally, consequences are weighed in determining an individual's decision-making capacity. This is the only feature of incapacity that does not relate to the individual's capacities per se, but is rather a factor that is considered when the individual's capacity is neither black nor white. Between the extremes of a comatose patient (who clearly lacks capacity) and a healthy, well-educated patient exist most patients who have their capacity formally assessed. Weighing the consequences of the decisions that need to be made is a way of acknowledging that declaring someone lacks capacity is not just a clinical-scientific determination but also an *ethical* act that deeply affects the individual.

While some ethicists have debated the practice, as a general rule, the standards for acknowledging an individual as competent to grant informed consent to participate in research will be lower when the risks are minimal and higher when the risks are greater than minimal (Wilks, 1997; Grisso & Appelbaum, 1998). While benefits are normally given weight in determining capacity in a therapeutic setting (e.g., even patients who are delusional are often allowed to sign themselves into treatment), because the primary aim of research is not therapeutic, benefits should not be given the same weight in determining capacity in a research setting. The National Bioethics Advisory Committee (NBAC) effectively concurred with this view when it recommended that ordinarily decision-making capacity should be formally assessed by an independent qualified professional when protocols present greater than minimal risk to populations that are at risk of being incompetent (National Bioethics Advisory Commission, 1998).

What precisely is meant by a sliding scale? At all levels of risks and benefits, potential participants should be expected to understand the information presented to them and to express a choice. Some have recommended that appreciation becomes particularly important when research involves greater than minimal risk research, and reasoning abilities are crucial when the risk-benefit ratio is most unfavorable (Delano, 2002).

Risk-benefit ratios have traditionally also played a significant role in determining whether to permit research involving a vulnerable population, which in a research setting has been defined as a population of people who are less capable of protecting their own interests (Levine, 1988; Weijer, 1999). Federal regulations provide a fixed scale of risk-benefit ratios with corresponding protections and exclusions for research involving children (45CFR46, subpart D), which is presented in chapter 6. NBAC has recommended a similar scale for research with persons who lack capacity (National Bioethics Advisory Commission, 1998). However, neither federal regulations nor the National Institutes of Health guidelines on this matter have adopted a fixed scale (National Institutes of Health, 1999).

ASSESSING CAPACITY: WHEN, WHO, AND HOW?

When Should Capacity Be Assessed?

Referring to the context of clinical health care, Grisso and Appelbaum write:

> Whether they recognize it or not, most clinicians assess their patients' decision-making abilities as part of every encounter. Ordinarily, this occurs unconsciously, as clinicians take notice of patients' dress, demeanor, communicative skills, intelligence, ability to attend to a conversation, apparent understanding, and ability to reach a decision. Since we all assume, appropriately, that the people with whom we deal are competent to make decisions about their own lives—indeed, the law makes a similar assumption—only when our unconscious monitoring detects something unexpected do we attend to it directly. (1998, p. 61)

Similarly, as a general rule, researchers should be sensitive to signs of incapacity in any research study. Such signs include an inability to paraphrase basic information about a study or to express a clear decision, evidence of intoxication, or a complete lack of interest in risks and benefits. Such signs should trigger a request for a formal capacity assessment or at the least—if the cause is fleeting, such as being overwhelmed by a new diagnosis or being intoxicated—the informed consent process should be rescheduled.

At the same time, in certain contexts IRBs may not want to leave determinations of capacity entirely up to the instincts of researchers, who may have varying degrees of training in this area and who may have conflicts of interest (see chapter 10). IRBs and others responsible for establishing consent policies need to walk a fine line between creating overly restrictive policies that stigmatize people with mental disorders by implying that they are likely to lack capacity (when evidence suggests otherwise) and overly permissive policies that enable researchers to obtain consent signatures from participants who genuinely lack capacity and are incapable of protecting themselves.

NBAC's report on capacity asserts that "all potential human subjects are pre-sumed to be capable of making decisions for themselves unless there is a par-ticular reason to suspect that a capacity assessment will be necessary" (National Bioethics Advisory Commission, 1998, recommendation 8). However, NBAC also notes that decisional impairment and incapacity may be more frequent among populations with certain mental disorders. When the risks of a research study are greater than minimal, NBAC suggests that capacity should be assessed, or else the researcher should be required to explain why an assessment is unnecessary with the particular participant group.

Who Should Assess Capacity?

As noted above, at an informal level, researchers should be trained to be sensitive to the decision-making capacity of potential participants. But when a formal as-sessment is required, who should conduct the capacity assessment?

NBAC declined to recommend that capacity be assessed by any particular group of professionals, such as psychiatrists. It rather explicitly acknowledged that a range of professionals may be qualified to assess capacity. This is increas-ingly true as standardized instruments are developed with scoring matrices.

NBAC's primary concern in addressing who should conduct capacity assess-ments was with potential conflicts of interests rather than formal qualifications. Particularly in research that presents greater than minimal risk, NBAC recom-mended the use of an independent professional to perform the capacity assess-ment; this was based on the conviction that "conflicts of interest can, in some cases, distort professional judgments, and that they should be eliminated wher-ever possible" (National Bioethics Advisory Commission, 1998, recommendation 8). NBAC acknowledged that considerations of feasibility might require IRBs to make exceptions; but it recommended that the burden fall on investigators to explain why an independent assessor is not feasible and how capacity would be assessed.

While NBAC's only example of infeasibility was a lack of qualified profes-sionals in the local area, Appelbaum suggests more compelling examples. He has observed that use of an independent assessor typically entails financially com-pensating a psychiatrist for travel and examination time. While some large well-funded studies might be able to absorb such costs, he observes that unfunded studies and most pilot studies conducted on small grants would lack such re-sources (Appelbaum, 2001). Moreover,

> most research today is conducted on an outpatient basis, with subjects recruited when they come for scheduled appointments. Recruitment in almost all research projects occurs sporadically and unpredictably. Unless a full-time capacity assessor were to be hired for a project (truly an extraordinary cost), the logistics of bringing potential subjects together with the assessor are formidable. . . . In many projects and for many subjects, requiring subjects to come for additional sessions unrelated to their care so that their capacity can be assessed by an independent person will simply preclude their enrollment. (p. 272)

Table 5.3 Capacity Assessment Commensurate With Risks and Population Traits

Form of Assessment	Risks Posed by Study	Population Traits
Informal, undocumented assessment	Lowest risk	Populations with no cognitive impairments expected
Formal, documented assessment by investigator	↓	↓
Formal, documented assessment and testing of actual comprehension and appreciation of study information by investigator	↓	↓
Formal, documented assessment and testing of actual comprehension and appreciation of study information by investigator—with a patient advocate or consent auditor present	↓	↓
Formal, documented screening and testing—by an independent assessor	Highest risk	Population with severe cognitive impairments expected

His last point is reinforced by surveys indicating that inconvenience is among the top reasons that potential participants decline to enroll in clinical trials (Getz & Borfitz, 2002).

We also need to ask whether real independence is usually possible to achieve. The whole point of insisting upon an independent capacity assessor is to eliminate the conflict of interest that researchers have insofar as they are interested both in ascertaining capacity and in enrolling participants efficiently. Yet no one would suggest that participants should shoulder the costs of hiring an independent assessor. It is rather researchers and sponsors of research who will pay the costs of independent assessors, which in turn makes "independent" assessors paid consultants to researchers and reintroduces a conflict of interest.

Using a Sliding Scale

Appelbaum suggests that a broad spectrum of assessment options may be acceptable, and the specific option chosen should correlate with the degree of risks—both the risks posed by the study and the risk that participants will lack capacity (Appelbaum, 2001). Table 5.3 expands upon his examples.

Restoring Accountability to Its Rightful Place

It may also be that we need to reassert the primary responsibility that investigators have for protecting the well-being of participants rather than delegating this task to others. Oversight is certainly needed, and conflicts of interests should be exposed and discussed; but research cannot be conducted in an ethical manner without researchers who are willing to act ethically and shoulder the burden of accountability, much as physicians shoulder the burden of practicing medicine according to standards of practice.

How Should We Assess Capacity?

Precisely how decision-making capacity should be evaluated has been the subject of much debate. NBAC declined to recommend an approach to assessment "since there is vigorous debate about methods, in part because of their different presuppositions" (National Bioethics Advisory Commission, 1998, recommendation 8). No guidance from any governmental body has subsequently been given. Further, very few standardized instruments for assessing capacity exist. In her review of existing assessment tools, Saks found only five.[3] Of the five, she focused on the MacArthur instrument because it appears "to be the most carefully constructed, best studied, and most discussed in the literature" (Saks, 1999, p. 59). For these same reasons, what follows focuses on the MacArthur Competence Assessment Tool for Clinical Research (MacCAT-CR) (Appelbaum & Grisso, 2001).

The MacCAT-CR is a 23-item instrument that was developed specifically to assess capacity in the context of clinical research. In contrast to some assessment batteries that can be extremely time consuming, it can be completed in 15–20 minutes. It is designed to assess directly the four key capacity functions—understanding, appreciation, reasoning, and ability to express a choice. It has been used successfully in nearly a dozen postvalidation studies (e.g., Carpenter et al., 2000; Casarett, Karlawish, & Hirschman, 2003; Karlawish et al., 2002; Kim, Cox, & Caine, 2002; Moser et al., 2004; Moser et al., 2002). While some authors have recommended the use of batteries of neurological tests to assess capacity (Grimes, McCullough, Kunik, Molinari, & Workman, 2000), in fact scores on the MacCAT-CR are strongly correlated with the psychiatric factors that such neurological testing aims to predict, such as apathy and avolition (Moser et al., 2002). Finally, in one study the MacCAT-CR identified significantly more capacity deficits than either the clinical evaluations of research staff or a formally administered Evaluation of Signed Consent (Carpenter et al., 2000).

Thus, while the MacCAT-CR and its predecessor instruments have been subjected to criticism based on assumptions that it makes, its emphasis on certain functional abilities, and the absence of a test of internal compulsion (Saks, 1999), it has proven to be a reliable instrument that is comparably simple to use and corresponds well with the dominant legal and clinical concepts of capacity.

WHEN POTENTIAL PARTICIPANTS LACK CAPACITY

How should researchers address potential participants who have been determined to lack decision-making capacity? If they are otherwise good candidates for participation and an IRB has approved a process for including participants who lack capacity, the following options should be considered.

3. These were (1) the Hopkins Competency Assessment Test (Janofsky, McCarthy, & Folstein, 1992; Orr & Janofsky, 1996); the Competency Interview Schedule (Bean, Nishisato, Rector, & Clancy, 1996); a test developed by Marson and colleagues (Marson, Cody, Ingram, & Harrell, 1995) based on the frameworks presented by Roth, Meisel, and Lidz (1977); and the Structured Interview for Competency and Incompetency Assessment Testing and Ranking Inventory (Tomada et al., 1997). As the dates of these articles suggest, efforts to standardize the assessment of capacity are still in their infancy.

Restoring Capacity

In an editorial, Paul Appelbaum observes that awareness of threats to decision-making capacity has increased in recent years, and there are many suggested responses. But he notes that "surprisingly little attention . . . has been given to means of restoring a situation that all involved recognize as ideal: competent patients making their own decisions about whether to enter a research study" (Applebaum, 1998, p. 1487). This recommendation is echoed in a more recent publication by Grimes and colleagues (Grimes, McCullough, Kunik, Molinari, & Workman, 2000).

Two studies of research participants with schizophrenia found that educational interventions were capable of increasing participant understanding to levels equal to those of non-ill participants. In one study, the intervention was reading the informed consent form to participants as often as necessary to enable participants to answer a questionnaire relating to the research protocol 100% correctly; 7-day retention of information was excellent (Wirshing, Wirshing, Marder, Liberman, & Mintz, 1998). In most cases, two readings were sufficient. A second study provided tailored education for participants including question and answer sessions, repeated presentation of material, a computer program that presented material on randomization and other research concepts, and an informational flip chart. The educational interventions were positively correlated with significant increases in understanding, appreciation, and reasoning scores (Carpenter et al., 2000). Using built-in "waiting periods" between the time information is conveyed and the time consent is obtained may also be useful in allowing participants to consider information and consult with others (National Institutes of Health, 1999).

In a study of boys and girls ages 7 to 20 years, Dorn, Susman, and Fletcher found that "emotional factors were more frequently related to understanding of research participants than age or cognitive development" (Dorn, Susman, & Fletcher, 1995, p. 185). They recommend that creating an environment that decreases anxiety and increases the individual's sense of control may enhance children's and adolescent's understanding of the research process. This recommendation is worth exploring with vulnerable adults as well.

Assent and Dissent

Even when participants lack capacity, there is general agreement that researchers generally should inform participants about the study, that participation is voluntary, and that they can leave at any time, and then seek their permission to participate. However, their permission should be viewed as "assent," not informed consent, and consent must either be waived or permission additionally obtained from a legally authorized representative.

Although the permission of an incapacitated individual is not sufficient to justify enrolling him or her in a study, NBAC has recommended that the objection or dissent of an individual "must be heeded in all circumstances" (National Bioethics Advisory Commission, 1998, recommendation 7). The reasoning NBAC provided is that "respect for persons must prevail over any asserted duty to serve the public good as a research subject" (National Bioethics Advisory Commission, 1998, recommendation

7). This rationale has been challenged for two reasons. First, by appealing to the Belmont Report's principle of respect for persons, it appears to appeal precisely to self-determination. Yet, as Baylis has observed, it is unclear why one would treat such dissent as though it were an autonomous, self-determining act (Baylis, 2001). Can one distinguish between morally valid and morally invalid acts of dissent just as one might distinguish between morally valid and morally invalid acts of granting consent? Second, there is no reason to assume that the only reason that people are included in research is to serve the public good: research can be a directly beneficial opportunity (Baylis, 2001). In such cases, is it sensible always to heed dissent? The National Commission, in its report on *Research Involving Those Institutionalized as Mentally Infirm*, recommended that courts be allowed to permit participation in research that is directly beneficial (National Commission for the Protection of Human Subjects of Biomedical and Behavioral Research, 1978, p. 7). Similarly, Koocher and Keith-Spiegel write that "unless the research holds out the prospect for benefiting the child participant in some way that is available only in the research context, the investigator appears to be obligated to excuse the child" (1990, p. 113). Although this articulates a presumption in favor of honoring the objection of a child, it also indicates an exceptional circumstance under which it might be overridden.

On the other hand, Koocher and Keith-Spiegel (1990) note that enrolling someone who is unwilling or hostile is not only difficult to justify but difficult to do and runs the risk of contaminating data. Similarly, Baylis (2001) acknowledges that objections are sufficient reason to interrupt or temporarily suspend an individual's participation. And in this regard, these authors approach the position of NBAC, for NBAC qualifies its position by stating that "an investigator, acting with a level of care and sensitivity that will avoid the possibility or the appearance of coercion, may approach people who previously objected to ascertain whether they have changed their minds" (National Bioethics Advisory Commission, 1998, recommendation 7). When one considers not only the practical challenges of enrolling someone against their objections, but also the extreme unlikelihood that direct benefits could be provided only in the context of research (given options of off-label prescriptions, for example), then NBAC's position should rarely if ever be violated. This position finds even greater support from the largest qualitative study of mental health consumers in California, which found that 47% avoided seeking traditional mental health services out of fear of involuntary commitment (Campbell & Schraiber, 1989). In the long run, the practice of imposing well-meaning therapy or research upon a patient may have the consequence that future beneficial encounters are avoided.

When assent rather than informed consent is sought from adults, efforts should be made to explain in a sensitive manner that they lack sufficient capacity to consent, and they should be given an opportunity to contest the decision, for example, soliciting a second evaluation (Delano, 2002; National Bioethics Advisory Commission, 1998, recommendation 9). An additional form of permission should then be sought using one of the following mechanisms.

Research Advanced Directives

Advanced directives are commonly used in health care to enable patients to express their wishes regarding various forms of life support should they become incapacitated with a poor prognosis for recovery. Research advanced directives are certainly less common but are one way for participants to express their preferences regarding participation in ongoing or future research studies (Levine, 1988). They have been used in studies of Alzheimer's patients as one way of enabling patients in the early stages of the disease to express a willingness to continue in a study as their disease progresses and they lose capacity (Sachs et al., 1994).

However, research advanced directives suffer from some of the same shortcomings as health care advanced directives. First, the meaning of any directive must be interpreted in the light of the concrete situation, which may give rise to disagreements. For example, an advanced directive may state that it becomes effective only when the patient becomes unable to make decisions; yet precisely when this occurs may be subject to debate, especially when capacities wax and wane. Dresser raises several additional concerns with research advanced directives:

> (1) Whether advanced decisions can be adequately informed; (2) how to safeguard the subject's right to withdraw from research; and (3) whether advance choice is a morally defensible basis for permitting otherwise prohibited levels of risks and burdens in research involving incapable subjects. (1999, p. 17)

Whatever the benefits and burdens of a research advanced directive, they are not commonly used, many researchers doubt that they are a workable solution, and scant research in this area suggests that patients dislike the idea of writing a "blank check" for participation in research (Dresser, 1999; Sachs et al., 1994).

Due to these limitations, instructive advanced directives are likely to be infeasible unless used together with a surrogate decision maker or participant advocate. However, advanced directives may be useful in providing surrogate decision makers with guidance.

Surrogate Decision Makers

As Dresser notes, existing federal policy "gives little direction on who should act as the incapable subject's personal representative in making decisions on research participation" (Dresser, 1999, p. 13). The Common Rule states that informed consent should be sought by the participant "or the subject's legally authorized representative" (45CFR46.111[a]); and the Belmont Report states that surrogate decision makers should "be those who are most likely to understand the incompetent subject's situation and act in that person's best interest" (National Commission, 1979, C.1). Surrogate decision makers are generally expected to exercise "substituted judgment," that is, to represent the previous wishes of the participant when these are known (Sunderland & Dukoff, 1999); but because these wishes may be unknown or ill informed with regard to the current situation, consideration of the participant's best interests must always be given. Table 5.4 summarizes the various ways that a surrogate decision maker may be identified with the pros and cons of each approach.

While some states specify who may serve as a legally authorized representative in a research context, most do not. The few states that do address consent to research commonly require guardians to obtain a specific court's authorization to

Table 5.4 Common Ways of Identifying a Surrogate Decision-Maker

Approach	Description	Pros	Cons
Follow legislation on research or clinical healthcare surrogate decision-making.	Typically next of kin; some states allow a friend who knows wishes of individual if no family is available.	Often easy. Does not require advanced directive or court order.	Next of kin or friends may not be available, willing to serve in role, or familiar with individual. Unclear whether this is permitted by law when state legislation is silent on consent for research.
Consult individual identified as research or healthcare durable power of attorney (DPA).	DPA form identifies who is legally authorized to make decisions when patient is incapacitated.	If document exists, it is easy to identify surrogate. Surrogate is chosen by individual, not by legislation or courts.	Most individuals have not completed a durable power of attorney. In some states it is unclear whether DPA for healthcare is authorized to make research decisions.
Seek court-appointed legal guardian.	Local court may appoint a legal guardian to make research decisions.	May reduce legal liability. May provide researchers with a clear decision-maker.	Can be costly. May take significant amount of time. May not succeed in appointing person familiar with individual.

grant consent to participation in research (Dresser, 1999). In the absence of specific guidance from states, many clinical researchers use the same guidelines that they use in clinical practice (e.g., relying on next of kin when they are involved in the care of the patient), though IRBs are free to determine whether such practices are acceptable to them. Unfortunately, in the absence of clear state legislation, the legality of following policies or laws that govern health care decision making in the context of research is unclear. However, traditionally, some level of legal protection is afforded by following best practices, and several high-level government policy bodies have sanctioned using health care surrogate decision makers as surrogates in the context of research (National Bioethics Advisory Commission, 1998, recommendation 15; National Institutes of Health, 1999). While IRBs and researchers currently appear concerned above all with the legal liability of accepting permission from a person whose decision-making authority is unclear, they should also bear in mind that they may also be legally at risk for unfairly excluding individuals from participation in research. NBAC and NIH have rightly urged states to clarify these matters with appropriate legislation.

A number of policy advocates have recommended that "consent auditors" or patient advocates be included in aspects of the ongoing consent process, including observing the consent process with surrogates and monitoring ongoing risks and benefits—at least when risks are greater than minimal (Bein, 1991; National Bioethics Advisory Commission, 1998; National Commission for the Protection of Human Subjects of Biomedical and Behavioral Research, 1978). In part, this is to assist surrogates in understanding information and their role; in part, it is to address a possible conflict of interest that surrogates may have (Skrutkowski et al., 1998). For example, research may be perceived as developing treatments for disorders that family members see themselves at risk of developing or that will eventually lighten their burden of giving care (Dresser, 1999). In any case, researchers have expressed concern that surrogates may not be adequately prepared for their roles, and have recommended education of surrogates on their roles prior to obtaining permission (Candilis, Wesley, & Wichman, 1993).

Precisely who should serve as a consent auditor and whether IRBs should have discretion to waive this requirement have been controversial, with recommendations ranging from mandatory inclusion of a federally employed advocate to optional institutionally appointed auditors (Dresser, 1999).

Community Permission for Individuals

The Common Rule provides that research with children that does not meet the risk-benefit ratio presented in the Common Rule may be approved by the Secretary of Health and Human Services "after consultation with a panel of experts in pertinent disciplines (for example: science, medicine, education, ethics, law) and following opportunity for public review and comment" (45CFR46.407[b]). Similarly, NBAC recommended that the Department of Health and Human Services create a Special Standing Panel (SSP) on research involving persons with mental disorders that may affect capacity. One of the tasks of the SSP was precisely to review "individual protocols that cannot otherwise be approved under the recommendations described in this report" (National Bioethics Advisory Commission, 1998, recommendation 2, A).[4]

Taking this kind of recommendation a step further, Thomasma has suggested that in research that involves greater than minimal risk, surrogates should not be allowed to grant permission; rather, "a committee representing the community of care" should be consulted (Thomasma, 1997, p. 240). This recommendation is far more demanding than the provisions of the Common Rule or the recommendation of NBAC insofar as it regards any research greater than minimal risk, but most importantly because this committee should be "composed of those who know and love the individual, and those who are touched by the disease most directly or are advocates for such persons" (p. 241). That is to say, a new committee would need to be created for each new participant.

Ethics and Feasibility

Ethical accountability only extends as far as our control over a situation; responsibility and freedom go hand in hand. In this world of limited resources, we often need to prioritize. Providing the best protections available may not only conflict with the autonomy of participants (by being overly paternalistic) but may be made impossible by limited time, money, and even limited patience on the part of participants and researchers alike. It is frequently asserted that the level of protections

4. This panel was never created.

offered in a study needs to be proportionate to risks and anticipated benefits; but it also needs to be feasible.

While Thomasma's suggestion that a committee be established to grant research permission in a broad range of scenarios sounds attractive in that it plugs the potential participant into a community of care and concern, it also raises questions of feasibility of the sort Appelbaum raised regarding NBAC's demands for an independent capacity assessor. The idea of establishing a unique, ad hoc committee for each participant enrolling in a study—a committee comprised not only of the surrogate but others who know and love the participant, as well as advocates and experts—does not reflect the real world of recruitment settings.

The worlds of "protectionist ideals" and actual research resources often collide. Nevertheless, Appelbaum concedes that most recommendations in the NBAC report would be "appropriate under some circumstances" (Appelbaum, 2001, p. 272). For example, some research centers have adopted a "tripartite" consent process that involves (1) an evaluation by a treatment team to assess whether an individual should be approached to participate; (2) an initial consent discussion with the researcher; and (3) a formal documented capacity assessment by an independent professional. But they use it—and shoulder the respective time and financial burdens—only in those studies that NBAC identified as especially controversial and in need of further study, namely, placebo-controlled, treatment withdrawal, and symptom provocation studies (Posever & Chelmow, 2001).

To be clear, these reflections on feasibility are not meant to defend what some might call pragmatic constraints on ethics. To the contrary, ethics requires that one consider matters of resources and feasibility; it requires that competing goals be weighed against each other. For as Appelbaum has observed, "to the extent that research is delayed or halted, people with mental disorders may suffer just as greatly as when their rights or interests are ignored in a research study" (Appelbaum, 2001, p. 271). Ethical analyses can never be conducted prescinding from facts, competing stakeholders, and values. It must aim always at the best solution—*all things considered.*

Case Study: Questionable Capacity

Twenty years ago, Roger was diagnosed with schizophrenia, paranoid type. Over the years, he has undergone many types of treatment with varying degrees of success. Roger found that although the treatments reduced his symptoms, often the side effects were more than he could bear. So he would take himself off medication, and his schizophrenic episodes would return. At times, Roger is so worn out by frightening all-night psychotic episodes that he considers suicide; but he still resists going back on medication.

Lately, Roger has been feeling a lot better. He hasn't had an episode in a month and his mind feels "clear." He has even been able to work on the next chapters of his mystery novel, which he had abandoned months ago when his episodes were particularly intense. Roger's mother, whom he visits regularly, notices his improvement and is delighted. However, they both know that it is only a matter of time before the symptoms return and the disorder consumes his life again.

Willing to try anything to avoid another episode, Roger decides to visit a psychic to get "advice from the heavens." His mother is not particularly bothered by Roger's visits to psychics. She's glad he's trying to find some source of hope. Upon visiting an astrologer, he is advised to seek out an experimental drug and is assured that the "universe will grant him a miracle cure" through this new medicine. Roger leaves the astrologer and heads to the local diner to read the newspaper. On the back page, he reads about a Phase II clinical trial of an antipsychotic agent that is enrolling adult patients with schizophrenia.

Roger immediately contacts the research director at the university-affiliated hospital. The researcher explains that this experimental drug is being tested for its efficacy and safety and might not improve his symptoms. The drug has shown modest success in previous trials but has potentially severe side effects. Roger expresses extreme interest in participating.

The research protocol involves administering a short assessment of decision-making capacity to all potential participants who are interested in the project. Those who are deemed incompetent are either not allowed to participate or need the permission of a legally authorized surrogate decision maker in addition to providing their own assent. Among other things, the assessment explores understanding of the protocol, appreciation of risks and benefits, and the reasoning processes used to decide whether to enroll. The evaluator finds that Roger is not in a psychotic episode and that he understands the risks and benefits extremely well. But he is concerned when Roger explains that he is certain he will receive benefits from the study and that he decided to enroll because an astrologer instructed him to seek out this study.

Should Roger be enrolled in the study, and if so, what procedure should be used?[5]

CASE COMMENTARY

Disallowing Roger's participation, or making it conditional upon someone else's permission, might be viewed by Roger as disrespecting his wishes, which are clear and strong. Conceivably, it would also be harmful to him as it might destroy the hope to which he is clinging; it will almost certainly cause him distress. However, reasons exist for doubting that he meets the criteria required to give informed consent, which raises both ethical and legal concerns.

The primary ethical task in this case is to clarify a fact: is Roger competent to make the decision? In many ways, his unusual belief regarding an astrologer's prediction stands at the center of this case. Because the clinician conducting the assessment determined that Roger is not in a psychotic episode, one might be tempted to dismiss this belief as unusual but not pathological. In fact, a recent Gallup poll found that 33 percent of Americans believe in astrology and Americans spend approximately $200 million per year on astrological services (Gillin, 2003). Seen from this perspective, Roger's belief might not be all that unusual within his society.

5. This case was developed with Angie Dunn.

However, two factors lead us to pause before finding him competent. First, Roger's level of certainty is disturbing. One might question whether your average citizens who consult astrologers would be willing to undertake risks to their health with no concern because they have absolute faith in the pronouncements of an astrologer. Second, referring to the prodromal and residual symptoms of schizophrenia, the *DSM-IV-TR* states that "individuals may express a variety of unusual or odd beliefs that are not of delusional proportions (e.g., ideas of reference or magical thinking)" (American Psychiatric Association, 2000, p. 302). That is to say, even though he is not episodic, his belief may not be wholly unrelated to his disorder.

However, neither the unusual belief in itself nor its etiology should be viewed as the primary cause for concern.[6] It is rather the consequences of his unusual belief that are problematic from the point of view of informed consent. He appears to fail to *appreciate* that he really might experience no benefit and that the study involves risks. This failure to appreciate adequately risks and benefits is more disconcerting given that the study is a Phase II trial that is designed to determine safety as well as efficacy. Moreover, Roger's ability to *reason* with the information is hampered by his strong conviction that the drug presents a miracle.

Thus, despite understanding the study and being able to articulate a clear decision, Roger's capacity is in doubt. As noted above, when a determination of capacity is not black-and-white, then it is important to take into account the consequences of the decision when determining capacity. Here we shift from viewing capacity in strictly psychological terms to viewing the act of declaring someone incompetent as an ethical judgment that involves a risk-benefit analysis. Typically, a lower bar is set for decisions that involve a high level of anticipated benefits and a low level of risks; a significantly higher bar is set when the anticipated consequences are different.

In this case, we know not only that there are risks of adverse reactions, but that in the past the side-effects of some antipsychotic medications were so severe that Roger preferred to live with the symptoms of schizophrenia, even when this led to suicidal ideation. Roger also has a history of taking himself off of medications. This can present a serious problem with antipsychotic drugs because symptoms may be exacerbated when withdrawal is sudden. The fact that Roger might withdraw himself from the experimental medication prevents us from knowing that he will actually receive the protection of close monitoring.

Finally, it is worth bearing in mind that the researcher, the psychiatric evaluator, and the research institution might be held liable if they permit Roger to consent to enroll in a greater than minimal risk study when evidence exists that he lacks decision-making capacity. This point is raised not because their interests should trump those of a participant, but because their actions could jeopardize their ability to serve other participants by wasting resources on a legal battle and undermining trust in the researchers.

6. In fact, a recent study found that poor neurological functioning and the symptoms of apathy and avolition were significantly negatively correlated with capacity, but psychotic symptoms—hallucinations and delusions—were not (Moser et al., 2002). Thus, even if Roger were actively delusional, one should not assume that he would lack capacity.

Several options exist. First, Roger could be recognized as competent to give informed consent and be allowed to enroll in the study. This option should be rejected on grounds that his capacity to make this decision is in question due to a lack of appreciation, inadequate reasoning, an uncertain risk-benefit ratio, and concerns of liability that would arise were one to choose to ignore these facts. A second option is to deny him the opportunity of enrolling in the study. Given that Roger wants to enroll in the study, and that he might actually benefit from it, this option should not be pursued until other options have been explored and found unsatisfactory (least infringement). Fortunately, a third option might be pursued with Roger that balances the concerns raised thus far.

The researcher should explain to Roger that the research team has an ethical and legal obligation to ensure that free and informed consent or surrogate permission is obtained from all participants prior to enrolling them, and that there are concerns that he is not able to give consent at this time. This is not because he has schizophrenia; in fact, the psychiatric evaluator believes he is capable of making decisions. However, because he does not reveal a sufficient appreciation of what the study involves, they recommend that he appoint a surrogate (which he is competent to do) who might grant permission for his participation in the study. His own assent would also be solicited to participate in the study. Moreover, given his history of taking himself off of medications against medical advice, his surrogate would be asked to provide support during his enrollment, assisting his participation in the monitoring process. The researchers should express a willingness to help him to leave the study and discontinue medications in a controlled fashion at any time he likes. If Roger finds this arrangement agreeable, he should be allowed to enroll in the study.

Is this approach a twofaced way of avoiding liability? After all, he is being told he is not competent to consent to participation, yet he would be treated as competent to appoint a surrogate. In fact, this approach simply takes into account the very different circumstances surrounding the two decisions that need to be made. The decision to appoint a surrogate is likely to be better appreciated, because it is somewhat removed from the astrologer's prediction; more important, the risk-benefit ratio is considerably more beneficial to Roger than allowing him to decide to enroll in research without the involvement of a surrogate.

Case Study: Waiving Parental Permission

A researcher is planning to conduct interviews to learn about the relationship between heroin use and high-risk sexual behaviors among street youth ages 12–18. He proposes to ask subjects about their knowledge, attitudes, and beliefs about heroin, where they get the drug, how they use it, their sexual practices, and their knowledge and practice of safer sex. Access to this population will be gained through locations where the teens hang out, including a youth drop-in center, a coffee shop, a park where they meet to shoot heroin, and a local needle exchange clinic.

While the primary purpose of the research is to gather information, he plans to use the data to design a public health intervention for the same group. He also plans to provide those who are poorly informed about safer sex practices with an informational brochure and to give every participant referral cards to drop-in addic-tion treatment centers. While he promises to maintain strict confidentiality, he also plans on informing participants that if they express suicidal intentions, he will both refer them to a crisis counseling center and will give their names to a state social worker who will try to get them some help.

The researcher knows from experience and the literature that many of these teens are homeless, and those who are not often come from abusive or neglectful homes. Obtaining parental permission might prove impossible in the case of those teens who are estranged from their parents and difficult or dangerous for those living with their parents. The researcher therefore believes that obtaining parental consent is neither feasible nor in the best interests of the adolescents, and he asks the IRB for a waiver of parental permission. Although the study will ask about private information and illegal activities that could put subjects at risk with the law, he thinks risks associated with the research interview are not greater in and of themselves than those that these teens would ordinarily encounter during the performance of routine physical exams or psychological tests.

Should the IRB require parental permission? If not, how should permission be obtained?

CASE COMMENTARY

This case presents a clear example of how our current legal framework leaves room for, and even requires, ethical thinking.

Our goal in this case is to enable teenagers to participate in this study, which may offer them direct benefits, while obtaining an appropriate form of permission for participation and offering adequate protections. However, obtaining an appro-priate form of permission is challenging for two reasons. First, the proposed par-ticipants are minors, so they cannot give informed consent.[7] Ordinarily, we would solicit "assent" from teenagers and "permission" from parents (45CFR46.408). But we have good reasons for questioning whether this standard practice is fea-sible and reasonable in this case. Second, the teens are being selected for the study because they have a history of using heroin, which may affect decision-making capacity. How likely is it that their assent will be free and informed?

As a first recommendation, we should require that the researcher develop a protocol for ascertaining whether the participants are competent to give assent, for example, by monitoring for signs that they are currently high and asking them to discuss or paraphrase parts of the informed consent document, for example, parts that discuss confidentiality protections (Brody & Waldron, 2000). But even if the participants are capable of granting assent, should they be allowed to participate without parental permission?

---

7. The analysis in this case assumes that minors are not able to give informed consent. However, some states allow adolescents to consent to substance abuse treatment, in which case they might be the most proper decision makers even from a legal perspective, and in some cases, seeking parental permission might violate privacy rules (Brody & Waldron, 2000). Whether such state laws extend to substance abuse research, especially research involving an anticipated direct benefit, also needs to be investigated.

Federal regulations state that an "IRB may . . . waive the requirements to obtain informed consent"[8] provided the IRB finds and documents that:

1. The research involves no more than minimal risk to the subjects;
2. The waiver or alteration will not adversely affect the rights and welfare of the subjects;
3. The research could not practicably be carried out without the waiver or alteration; and
4. Whenever appropriate, the subjects will be provided with additional pertinent information after participation.[9] (46.116[d])

In analyzing this protocol, only the first three criteria are relevant because the study design does not require deception or the withholding of information. The easiest criterion to meet is the third: the research would not be feasible because contacting the parents is not consistently possible due to estrangement, and many teens who might be able to contact their parents would be reluctant to solicit their permission.[10] The second criterion is also fairly easy to meet. We have good reason to believe that the rights and welfare of the teens will be better protected by waiving parental permission. Disclosure of their behavior to their parents might put them at risk; and the study appears likely to offer benefits to participants.

The first criterion, however, poses a challenge. Minimal risk means "that the probability and magnitude of harm or discomfort anticipated in the research are not greater in and of themselves than those ordinarily encountered in daily life or during the performance of routine physical or psychological examinations or tests" (46.102[i]). One might argue that a routine physical exam might turn up needle marks and a routine psychological exam might reveal signs of substance abuse and high-risk sexual behavior. Because HIPAA regulations offer the same level of protection of identifiable protected health information in the context of research as in therapy, arguably the risks of this study are not higher than those that *these* participants might ordinarily encounter in daily life.

This judgment, however, might be challenged on certain interpretations of the regulations. Some policy analysts and scholars have suggested that the risks "ordinarily encountered in daily life" should be viewed as those ordinarily encountered by a *normal, healthy* individual (National Human Research Protections Advisory Committee, 2002; Penslar, 1993). But here we need to distinguish between exposing

---

8. While section 46.116 speaks of "legally informed consent of either the subject or the subject's legally authorized representative," subpart D, which addresses research involving children, speaks of parental permission rather than informed consent. The idea is that informed consent can only be granted by a competent participant for him or herself; every other form of permission should be called by another name (assent of a minor, permission of a parent, consultation of a community, etc.).

9. It is interesting to note how these four criteria for waiving informed consent mirror the criteria presented in chapter 4 for justifying decisions when two or more values or norms conflict: the first and second criteria address proportionality, the third addresses necessity, and the fourth addresses least infringement. The "effectiveness" test is tacitly present insofar as it is presumed that a waiver will make the study feasible and thereby able to offer the anticipated benefits.

10. See Diviak, Curry, Emery, and Mermelstein (2004) for discussion of similar concerns in smoking cessation research.

a participant to a greater than minimal risk procedure due to his or her situation (e.g., experimental antipsychotic medication, when similar medications are used daily due to the participant's diagnosis) and exposing a participant to a procedure that is in itself minimal risk (e.g., a survey) but includes a higher risk due to the person's situation (e.g., being a heroin user). The latter is certainly a more plausible reading of risks "ordinarily encountered in daily life" than the former, even though both involve interpreting ordinary risks within the context of the individual's real life situation.

As the *IRB Guidebook* notes, "the concept of minimal risk is evaluative rather than objective" and "considerable room for interpretation exists" (Penslar, 1993, ch. 6). As noted in chapter 2, where considerable room for interpretation exists, community consultation is often helpful. But consulting the community of participant parents would be extraordinarily difficult, and consulting minors would not resolve the ethical issue.

As an alternative, we might recommend the test that Osher and Telesford propose for researchers who work with minors: "Would I gladly and willingly subject my own children, my own family, or myself to the procedures to be undertaken by this inquiry?" (Osher & Telesford, 1996, p. 39). Researchers or IRB members might ask, if my child were estranged, living on the streets, and addicted to heroin, would I prefer that he be denied the opportunity to participate in this study without my permission or that he be allowed to enroll with his own assent? Assuming adequate protections are put in place, many reasonable parents would find the latter option preferable.

While this "Golden Rule" test will not solve all problems, largely because different people want to be treated differently, in the absence of evidence that those affected actually embrace contradictory values, it presents a reasonable minimum standard. The exceptions to the norm of informed consent that such a standard would sanction will stand in sharp contrast to exceptions that are patently unethical or exploitive, such as the deviations found in the Tuskegee syphilis study.

These considerations about the minimal risk standard are certainly relevant to determining the ethics of research with minors without parental consent. However, the specific subpart of the federal regulations that addresses research with children grants even more room for discretion than does the subpart A (Porter, 1996). Subpart D, "Additional DHHS Protections for Children Involved as Subjects in Research," states that:

> In addition to the provisions for waiver contained in 46.116 of Subpart A, if the IRB determines that a research protocol is designed for conditions or for a subject population for which parental or guardian permission is not a reasonable requirement to protect the subjects (for example, neglected or abused children), it may waive the consent requirements . . . provided an appropriate mechanism for protecting the children who will participate as subjects in the research is substituted, and provided further that the waiver is not inconsistent with Federal, State, or local law. The choice of an appropriate mechanism would depend upon the nature and purpose of the activities described in the protocol, the risk and anticipated benefit to the research subjects, and their age, maturity, status, and condition. (45cfr46.408[d])

That is to say, if parental permission is unlikely to yield additional protections to a child, it may be substituted by putting appropriate additional safeguards in place. Given the age and independence of the population under consideration, one such protection would be to require informed assent with assessment of decision-making capacity. Additionally, given that the researcher will be asking participants to discuss sensitive and illegal behaviors, he should be required to obtain a Certificate of Confidentiality, which will protect him from having his data subpoenaed by a court. His "informed assent" discussion with participants should explain to participants any conditions under which he might voluntarily breach confidentiality.[11]

Is this solution satisfactory? Not entirely, but it may be the best we can do with a very imperfect situation (for no teen should live on the streets and shoot heroin—but the researcher cannot fix that problem). It is also unsatisfactory because ordinarily researchers should seek to build partnerships with families (Osher & Telesford, 1996); yet this scenario sets precedent for bypassing parental rights to give permission for health and research interventions.

Philosophers have offered several arguments why it is generally appropriate to recognize parental rights to make decisions related to the participation of their children in research or health care:

1. Parents usually know their children well and are interested in their well-being.
2. Families typically bear the consequences of choices made on behalf of their child.
3. Children learn from their families the values and standards that often guide important decisions. This education in values is important both to individuals and societies.
4. To function well, families need to have an intimate sphere recognized by the state that limits the state's power to intrude. (Buchanan & Brock, 1989)

However, while these moral considerations can be compelling in ordinary circumstances, they are of limited applicability in cases of estranged children or of abusive relationships.

Nevertheless, based on the facts we have been given in the case at hand, we cannot rule out the possibility that some teens who would qualify for inclusion in the study live with parents who are caring. In order to minimize the infringement on parental rights, we might recommend that the researcher produce an information sheet for parents that could be given to participants who request it. The researcher might routinely ask the teens whether they live with their parents, whether they think their parents know about their drug use and would want to be informed about their participation. Those who answer yes to all of

11. A case in chapter 9 discusses when a researcher might consider breaching confidentiality, for example, if a participant poses a direct and serious harm to another. In the case under discussion here, it is easy to imagine such a scenario, for example, if a participant informs him that he or she is HIV positive and is having unprotected sex and sharing needles. Alternately, the participant might report being abused by a parent, which would be a reportable offense.

these questions could be provided with the information sheets to give to their parents; or the researcher could offer to mail the information sheet. Providing information to parents who are involved and are not abusive—with the teen's permission—shows respect for parents and might provide an appropriate form of transparency.[12]

Further EMHR Resources

- Unit four of the *Dialogues* DVD contains an interview with Philip Candilis and excerpts of a focus group with mental health consumers on decision-making capacity
- www.emhr.net contains a bibliography and case studies on decision-making capacity and surrogate decision making

REFERENCES

American Psychiatric Association. (2000). *Diagnostic and statistical manual of mental disorders*. 4th ed., text revision (*DSM-IV-TR*). Washington, DC: American Psychiatric Association.

Appelbaum, P. S. (1998). Editorial: Missing the boat: Competence and consent in psychiatric research. *American Journal of Psychiatry*, *155*(11), 1486–1488.

Appelbaum, P. S. (2001). Competence to consent to research: A critique of the recommendations of the National Bioethics Advisory Committee. *Accountability in Research*, *7*, 265–276.

Appelbaum, P. S., & Grisso, T. (1995). The MacArthur treatment competence study, I: Mental illness and competence to consent to treatment. *Law and Human Behavior*, *19*, 105–126.

Appelbaum, P. S., Grisso, T., Frank, E., O'Donnell, S., & Kupfer, D. J. (1999). Competence of depressed patients for consent to research. *American Journal of Psychiatry*, *156*(9), 1380–1384.

Appelbaum, P. S., & Grisso, T. (2001). MacArthur Competence Assessment Tool for Clinical Research (MacCAT-CR). Sarasota, FL: Professional Resource Press.

Baylis, F. (2001). IRBs: Protecting the well-being of subject-participants with mental disorders that may affect decisionmaking capacity. *Accountability in Research*, *7*, 183–199.

Bean, G., Nishisato, S., Rector, N., & Clancy, G. (1996). The assessment of competence to make a treatment decision: An empirical approach. *Canadian Journal of Psychiatry*, *41*, 85.

Bein, P. M. (1991). Surrogate consent and the incompetent experimental subject. *Food Drug Cosmetic Law Journal*, *46*(5), 739–771.

Berg, J. W., & Appelbaum, P. S. (1999). Subjects' capacity to consent to neurobiological research. In H. A. Pincus, J. A. Lieberman, & S. Ferris (Eds.), *Ethics in psychiatric research: A resource manual for human subjects protection* (pp. 81–106). Washington, DC: American Psychiatric Association.

12. The recent survey of Wagener and colleagues suggests that many IRBs are unaware of the possibility of waiving consent or are reluctant to waive consent even when it may be appropriate. Researchers need to be prepared to work with IRBs and to educate IRB members when necessary (Wagener et al., 2004).

Brody, J. L., & Waldron, H. B. (2000). Ethical issues in research on the treatment of adolescent substance abuse disorders. *Addictive Behaviors*, *25*(2), 217–228.

Buchanan, A. E., & Brock, D. W. (1989). *Deciding for others: The ethics of surrogate decisionmaking*. New York: Cambridge University Press.

Campbell, J., & Schraiber, R. (1989). *The well-being project: Mental health clients speak for themselves (A report of a survey conducted for the California Department of Mental Health, Office of Prevention)*. Sacramento, CA: California Network of Mental Health Clients.

Candilis, P. J., Wesley, R. W., & Wichman, A. (1993). A survey of researchers using a consent policy for cognitively impaired human research subjects. *IRB: A Review of Human Subjects Research*, *15*(6), 1–4.

Carpenter, W. T., Jr., Gold, J. M., Lahti, A. C., Queern, C. A., Conley, R. R., Bartko, J. J., et al. (2000). Decisional capacity for informed consent in schizophrenia research. *Archives of General Psychiatry*, *57*(6), 533–538.

Casarett, D., Karlawish, J. H. T., & Hirschman, K. B. (2003). Identifying ambulatory center patients at risk of impaired capacity to consent to research. *Journal of Pain and Symptom Management*, *26*, 615–624.

Delano, S. J. (2002). Research involving adults with decisional impairment. In R. J. Amdur & E. A. Bankert (Eds.), Institutional review board. *Management and function* (pp. 389–393). Boston: Jones and Bartlett.

Diviak, K. R., Curry, S. J., Emery, S. L., & Mermelstein, R. J. (2004). Human subjects' challenges in youth tobacco cessation research: Researchers' perspectives. *Ethics and Behavior*, *14*(4), 335–349.

Dorn, L. D., Susman, E. J., & Fletcher, J. C. (1995). Informed consent in children and adolescents: Age, maturation and psychological state. *Journal of Adolescent Health*, *16*(3), 185–190.

Dresser, R. (1999). Research involving persons with mental disabilities: A review of policy issues and proposals. In National Bioethics Advisory Commission (Ed.), *Research involving persons with mental disorders that may affect decisionmaking capacity: Commissioned papers* (pp. 5–28). Rockvillle, MD: National Bioethics Advisory Committee.

Getz, K., & Borfitz, D. (2002). *Informed consent: A guide to the risks and benefits of volunteering for clinical trials*. Boston: CenterWatch.

Gillin, B. (2003, January 22). Our stars, our selves. Philadelphia Inquirer.

Grimes, A. L., McCullough, L. B., Kunik, M. E., Molinari, V., & Workman, R. H., Jr. (2000). Informed consent and neuroanatomic correlates of intentionality and voluntariness among psychiatric patients. *Psychiatric Services*, *51*(12), 1561–1567.

Grisso, T., & Appelbaum, P. S. (1998). *Assessing competence to consent to treatment: A guide for physicians and other health professionals*. New York: Oxford University Press.

Holder, A. R. (1983). Involuntary commitment, incompetency, and consent. *IRB: A Review of Human Subjects Research*, *5*(2), 6–8.

Janofsky, J. S., McCarthy, R. J., & Folstein, M. F. (1992). The Hopkins competency assessment test: A brief method for evaluating patients' capacity to give informed consent. *Hospital and Community Psychiatry*, *43*, 132.

Karlawish, J. H. T., Knopman, D., Clark, C. M., Morris, J. C., Marson, D., Whitehouse, P. J., et al. (2002). Informed consent for Alzheimer's disease clinical trials: A survey of clinical investigators. *IRB: Ethics & Human Research*, *24*(5), 1–5.

Kim, S. Y. H., Cox, C., & Caine, E. D. (2002). Impaired decision-making ability in subjects with Alzheimer's disease and willingness to participate in research. *American Journal of Psychiatry*, *159*, 797–802.

Koocher, G. P., & Keith-Spiegel, P. C. (1990). *Children, ethics, and the law: Professional issues and cases*. Lincoln: University of Nebraska Press.

Levine, R. J. (1988). *Ethics and regulation of clinical research* (2nd ed.). New Haven, CT: Yale University Press.

Marson, D. C., Cody, H. A., Ingram, K. K., & Harrell, L. E. (1995). Neuropsychologic predictors of competency in Alzheimer's disease using a rational reasons legal standard: A prototype instrument. *Archives of Neurology, 52*, 955.

Menikoff, J. (2001). *Law and bioethics: An introduction*. Washington, DC: Georgetown University Press.

Miller, V. A., Drotar, D., & Kodish, E. (2004). Children's competence for assent and consent: A review of empirical findings. *Ethics & Behavior, 14*(3), 255–295.

Moreno, J. D. (1999). Critical issues concerning research involving decisionally impaired persons. In National Bioethics Advisory Committee (Ed.), *Research involving persons with mental disorders that may affect decisionmaking capacity: Commissioned papers* (pp. 51–59). Rockvillle, MD: National Bioethics Advisory Committee.

Moser, D. J., Arndt, S., Kanz, J. E., Benjamin, M., Bayless, J. D., Reese, R. L., et al. (2004). Coercion and informed consent in research involving prisoners. *Comprehensive Psychiatry, 45*, 1–9.

Moser, D. J., Schultz, S. K., Arndt, S., Benjamin, M. L., Fleming, F. W., Brems, C. S., et al. (2002). Capacity to provide informed consent for participation in schizophrenia and HIV research. *American Journal of Psychiatry, 159*(7), 1201–1207.

National Bioethics Advisory Commission. (1998). *Research involving persons with mental disorders that may affect decisionmaking capacity: Vol. 1. Report and recommendations*. Rockville, MD: National Bioethics Advisory Commission.

National Commission. (1979). *The Belmont report: Ethical principles and guidelines for the protection of human subjects of research*. Washington, DC: Department of Health, Education, and Welfare.

National Commission for the Protection of Human Subjects of Biomedical and Behavioral Research. (1978). *Research involving those institutionalized as mentally infirm: Report and recommendations*. Washington, DC: Department of Health, Education, and Welfare.

National Human Research Protections Advisory Committee. (2002). *Report from NHRPAC Clarifying Specific Portion of 45 CFR 46 Subpart D that Governs Children's Research*. Retrieved January 11, 2007, from http://www.hhs.gov/ohrp/nhrpac/documents/nhrpac16.pdf.

National Institutes of Health. (1999). Research involving individuals with questionable capacity to consent: Points to consider. *Biological Psychiatry, 46*, 1014–1016.

Orr, W. B., & Janofsky, J. S. (1996). Clinicians' judgment of capacity of nursing home patients to give informed consent. *Psychiatric Services, 47*, 956.

Osher, T. W., & Telesford, M. (1996). Involving families to improve research. In K. Hoagwood, P. S. Jensen, & C. B. Fisher (Eds.), *Ethical issues in mental health research with children and adolescents* (pp. 29–39). Mahwah, NJ: Lawrence Erlbaum Associates.

Penslar, R. L. (1993). *Institutional review board guidebook*. Washington, DC: Office for Human Research Protections, Department of Health and Human Services. Retrieved January 11, 2007, from http://www.hhs.gov/ohrp/irb/irb_guidebook.htm.

Porter, J. P. (1996). Regulatory considerations in research involving children and adolescents with mental disorders. In K. Hoagwood, P. S. Jensen, & C. B. Fisher (Eds.), *Ethical issues in mental health research with children and adolescents* (pp. 15–28). Mahwah, NJ: Lawrence Erlbaum Associates.

Posever, T. A., & Chelmow, T. (2001). Informed consent for research in schizophrenia: An alternative for special studies. *IRB: Ethics & Human Research, 23*(1), 10–15.

President's Commission. (1982). *Making health care decisions: A report on the ethical and legal implications of informed consent in the patient-practitioner relationship* (Vol. 1). Washington, DC: President's Commission for the Study of Ethical Problems in Medicine and Biomedical and Behavioral Research.

Roth, L. H., Meisel, A., & Lidz, C. W. (1977). Tests of incompetency to consent to treatment. *American Journal of Psychiatry, 134*, 279.

Sachs, G. A., Stocking, C. B., Stern, R., Cox, D. M., Hougham, G., & Sparage Sachs, R. (1994). Ethical aspects of dementia research: Informed consent and proxy consent. *Clincal Research, 42*(3), 403–412.

Saks, E. R. (1999). Competency to decide on treatment and research: The MacArthur capacity instruments. In National Bioethics Advisory Committee (Ed.), *Research involving persons with mental disorders that may affect decisionmaking capacity: Commissioned papers* (pp. 59–78). Rockvillle, MD: National Bioethics Advisory Committee.

Skrutkowski, M., Weijer, C., Shapiro, S., Fuks, A., Langleben, A., & Freedman, B. (1998). Monitoring informed consent in an oncology study posing serious risk to subjects. *IRB: A Review of Human Subjects Research, 20*(6), 1–5.

Sunderland, T., & Dukoff, R. (1999). Surrogate decision making and advance directives with cognitively impaired research subjects. In H. A. Pincus, J. A. Lieberman, & S. Ferris (Eds.), *Ethics in psychiatric research: A resource manual for human subjects protection* (pp. 107–119). Washington, DC: American Psychiatric Association.

Thomasma, D.C. (1997). A communal model for presumed consent for research on the neurologically vulnerable. In A. E. Shamoo (Ed.), *Ethics in neurobiological research with human subjects: The Baltimore Conference on Ethics* (pp. 239–252). Amsterdam: Gordon and Breach.

Tomada, A., Sumiyama, T., Tsukada, K., Hayakawam, T., Matsubara, K., Kitamura, F., et al. (1997). Structured interview for competency and incompetency assessment testing and ranking inventory. *Journal of Clincal Psychology, 53*, 443.

Wagener, D. K., Sporer, A. K., Simmerling, M., Flome, J. L., An, C., & Curry, S. J. (2004). Human subjects challenges in youth-focused research: Perspectives and practices of IRB administrators. *Ethics and Behavior, 14*(4), 335–349.

Weijer, C. (1999). Research involving the vulnerable sick. *Accountability in Research, 7*, 21–36.

Wilks, I. (1997). The debate over risk-related standards of competence. *Bioethics, 11*(5), 413–426.

Wirshing, D. A., Wirshing, W. C., Marder, S. R., Liberman, R. P., & Mintz, J. (1998). Informed consent: Assessment of comprehension. *American Journal of Psychiatry, 155*(11), 1508–1511.

6

Thinking About Harms and Benefits

Nothing learned will prevent, find, or cure a single case.
—James Jones, *Bad Blood: The Tuskegee Syphilis Experiment*

This chapter presents a general framework for considering risks and benefits in the design and review of research. Subsequent chapters examine specific risks and benefits in the context of a variety of study designs in mental health research.

WHY AUTONOMY IS INSUFFICIENT TO JUSTIFY PARTICIPATION IN RESEARCH

After being criticized for conducting studies of obedience to authority in which participants were deceived and led to believe they had administered terrible electrical shocks to other alleged participants (Baumrind, 1964), Stanley Milgram defended himself by citing a subsequent survey of the participants in which less than 2% were sorry to have taken part in the experiment (Milgram, 1964). A more recent survey of healthy children and children with major depressive disorder who had participated in a multi-day sleep and neuroendocrine study that involved indwelling intravenous catheters and all-night electroencephalography found that no child or parent regretted participation (Townsend et al., 1988). How significant should such considerations of participant attitudes be in evaluating whether a study design should be considered ethical or approved by review boards? Does participant consent justify exposing people to various harms?

The Nuremberg Code's first principle is, "The voluntary consent of the human subject is absolutely essential." Virtually every code of research ethics written since 1949 has echoed this call for consent, at least for research that involves any significant level of risk.[1] But then these same codes go on to demand much more. They require that research be designed to offer important benefits and that steps be taken to minimize risks. Consent is necessary, but why is it not considered sufficient to justify including human beings in a study?

Put in other words, should respect for autonomy alone suffice to justify a person's participation in a study? We could go further and ask whether it is

---

1. The regulations do not require informed consent for all kinds of research (DuBois, 2002). For example, certain kinds of minimal risk research—research with existing data or public observation—may be exempt from regulatory required informed consent and may not ethically require consent depending on circumstances.

even possible to respect autonomy while denying a person the opportunity to participate in high-risk studies. Some ethicists have argued along such "libertarian" lines. For example, Engelhardt—one of the original philosophical consultants to the National Commission—has argued that "if it is morally proper for individuals freely to volunteer for service in the armed forces, it should be morally proper as well to volunteer for service in research forces," even when this involves dangerous research (Engelhardt, 1996, p. 333). Likewise, he argues that even in cases of risky research that is based on "nonorthodox approaches to health care"—that is, research that is not based on Western concepts of scientific evidence—participation should be allowed if the individuals involved understand and appreciate the risks: "One should be as tolerant of martyrs for unconventional understandings of science as one is of martyrs for what others may hold to be unconventional religious viewpoints (e.g., an adult Jehovah's Witness deciding to die rather than accept a blood transfusion …)" (Engelhardt, 1996, p. 334).

We can offer at least two arguments against a libertarian approach to research approval: the first is based on the larger principle of respect for human beings; the second is based on the unfeasibility of implementing a libertarian ethic in research.

In chapter 2, it was argued that one way of understanding how the Belmont Report's principles are not completely arbitrary is to look at what respect for human beings requires. We noted that respecting another person requires respecting five key aspects of human beings, not just one. A libertarian position emphasizes respect for human beings as rational and self-determining. But human beings are also vulnerable to harms and in need of basic goods. Unless these dimensions are respected, we cannot meet our basic needs, much less flourish.

Moreover, a libertarian justification of participation in research is naïve and unfeasible. The autonomy—the rationality and self-determination—of people is often severely limited. As noted in chapters 4 and 7, many threats to the voluntariness of informed consent exist, including low reading or comprehension levels, desperate needs for compensation or free medical care, and therapeutic misconceptions. When these threats to informed consent are combined with the strong motives that researchers often have to enroll participants, a risk of exploitation arises. Moreover, a review of the empirical literature on the medical decision making of patients suggests that while most want information on procedures, they also want to rely on others—both family and physicians—in making important medical decisions (Schneider, 1998).

Thus, while consent is necessary to justify subjecting a person to risks for the sake of research, it is not sufficient. Additionally, we need to consider the requirements of the principles of beneficence, nonmaleficence, justice, and relationality.

THE DUTY TO BE BENEFICENT

Beneficence provides the driving impetus behind the entire research enterprise. Research is meant to serve a purpose, to benefit people in a variety of ways. In fact, to the extent that we view respect for autonomy as a *valid reason* for permitting research, we do not esteem autonomy simply as arbitrary volition but as the exercise of *rational* choice, a choice to participate in an endeavor that individuals believe will yield benefits to themselves or others.

It is often said that there are no duties to be beneficent, only duties not to harm. And indeed, in using the term "beneficence," the Belmont Report focused much more on minimizing harms than on providing benefits. Nevertheless, in chapter 2, it was argued that beneficence is a form of respect for persons as finite beings with basic needs. Aristotelians (Aristotle, 1980), communitarians (Etzioni, 1998; C. Taylor, 1989), feminists (Tong, 1998), and personalists (Mounier, 1950/1979) have long emphasized that human beings are not best understood as autonomous isolated individuals, but rather as interdependent members of communities. This is in part because we cannot meet our basic needs alone.

If human beings cannot survive or thrive without the beneficent actions of others, then it is reasonable to embrace the idea that respect for human beings requires at least some effort to meet their basic needs. But two important qualifications need to be made. First, "at least some effort" should be made, but this effort should be context specific. In contrast to duties not to harm, our beneficent actions need not be directed toward others in the same impartial manner (Beauchamp & Childress, 2001). Special roles or relationships to others—for instance, being a parent or a personal physician—may not only justify special beneficent treatment but obligate it. This would apply to societal as well as individual relationships: nations may show some partiality toward their citizens; professional societies may provide special benefits to members. Second, both societal and individual *duties* to be beneficent arguably relate only to certain basic human needs. For example, many people recognize a duty to redistribute staple foods or the goods needed to buy or produce staple foods; but most people would say there is not a duty to interfere with the naturally occurring distribution of Champagne or caviar. The intuition behind such widely held ideas is that there are basic human needs that we ought to help people meet, but we have no duty to satisfy their every desire.

While it may be difficult to get a strong consensus on the specific details of a list of basic human needs, we see certain needs repeatedly occurring in the writings of humanists, ethicists, and human rights advocates. Table 6.1 summarizes areas of significant convergence across these three fields.

Table 6.1 A List of Basic Human Needs Recognized by Diverse Traditions

Maslow's Hierarchy (Maslow, 1970)	Basic Goods (Finnis, 1980)	Universal Declaration of Human Rights (United Nations General Assembly, 1948)
Self-actualization	Knowledge, religion (or reflection on ultimate reality), self-integration; skill in work or play	Right to rest and leisure, to participate in cultural life of the community, to education, to choose and manifest religion
Love/esteem	Friendship (including marriage) and sociability	Right to marry, to peaceful assembly and association, to be free from arbitrary attacks upon honor and reputation
Safety	Life, self-integration (including psychological security)	Right to be free of torture, arbitrary arrest, cruel treatment
Physiological	Life	Right to life, to just remuneration for work, to food, clothing, housing, medical care

Clearly, these needs—even if universal—can be met in a wide variety of ways; some variation may be explained at the cultural level, some at the individual level. People in one culture may live reasonably well without being able to read, without access to private transportation, and without high-tech medical care. Others may need to read and have transportation in order to earn a living wage, and they may be exposed to health hazards that require high-tech medical solutions. Thus, it is reasonable to view duties of beneficence as limited not only by special relationships, but also by the ways that cultural and individual differences influence needs, and by the resources we have to meet the needs of others.

To summarize, depending on society's or an individual's relationship to others, duties may exist to meet certain basic needs in culturally and individually appropriate ways. Now we may ask: What kinds of benefits can researchers be expected to provide? And to whom are they expected to provide benefits?

THE VARIETY OF RESEARCH BENEFITS

In professional ethics, the goals or purposes of a profession determine the specific duties that professionals have. The goal of "pure" research is simply knowledge. The goals of applied sciences, like medical research, are to gain knowledge that will improve human lives in a variety of ways, for example, by improving medical care. Interestingly, the Belmont Report states that the term "benefit" "is used in the research context to refer to something of positive value related to health or welfare" (C2). While this sounds like a reductionistic view of research benefits, arguably knowledge itself improves human welfare.[2] Understood in this fashion, even pure research contributes to respect for human beings.

Apart from knowledge and the one aspect of human welfare that the Belmont Report specifically names (health), what other benefits can research confer? Joan Sieber identifies seven different kinds of benefits that can be offered in research. Not all research will be able to offer all seven kinds of benefits. Her focus is on community-based social and behavioral research, and accordingly she refers to benefits to communities; but all kinds of research should be expected to provide at least some of these benefits, even if the beneficiaries are not always communities. She proposes that the following benefits are listed in a descending order of difficulty to provide. Ironically, she suggests that the most common goal of scientific research—scientific outcomes in the sense of an original contribution to the scientific field—may be the most difficult to provide.

This broad conception of the kinds of benefits research can offer overlaps with the full range of basic needs delineated below in table 6.2.

Especially as we review research that goes beyond the narrow scope of biomedical research, it is important to adopt a broad view of benefits in reviewing the merits of a project.

---

2. Whether or not this takes liberty with the definition can be debated. However, even commentators who focus on clinical research note that health is often interpreted in a broad biopsychosocial sense and that some research may be of immediate value, whereas more basic research may be said to have future value insofar as useful applied research may eventually be built upon it (Casarett et al., 2002).

Table 6.2 A Taxonomy of Benefits in Research

Kind of Benefit	Example From Community-Based Research
Valuable relationships	The community establishes ties with helping institutions and funders.
Knowledge or education	The community develops a better understanding of its own problems.
Material resources	The community makes use of research materials, equipment, and funding.
Training, employment, opportunity for advancement	Community members receive training and continue to serve as professionals or paraprofessionals within the ongoing project.
Opportunity to do good and to receive the esteem of others	The community learns how to better serve its members.
Empowerment	The community uses findings for policy purposes, gains favorable attention of the press, politicians, and the like.
Scientific/clinical outcomes	The community provides treatment to its members (assuming the research or intervention is successful).

Derived from Sieber (1992).

Nevertheless, a broad view of benefits when combined with a broad view of beneficiaries can yield a very complex picture. In addition to the seven kinds of benefits, Sieber identifies seven common beneficiaries of research: (1) participants, (2) the participants' communities, (3) the researcher, (4) the research institution, (5) the funding agency, (6) scientific disciplines, and (7) the larger society. "The conjunction of seven kinds of benefits and seven kinds of beneficiaries yields a 49-cell matrix that is useful in research planning" (Sieber, 1992). It is particularly useful in attempts to maximize benefits: opportunities abound when research is viewed in this fashion. However, such a matrix may be unwieldy in weighing benefits against risks. Above all, it might give the impression that the scales are loaded as we weigh risks to participants against 49 categories of goods.

The National Bioethics Advisory Commission (NBAC) distinguished between three different kinds of potential benefits that research might offer to participants: (1) intended direct benefits such as access to experimental therapies; (2) unanticipated benefits such as identifying non–study-related health problems; and (3) indirect benefits such as increased social contact. Similarly, NBAC sharply distinguished between benefits to participants and benefits to all others. When conducting risk-benefit analyses, NBAC encouraged IRBs to focus only on the balance of risks to participants and potential direct benefits (not indirect or unintended) to participants (not researchers, communities, society, or other groups) (National Bioethics Advisory Commission, 2001).

Perhaps wisdom lies in striking a balance between these two approaches. On the one hand, NBAC's approach is likely to prevent exploitation of vulnerable participants in greater than minimal risk research. On the other hand, it downplays the significance of indirect benefits and benefits to important stakeholders, and it puts forward its recommendation as a one-size-fits-all approach that may be inappropriate in the context of minimal risk research such as quality improvement surveys that may offer little direct benefit to participants but much to communities and institutions. If altruism is a legitimate motive for research, then other kinds of benefits and other beneficiaries should be taken into account when considering the balance of risks to benefits, especially in research that is minimal risk or that involves less vulnerable populations. Furthermore, if we deny that research can be conducted with the primary aim of gaining knowledge or benefiting a community, then it is impossible to dispel the therapeutic misconception (chapter 4) in the context of clinical research: all research would be aimed first and foremost at providing direct benefits to participants (presumably, therapeutic benefits in the clinical context).

EVALUATING RISKS

Early in his discussion of risks in research, Levine states that "empirical data have become available that indicate that, in general, it is not particularly hazardous to be a research subject" (1988, p. 39). For example, he cites data on one of the riskiest forms of research—phase I (safety) drug testing—that indicate risks are about the same as working as a secretary and are 1/7th of those of working as a window washer. He also observes that in a review of "805 protocols involving 29,162 prisoner subjects over 614,534 days, there were 58 adverse drug reactions, of which none produced death or permanent disability" (p. 39). Similarly, in discussing risks in research with children in behavioral science, Koocher and Keith-Spiegel (1990) state that such research "does not typically present the more serious consequences to participants, such as pain or a worsening of a physical condition, that can arise in biomedical research. In fact, the risks in social and behavioral research often appear trivial" (p. 125).

On the one hand, statements like these provide needed perspective. The press reports on deaths and scandals in research; research ethics textbooks regularly revisit the worst chapters in the history of research; and research regulations often require elaborate systems of protection—all reinforcing the belief that research is a very dangerous enterprise. In fact, most people who have participated in clinical trials not only do not experience significant harms but report satisfaction with their experience and a willingness to participate in research again (Getz & Borfitz, 2002).

On the other hand, the reason that research is, today, relatively safe is because of heightened vigilance on the part of researchers and oversight bodies (IRBs, government agencies, funding agencies, advocates, and others). In fact, both Levine (1988) and Koocher & and Keith-Spiegel (1990) go on to highlight the variety of harms that are possible in research.

The concept of risk refers to the probability and magnitude of harms. Table 6.3 summarizes the five primary forms of harm identified in the Belmont Report.[3]

---

3. Koocher (2002) has developed "CABLES" as an acronym and metaphor for conceptualizing risks in research. CABLES stands for cognitive, affective, biological, legal, economic, and social/cultural harms.

Table 6.3 The Five Primary Forms of Harm Identified in the Belmont Report

Kind of Harm	Examples
Psychological	Boredom, anxiety, embarrassment, or psychotic relapse
Physical	Sexual dysfunction, high blood pressure, or death
Legal	Fines or imprisonment
Social	Stigmatization, harm to reputation, or divorce
Economic	Lost time at work, loss of employment, legal fees or medical bills for harms incurred in research

Derived from National Commission (1979).

As we have seen, the duty not to harm (nonmaleficence) closely relates to beneficence. One reason is that both relate to the basic human needs listed in table 6.1. We may understand the various harms as forms of damage to our enjoyment of, or ability to obtain, the goods that meet our basic needs.

Levine has observed that the very same kinds of risks that threaten individuals may also threaten society. For example, when the results of poorly conducted research find their way into peer-reviewed literature and eventually into public media, they can contribute to widespread poor health practices, stigmatization of groups, wasted research and health dollars, and mental anguish among those affected by these harms (Levine, 1988). The development of antipsychotic medications, discussed in the introduction, may provide a powerful example of this phenomenon (Whitaker, 2002). These risks certainly deserve consideration, even if risks to participants should be given primary regard.

Research regulations and IRBs typically categorize risk as either minimal risk or greater than minimal risk. The regulatory definition of minimal risk is "the probability and magnitude of harm or discomfort anticipated in the research are not greater in and of themselves than those ordinarily encountered in daily life or during the performance of routine physical or psychological examinations or tests" (45CFR46.102[i]). While much rests upon this definition—for example, decisions whether research may be exempt from ongoing IRB review or whether consent may be waived or deception allowed—its interpretation has been subject to controversy, and the literature on the subject reveals no consensus (Kopelman, 2000).

By considering both the probability and the magnitude of harm, it seems that we arrive at the counterintuitive idea that minimal risk research may in fact involve either a high probability of harm or a high magnitude of harm (but not both). For example, in the United States, the risk of death driving to work is one that is ordinarily encountered in daily life (low probability, high magnitude of harm). Likewise, the risk of boredom in performing repetitive tasks is commonly encountered in daily life (high probability, low magnitude of harm). At what point does a combined probability and magnitude of harm exceed minimal standards? Using standards of "daily life" is of only limited use because different individuals encounter radically different risks in everyday life, depending on factors such as medical diagnoses and socioeconomic status (Barnbaum, 2002).

Some have argued for a context-dependent interpretation of minimal risk that takes into account the actual risks individuals face in daily life (Freedman et al., 1993). Others have argued that the risks of daily living should be determined with reference to those faced by healthy, general populations; otherwise, some will be subjected to greater risks than others, and the minimal risk standard becomes relative (Kopelman, 1995; National Bioethics Advisory Commission, 2001).

From an ethical perspective, we can ask whether such discrepancies would be unjust or simply unfortunate (to borrow a distinction from Engelhardt [1996]). But more important, we need to ask whether a relative standard of minimal risk is likely to lead to exploitation (i.e., using others merely as means to an end, with no regard for their best interests). Two guidelines might be offered to avoid exploitation. First, because informed consent enables participants to weigh risks and benefits themselves, whenever informed consent will be waived, the "safer" interpretation of minimal risk should be used. Second, when risks appear to be outside the scope of those risks encountered in the daily life of healthy people, community members should be consulted to provide transparency and to take into account the fact that different people subjectively experience risks differently (Martin et al., 1995; Meslin, 1990).

HOW ART THOU VULNERABLE? LET ME COUNT THE WAYS

Chapter 2 suggested that the principle of nonmaleficence refers to respect for human beings insofar as we are vulnerable to harms—and we are all vulnerable to harms both small and great. However, in a regulatory context, Levine has argued that the term refers above all to "those who are relatively (or absolutely) incapable of protecting their own interests" (Levine, 1988, p. 72). The Common Rule identifies several groups as vulnerable, including "children, prisoners, pregnant women, mentally disabled persons, or economically or educationally disadvantaged persons" (45CFR46.111[a][3]). However, specific rules exist in subparts B–D to protect only three of these groups: pregnant women, fetuses, and neonates; prisoners; and children.[4] Table 6.4 presents the additional protections that the Common Rule has put in place for research involving children or participants who have not yet reached the legal age required to give informed consent. (Information on the specific protections afforded to prisoners and pregnant women, fetuses, and neonates can be found in the regulations section of www.emhr.net.)

However, this group-based approach to vulnerability was rejected by NBAC in its 2001 report on "Ethical and Policy Issues in Research Involving Human Participants." They rejected it on several grounds: that a group-based approach may become unwieldy if we seek to craft special regulations for each group; many groups require the same kinds of protections; some individuals may belong to more than one vulnerable group; the status of groups changes with time; and it fails to take into account ways in which members of groups may be particularly

---

4. Interestingly, the men in the Tuskegee syphilis study were vulnerable in multiple ways using NBAC's framework; yet using the framework of the Common Rule, no specific additional protections exist to protect similar men or women.

Table 6.4 Protections and Risk-Benefit Ratios in Research With Children

Risk-Benefit Description	Special Required Protections
Not greater than minimal risk	Assent of children and permission of parents
Greater than minimal risk with prospect of direct benefit to individual subjects	Same as above plus . . . • Risk is justified by anticipated benefits to subjects • Risk-benefit ratio at least as favorable as that of alternative approaches
Greater than minimal risk with no prospect of direct benefit to individual subjects, but likely to yield generalizable knowledge about subject's disorder or condition	Same as above plus . . . • Risk may be only a minor increase over minimal risk • Research procedures must present experiences that are commensurate with those inherent in subject's actual or expected medical . . . or psychological . . . situations • Expected knowledge should be of vital importance in understanding or ameliorating the disorder
Research not otherwise approvable that presents an opportunity to understand, prevent, or alleviate a serious problem affecting the health or welfare of children	Secretary of Health and Human Services, after consulting with expert panel and opportunity for public comment, determines that study will be conducted in accordance with sound ethical principles. Assent of children and permission of parents.

Based on Federal Regulations 45CFR46 sections 404–407of subpart D.

vulnerable only to certain kinds of research harms (National Bioethics Advisory Commission, 2001). In place of a group-based approach, NBAC argued that six kinds of vulnerability should be considered when reviewing research. Each one of these vulnerabilities refers to a factor that either threatens voluntary, informed consent or increases the likelihood of exploitation. Table 6.5 summarizes the kinds of vulnerabilities and the corresponding heightened risks.

Each of the six vulnerabilities calls for special safeguards, although these will need to be tailored to the specific study and the specific heightened risks. For example, participants with cognitive vulnerability may need an assessment of decision-making capacity, and their wishes or interests may need to be protected using advanced directives or surrogate decision makers. Communicative vulnerabilities may require special accommodations using oral communication, closed captioning, or translation services. Medical vulnerability may be addressed by using an impartial third party to obtain informed consent in order to reduce the risk that a research will be confused with therapy. Separating the roles of treating physician and investigator may serve the same purpose and eliminate a conflict of interest.

ARE PEOPLE WITH MENTAL DISORDERS A VULNERABLE GROUP?

Why would we ask whether people with mental disorders are a vulnerable group if we just considered good reasons for taking a non-group-based approach to

Table 6.5 NBAC's Six Types of Vulnerability and Corresponding Heightened Risks

Type	Description of Participant	Heightened Risks
Cognitive or communicative vulnerability	Insufficiently able to comprehend information, deliberate, make or express decisions	Informed consent will not be properly obtained; participant less able to protect interests
Institutional vulnerability	Subjected to formal authority of others—e.g., prisoners and students	Participation will not be truly voluntary; participant may be exploited
Deferential vulnerability	Informally subordinate to another—e.g., due to gender or roles	Participation will not be truly voluntary; participant may be exploited
Medical vulnerability	Has serious health condition for which there is no satisfactory standard treatment	Trouble weighing risks and benefits; participant may be exploited due to therapeutic misconception
Economic vulnerability	Lacks access to adequate income, housing, or health care	Potential benefits from participation may be unduly influential and threaten voluntariness
Social vulnerability	Others may disvalue participant and his or her interests, welfare, and contributions to society	Discrimination may lead to unfair treatment and stigmatization

Derived from National Bioethics Advisory Commission (2001).

vulnerability? First, as noted above, current regulations identify "mentally disabled persons" as vulnerable and in need of additional safeguards (45CFR46.111[b]). Moreover, NBAC—the very commission that argued against taking a group-based approach to vulnerabilities—issued a lengthy report specifically on "Research Involving Persons With Mental Disorders That May Affect Decisionmaking Capacity" (National Bioethics Advisory Commission, 1999)—admittedly, two years prior to its general report on research with human participants. In this report, NBAC offers two reasons for focusing on this group: (1) "this population's difficult history of involvement in medical research" and (2) that research involving subjects with such disorders "should be governed by specific further regulations." This is reminiscent of the work of the National Commission, which issued the Belmont Report. Among the 17 reports the National Commission produced was one dedicated to "Research Involving Those Institutionalized as Mentally Infirm" (National Commission for the Protection of Human Subjects of Biomedical and Behavioral Research, 1978).[5] Whereas NBAC focused upon the cognitive vulnerability of people with mental disorders, the National Commission focused on institutional vulnerability.

However, the different focuses of these two reports should suffice to remind us why addressing vulnerability in terms of groups was rejected by NBAC: members

---

5. For a summary of this report, see Levine, 1988, pp. 266–267. For a commentary on why the report "remains the only study of the National Commission to be ignored," see Jonsen, 1998, pp. 104–105.

of other groups share cognitive and institutional vulnerability and require similar protections; and members of groups (such as "persons with mental disorders") do not all share the same vulnerabilities. To these reasons we can add at least two. First, a group-based approach can reinforce certain social stereotypes or stigmas. As noted in chapter 5, most people diagnosed with a mental disorder are competent to make decisions, and most are not institutionalized. Second, it encourages us to focus on just one area of vulnerability—for instance, cognitive or institutional vulnerability—when individuals may be vulnerable in multiple ways. A person diagnosed with a severe mental disorder who moves in and out of institutions may suffer from all six vulnerabilities. However, while a mental health diagnosis may present a risk factor for these vulnerabilities, it is only a risk factor; it might justify assessing individuals but not labeling them in blanket fashion (Grisso & Appelbaum, 1998).

Rather than crafting special regulations for each group that is at risk for being vulnerable in one or more ways, it would seem prudent to require that researchers and those involved in research oversight (e.g., IRBs, institutions, and funding agencies) identify whether the research population they plan to involve is at risk for any of the six vulnerabilities, and if so, to establish proper safeguards and a proper level of stakeholder involvement (e.g., oversight representation by community members or advocates). As we will see, these recommendations are neither novel nor uniquely tailored to mental health research; they should be part of any standard risk-benefit analysis.

INSTEAD OF BALANCING RISKS AND BENEFITS

The Belmont Report observes that in speaking of "balancing" risks and benefits, one is speaking metaphorically (C2). Sieber provides a few reasons that it can only be understood metaphorically: most risks and benefits cannot be quantified; some risks and benefits cannot be identified accurately before research is conducted; it is impossible to consider all possible risks and benefits (e.g., new friendships made during research); and it is impossible to consider risks and benefits to each participant (Sieber, 1992).

The following is a list of general guidelines that have been gleaned from the Belmont Report's treatment of risks and benefits in research (section C.2). In an effort to show how these guidelines are not haphazard or arbitrary, following each guideline is a statement of how it can be derived from at least one of the ethical justification criteria presented in chapter 3.

First, the anticipated benefits of research should be significant enough to justify conducting the study. At a very minimum, this requires that studies are scientifically valid (Freedman, 1987). Benefits to participants should be given special consideration, especially in greater than minimal risk research or research involving participants with vulnerabilities. This set of guidelines derives from the proportionality test and the related effectiveness test.

Second, brutal or inhumane treatment of human participants is never morally justified. The Nazi experiments provide rare but compelling examples of such research, including high altitude, freezing, mustard gas, typhus, poison, and sterilization experiments conducted without consent and with harms intentionally inflicted (T. Taylor, 1992). This guideline treats a prohibition on intentionally maleficent behavior as a greater than prima facie norm. Inhumane treatment should not be tested for justification; it should be ruled out absolutely.

Third, reduce risks to those necessary to achieve the research objective. As the Nuremberg Code suggests, this should involve considering whether human participants are needed at all (Annas & Grodin, 1992). Within the context of clinical trials, NIH and FDA policies require the use of additional risk minimization strategies, such as data and safety monitoring boards (Gordon et al., 1998). IRBs or investigators may use the information gathered by these boards to modify informed consent during a study, to allow crossover to the experimental treatment when research results are therapeutically promising, or to close down a study deemed inadequately safe. Additionally, protocols that run risks of exacerbating symptoms or leaving symptoms untreated may include a "rescue arm," that is, a plan to provide short-term treatment of acute symptoms and to remove participants from a study if short-term treatment is unsuccessful or insufficient (Oquendo et al., 2004b). (The case studies found in this chapter and in chapter 8 discuss these and other risk-reducing strategies in more detail.) This guideline derives from the necessity and least infringement tests.

Fourth, give special consideration to participant vulnerabilities. Should vulnerable participants be included in the study at all—does the research concern their needs, is it expected to benefit them or people who share their vulnerabilities (National Commission, 1979, C3)? If so, are special protections needed? At face value, this expresses a commitment to justice in justifying risks. But it also derives from the proportionality and necessity tests: vulnerable people may be at greater risk (making justification more difficult), and it may not be necessary to subject people to heightened risks.

Fifth, present relevant risks and benefits in the informed consent documents and procedures. Greater risks require greater justification, including more manifest voluntariness on the part of participants (National Commission, 1979, C2). This derives from the "proper process" test. Due process in research involves getting informed consent.

To these five criteria, we can add a guideline that has become emphasized and expanded in recent years: use appropriate processes to evaluate risks and benefits. This will involve (a) drawing from existing scientific evidence (National Commission, 1979, C2), (b) submitting to IRB review as appropriate (45CFR46), and (c) including community members as appropriate in identifying and evaluating risks and benefits (Centers for Disease Control and Prevention et al., 1998; National Bioethics Advisory Commission, 1999). This is nothing other than a statement that proper process should be followed—partly out of respect for stakeholders and partly to draw from community wisdom in implementing the other tests (e.g., identifying and evaluating risks).

Thus far, our discussion of risks and benefits has been very general. In subsequent chapters, we will look at several important applied topics: identifying and managing the risks and potential benefits that arise within specific study designs, ranging from community-based qualitative research to placebo-controlled clinical trials (chapter 8); risks of privacy violations and breaches of confidentiality (chapter 9); and conflicts of interest, which are a growing source of heightened risks for participants (chapter 10).

Case Study: A Study of Suicidality With At-Risk Teens

In the year 2000, nearly 30,000 people in the United States committed suicide, and various sources estimate that there are 8 to 25 times as many suicide attempts for every suicide death. Nevertheless, despite the public health and personal burdens associated with suicide, "the empirically validated knowledge base is limited," and "clinical wisdom and empirical evidence have minimal overlap when it comes to interventions with persons at high risk for suicidality" (Pearson et al., 2001). There are at least two reasons for this. First, suicidal behaviors are relatively rare and are often difficult to predict; this makes it difficult to conduct studies with sufficiently large samples and statistical power to determine the efficacy of interventions. Second, people at high risk for suicide are frequently excluded from participation in clinical trials, and few trials are designed specifically to target people at high risk for suicide. This is due largely to perceived risks to investigators, institutions, and sponsors (Pearson et al., 2001).

Suicide among youths is a growing problem. Suicide is the third leading cause of death among 10- to 24-year-olds (National Institute of Mental Health, 2006). Depression is a major risk factor for suicide among youth (Gould et al., 2003) and the general population (Oquendo et al., 2004a); for example, major depression involves a 15% suicide rate (Hahn et al., 2003).

Standard clinical practice has involved treating depressed teens with antidepressants, even though most antidepressants on the market have not been approved for use with people under 18 years old. Whether the use of antidepressants in teens is associated with increased or decreased risk of suicide is currently debated (Simon, 2006).

A clinical trial is now being proposed to determine the safety of a commonly prescribed antidepressant with children ages 12–17. Because some controversy has arisen regarding suicide risk and the use of antidepressants, the investigators will treat suicidality as an outcome measure. The investigators define suicidality to include suicidal ideation, attempted suicide, or death by suicide. Moreover, whereas psychopharmaceutical clinical trials frequently exclude patients who are at high risk of suicidality from participation, this trial proposes to include such patients.

Investigators will randomize participants to one of four treatment arms: the experimental drug (FDA approved for adult use only); cognitive-behavioral therapy, which has been proven effective in treating depression; the experimental drug and cognitive behavioral therapy; and a competitor drug (FDA approved for adult use only) that has greater side effects with adults but is widely used.

When the study is presented to the IRB, the Vice President of Research Administration resolutely states that there is no way the IRB can approve the study as proposed. He recommends that suicide be treated merely as an unforeseen adverse event and that persons at high risk for suicidality be excluded. Otherwise, he fears that liability to the institution will be unacceptably high. However, members of the department of psychiatry point out that a trial sponsor is undertaking risks to generate knowledge that is important to preventing teen suicide, and the institution ought to be at least as willing to undertake risks. Others suggest that the study might be approved but that special protections should be offered both because the participants are minors and because the study involves a risk of death.

Would you recommend that this study be approved with suicidality as an outcome variable? If so, what special protections would you want to see in place?

CASE COMMENTARY

Suicide research potentially poses one of the sharpest dilemmas in human research ethics based on conflicting goals and values. Given that death by suicide is an outcome measure in suicide prevention research—rather than merely an unforeseen adverse event—therapeutic and research aims conflict. In theory, if all participants in a study received an effective therapeutic intervention, the study would be unable to determine whether an experimental intervention reduced incidences of suicide.

Nevertheless, death and morbidity are commonly measured outcomes in biomedical clinical trials, for example, in cancer or cardiology research. So why does suicide research generate so much discomfort within the research community? People may—rightly or wrongly—believe that suicide is more easily prevented than death from cancer or heart disease. Moreover, death is rarely a result of mental disorders—except through suicide and substance abuse. Mental health researchers and clinicians may therefore be less accustomed to encountering death in the course of their work than oncologists and cardiologists. Finally, in this case, we are discussing the death of teens at their own hands. Such deaths are premature and tragic. Even the philosophers who argued on behalf of a U.S. constitutional right to physician-assisted suicide explicitly sought to exclude collaboration with teenage suicidal intentions resulting from unrequited love or any suicidal intention resulting from depression or mental disorders (Dworkin et al., 1997).

Because this case has so many facets that deserve exploration, I will follow closely the analytic and justification framework presented in chapter 3.

Analysis

The stakeholders in this case include the proposed participants, their family members, the researchers, the population of people at risk for suicide, the research sponsor (the pharmaceutical company), and the research institution. All of these stakeholders share an interest in gaining new knowledge about antidepressants in the hopes of eventually reducing the prevalence of suicide. For some, the interest is immediate and personal; for others, secondary interests exist. The sponsor and researchers may be interested in designing the study to achieve statistically significant results in the shortest amount of time necessary. Withholding all treatment from at least one experimental group would likely facilitate this. Yet this is not in the interests of participants. Similarly, the sponsor has an interest in publishing results that will make its drug appear in the best light possible. Yet people at risk for suicide will be best served by a full disclosure of both positive and negative results. In what follows, we will assume that the interests of participants should be put above the interests of researchers and sponsors insofar as these conflict.

Many facts are relevant to our analysis of this case. The prevalence of suicide among teens and our lack of knowledge about whether antidepressants increase or decrease suicidality suggest the significance of this research. The study will not involve placebo; no known effective suicide-preventing treatment will be withheld. All participants will receive some form of treatment that has found some level of acceptance among practitioners. While we made the decision above to put the interests of participants above the interests of others, a perceived legal risk to conducting such research may prevent investigators from conducting the study. However, most cases in which courts found practitioners or hospitals culpable for a patient's suicide involved hospitalized patients (on the assumption that health care providers then have greater control over patients) and negligent care, such as failing to investigate a patient's history, ignoring evidence of suicidal tendencies, or discharging an acutely suicidal patient (Pearson et al., 2001). These "legal risks" thus can be managed with a careful protocol and responsible practice. Other relevant facts are discussed below.

All of the "intermediate" ethical principles presented in chapter 2 are relevant to this discussion. Beneficence requires that we make efforts to reduce the prevalence of suicide among teens. While beneficence may not always require that research offer direct benefits to all participants (e.g., to healthy participants in a survey), research involving minors with therapeutic needs ordinarily should offer direct benefits (though the subpart D of the Common Rule allows for some exceptions to this norm). Nonmaleficence requires that the study design minimize harms to the participants as far as possible. It also requires that we address the status quo in which teens are regularly prescribed medications with risks unknown for their population. Autonomy requires that investigators make extra efforts to enable the teens to understand the study and to be capable of giving their assent. It additionally requires working closely with parents to educate them about treatment alternatives and to obtain permission. Given the risks involved in the study, extra efforts to avoid undue influence are appropriate. Investigators should offer either no financial reimbursement or only modest reimbursement for participants' time; money should not be used as an incentive or prospective benefit. Justice requires that no participants be denied a readily available known effective treatment when their lives may be at stake. It also requires that people at risk for suicide not be systematically excluded from participation in research. The institution should consider this as it weighs its potential liability, which, as noted above, could be reduced through development and implementation of an appropriate protocol.[6] Finally, relationality is relevant insofar as the participants depend upon

---

6. In the analysis of the first case study in chapter 5, considerations of legal liability were given weight. This can be legitimate insofar as lawsuits may jeopardize an institution's ability to carry out its research and healing mission and may undermine public trust in the institution. However, legal risk management becomes problematic when it significantly compromises the benefits offered to patients or research participants.

others—especially family and guardians—to foster their well-being. Moreover, suicide often deeply scars loved ones. Limits to confidentiality should be put in place and disclosed to participants in order to enable researchers to contact family or caregivers directly in monitoring participants' suicidality and ensuring compliance with care plans (e.g., attending counseling sessions or taking prescribed medications).

Options: the study could be conducted as designed. It could be disapproved as designed on grounds of institutional risk management or participant safety. It could be approved with a variety of additional safeguards in place.

Justification

I argue that the study should be approved with a series of safeguards in place. This choice seeks to balance the aims of gaining important knowledge about the relationship of antidepressants to suicidality and protecting participants to the best of our ability.[7]

In this case, everything hinges on the least infringement test. Can we minimize the risk of suicide sufficiently well while gaining the knowledge we seek?[8] The details provided in the case already include very significant minimizations of risk. First, no one is being denied a known effective treatment, and everyone is receiving some form of treatment. While this is important in itself, it also satisfies the regulatory requirement that research involving children and greater than minimal risks offer direct benefits to participants (or meet the heightened standards of protection presented in table 6.4 above). Second, by focusing on suicidality (including suicidal ideation) rather than completed suicide as an outcome, investigators are able both to increase the likelihood of finding statistically significant differences across treatment arms and to intervene much sooner with additional preventative interventions.[9]

7. Throughout this section, I am highly indebted to the recommendations of Pearson, Stanley, King, and Fisher (2001) and Oquendo, Stanley, Ellis, and Mann (2004b). Both resources should be consulted for further detail on providing protections in suicide research. Moran (2004) summarizes many of their recommendations in a brief report for clinical researchers.

8. As an aside, it should be noted that the primary aim of this study is not suicide prevention, but rather to study the effects of antidepressants on suicidality. A study aimed at preventing suicide might involve even riskier designs. For example, in locations where unsatisfactory suicide prevention programs exist, researchers might be tempted to randomize a group to "standard treatment," which might include little more than providing access to a hotline and close monitoring with in-patient treatment as a "rescue arm." Given the risk of death, such designs are significantly more difficult to justify even though (a) they do not deny participants a readily available gold standard and (b) they may generate greater statistical power (because the control group is likely to do significantly worse than experimental groups). In part, this is because alternative designs are feasible even if they would require more resources. Additionally, insofar as such research involves minors, it involves greater than minimal risks without the prospect of direct benefits to all participants and likely would fail the specific requirements of 45CFR46 subpart D.

9. In fact, in a recent study of treatment with Clozapine to reduce suicidality, very few high-risk patients actually died of suicide. Moreover, even though the experimental arm included more deaths by suicide than the control arm (5 vs. 3, a statistically insignificant difference), the study demonstrated that it significantly reduced suicidality (Meltzer et al., 2003).

Nevertheless, investigators should put into place additional protections that are not mentioned in the case. First, investigators should monitor all participants for signs of increased suicidality. Second, clear criteria should be established for withdrawal from the trial, for example, experiencing significant treatment side effects. Third, criteria should be established for "rescue treatment." This should involve providing emergency coverage and a protocol for hospitalization. Emergency treatment need not require withdrawal from the study; participants might be followed even during in-patient treatment. This enhances the scientific design by reducing attrition and enables investigators to provide potentially beneficial monitoring and experimental treatments. Additional emergency treatments can be treated as "outcomes" rather than confounding variables that require exclusion from the data set. Researchers should solicit family involvement in monitoring for suicidality and encouraging compliance with treatment. The informed consent process should include additional efforts to foster decision-making capacity. For example, participants and their family members might be given a "quiz" on crucial information regarding treatment options, monitoring procedures, and emergency treatment within the study. Aspects of the study that are inadequately understood should be reviewed until understood. "Cross-over" and "stopping rules" should also be established. That is, if one arm of the study proves to be superior prior to completion of the study, investigators should give participants the option of receiving the effective treatment. Similarly, if one arm of the study proves significantly less effective, it should be discontinued. These and related protections are discussed at greater length in recent publications (Oquendo et al., 2004a; Oquendo et al., 2004b; Pearson et al., 2001). Finally, appropriate community consultation should shape the development and review the protocol. At a minimum, either the sponsor or the local institution should include community members (e.g., parents of teens with depression) in the design and approval of research protections.

With these protections and processes in place, the remaining risks of suicide appear unavoidable (thus passing the necessity test).

By treating suicidality rather than completed suicide as an outcome variable, by involving family or guardians in monitoring and compliance, and by including individuals at heightened risk of suicide, this study is also likely to have statistical effect sizes large enough to generate new knowledge about the treatment of depression and minimization of suicidality.

The above considerations suggest that the benefits of this study are proportionate to the risks.

Further EMHR Resources

- Unit two of the *Dialogues* DVD contains an interview with Joan Sieber and excerpts of a focus group with mental health consumers on risks and benefits in research
- www.emhr.net contains a bibliography and case studies on risk-benefit analyses in research

REFERENCES

Annas, G. J., & Grodin, M. A. (Eds.). (1992). *The Nazi doctors and the Nuremberg Code: Human rights in human experimentation*. New York: Oxford University Press.

Aristotle. (1980). *The Nicomachean ethics* (D. Ross, Trans.). Oxford: Oxford University Press.

Barnbaum, D. (2002). Making more sense of "minimal risk." *IRB: Ethics & Human Research, 24*(3), 10–13.

Baumrind, D. (1964). Some thoughts on ethics of research: After reading Milgram's "'behavioral study of obedience.'" *American Psychologist, 19*, 421–423.

Beauchamp, T. L., & Childress, J. F. (2001). *Principles of biomedical ethics* (5th ed.). New York: Oxford University Press.

Casarett, D. J., Karlawish, J. H. T., & Moreno, J. D. (2002). A taxonomy of value in clinical research. *IRB: Ethics & Human Research, 24*(6), 1–6.

Centers for Disease Control and Prevention, Department of Health and Human Services, National Institutes of Health, Food and Drug Administration, Human Resources and Services Administration, Substance Abuse and Mental Health Services Administration, et al. (1998). *Building community partnerships in research: Recommendations and strategies*. Washington, DC: DHHS.

DuBois, J. M. (2002). When is informed consent appropriate in educational research? *IRB: Ethics & Human Research, 24*(1), 1–8.

Dworkin, R., Nagel, T., Nozick, R., Rawls, J., Scanlon, T., & Thomson, J. J. (1997). Assisted suicide: The philosophers' brief. *New York Review of Books, 44*(5), 41–47.

Engelhardt Jr., H. T. (1996). *The foundations of bioethics*. New York: Oxford University Press.

Etzioni, A. (Ed.). (1998). *The essential communitarian reader*. Lanham, MD: Rowman & Littlefield.

Finnis, J. (1980). *Natural law and natural rights*. Oxford, England: Clarendon Press.

Freedman, B. (1987). Scientific value and validity as ethical requirements for research: A proposed explication. *IRB: A Review of Human Subjects Research, 9*(6), 7–10.

Freedman, B., Fuks, A., & Weijer, C. (1993). In loco parentis: Minimal risk as an ethical threshold for research upon children. *Hastings Center Report, 23*(22), 13–19.

Getz, K., & Borfitz, D. (2002). *Informed consent: A guide to the risks and benefits of volunteering for clinical trials*. Boston: CenterWatch.

Gordon, V. M., Sugarman, J., & Kass, N. (1998). Toward a more comprehensive approach to protecting human subjects: The interface of data safety monitoring boards and institutional review boards in randomized clinical trials. *IRB: A Review of Human Subjects Research, 20*(1), 1–5.

Gould, M. S., Greenberg, T., Velting, D. M., & Shaffer, D. (2003). Youth suicide risk and preventive interventions: A review of the past 10 years. *Journal of the American Academy of Child and Adolescent Psychiatry, 42*(4), 386–405.

Grisso, T., & Appelbaum, P. S. (1998). *Assessing competence to consent to treatment: A guide for physicians and other health professionals*. New York: Oxford University Press.

Hahn, R. K., Albers, L. J., & Reist, C. (2003). *Current clinical strategies: Psychiatry*. Laguna Hills, CA: Current Clinical Strategies.

Jones, J. H. (1993). *Bad blood: The Tuskegee syphilis experiment* (2nd revised ed.). New York: Free Press.

Jonsen, A. R. (1998). *The birth of bioethics*. New York: Oxford University Press.

Koocher, G. P. (2002). Using the CABLES model to assess and minimize risk in research: Control group hazards. *Ethics & Behavior, 12*, 75–86.

Koocher, G. P., & Keith-Spiegel, P. C. (1990). *Children, ethics, and the law: Professional issues and cases*. Lincoln: University of Nebraska Press.

Kopelman, L. M. (1995). Children: III. Health care and research issues. In W. T. Reich (Ed.), *Encyclopedia of bioethics* (Vol. 1, pp. 357–368). New York: Simon & Schuster Macmillan.

Kopelman, L. M. (2000). Moral problems in assessing research risk. *IRB: A Review of Human Subjects Research, 22*(5), 3–6.

Levine, R. J. (1988). *Ethics and regulation of clinical research* (2nd ed.). New Haven, CT: Yale University Press.

Martin, D. K., Meslin, E. M., Kohut, N., & Singer, P. A. (1995). The incommensurability of research risks and benefits: Practical help for research ethics committees. *IRB: A Review of Human Subjects Research, 17*(2), 8–10.

Maslow, A. (1970). *Motivation and personality* (2nd ed.). New York: Harper & Row.

Meltzer, H. Y., Alphs, L., Green, A. I., Altamura, A. C., Anand, R., Bertoldi, A., et al. (2003). Clozapine treatment for suicidality in schizophrenia: International suicide prevention trial. *Archives of General Psychiatry, 60*, 82–91.

Meslin, E. M. (1990). Protecting human subjects from harm through improved judgements. *IRB: A Review of Human Subjects Research, 12*(1), 7–10.

Milgram, S. (1964). Issues in the study of obedience: A reply to Baumrind. *American Psychologist, 19*, 848–852.

Moran, M. (2004). Research designs need not exclude suicide risk. *Psychiatry News, 39*(19), 26–41.

Mounier, E. (1950/1979). *Personalism* (P. Mairet, Trans.). Southbend, IN: University of Notre Dame Press.

National Bioethics Advisory Commission. (1999). *Research involving persons with mental disorders that may affect decisionmaking capacity: Vol. 2. Commission papers*. Bethesda, MD: National Bioethics Advisory Commission.

National Bioethics Advisory Commission. (2001). *Ethical and policy issues in research involving human participants*. Bethesda, MD: National Bioethics Advisory Commission.

National Commission. (1979). *The Belmont report: Ethical principles and guidelines for the protection of human subjects of research*. Washington, DC: Department of Health, Education, and Welfare.

National Commission for the Protection of Human Subjects of Biomedical and Behavioral Research. (1978). *Research involving those institutionalized as mentally infirm: Report and recommendations*. Washington, DC: Department of Health, Education, and Welfare.

National Institute of Mental Health. (2006). *In harm's way: Suicide in America*. Revised. Retrieved January 12, 2007, from http://mentalhealth.gov/publicat/harmsway.cfm.

Oquendo, M. A., Galfalvy, H., Russo, S., Ellis, S. P., Grunebaum, M. F., Burke, A., et al. (2004a). Prospective study of clinical predictors of suicidal acts after a major depressive episode in patients with major depressive disorder or bipolar disorder. *American Journal of Psychiatry, 161*(8), 1433–1441.

Oquendo, M. A., Stanley, B., Ellis, S. P., & Mann, J. J. (2004b). Protection of human subjects in intervention research for suicidal behavior. *American Journal of Psychiatry, 161*(9), 1558–1563.

Pearson, J. L., Stanley, B., King, C., & Fisher, C. B. (2001). *Issues to consider in intervention research with persons at high risk of suicidality*. Updated 2004. Rockville, MD: National Institute of Mental Health. Retrieved on January 12, 2007, from http://www.nimh.nih.gov/suicideresearch/highrisksuicide.cfm.

Schneider, C. E. (1998). *The practice of autonomy: Patients, doctors and medical decisions.* New York: Oxford University Press.

Sieber, J. E. (1992). *Planning ethically responsible research: A guide for students and internal review boards* (Vol. 31). Newbury Park, CA: Sage Publications.

Simon, G. E. (2006). The antidepressant quandary—considering suicide risk when treating adolescent depression. *New England Journal of Medicine, 355*(26), 2722–2723.

Taylor, C. (1989). *Sources of the self: The making of the modern identity.* Cambridge, MA: Harvard University Press.

Taylor, T. (1992). Opening statement of the prosecution. December 9, 1946. In G. J. Annas & M. A. Grodin (Eds.), *The Nazi doctors and the Nuremberg code: Human rights in human experimentation* (pp. 67–93). New York: Oxford University Press.

Tong, R. P. (1998). *Feminist thought: A more comprehensive introduction.* Boulder, CO: Westview Press.

Townsend, E. M., Puig-Antich, J., Nelson, B., & Krawiec, V. (1988). Well-being of children participants in psychobiological research: A pilot study. *Journal of the American Academy of Child and Adolescent Psychiatry, 27*(4), 483–488.

Universal declaration of human rights, General Assembly Resolution 217 A (III) (1948).

Whitaker, R. (2002). *Mad in America.* Cambridge, MA: Perseus.

7

Justice in Recruitment and Research

When notions of right and wrong, justice and injustice, are examined not from an abstract position but from the position of groups who have suffered through history, moral relativism recedes and identifiable normative priorities emerge.
    —Mari Matsuda, cited in Patricia A. King, "Race, Justice, and Research"

Inequalities are rampant in research. Some inequalities are intentionally built into studies. Randomized experiments, for example, may assign some participants to receive a placebo, while others receive the gold standard treatment or a treatment of unknown value. Other inequalities arise from the contingencies of the population involved: some participants are allowed to give consent for themselves, while others are not due to age or cognitive capacities. Still other inequalities are virtually intrinsic to the enterprise. For example, researchers generally have more knowledge and power than participants.

Engelhardt (1996) suggests that some inequalities are simply unfortunate, not unfair or unjust (p. 108). We typically say inequalities are unfortunate when they cannot be remedied (or cannot be remedied without creating new concerns about justice). For example, we cannot prevent or cure all diseases, so some occurrences of disease fall in the category of the unfortunate. Yet other diseases can be treated, but not all people receive the treatment. For example, whether an individual will receive dialysis or a renal transplant for kidney disease depends largely upon what country one lives in and, in some countries, upon one's ability to pay for treatment or one's age. In countries that use age-based rationing, it is argued that the state cannot pay to treat everyone, and age-based criteria are justified through cost-benefit analyses. Should we also say things are simply unfortunate when we could remedy the inequality but believe it is most prudent not to do so given limited resources? When is it ethical to leave an inequality unremedied?

Such questions lead us into the tangled realm of justice theories. The Belmont Report cited the most general (or formal) principle of justice, which was articulated by Aristotle over 2,300 years ago: "equals ought to be treated equally" (National Commission, 1979, B.1). Yet this simply generates the question "who is equal and who is unequal?" Chapter 2 presented a humanized principle of justice that refers to the fact that all humans are of equal value. Yet even if all people are of equal worth, the Belmont Report observes that we may depart from equal treatment when people differ in relevant ways. So-called "material principles" of justice propose competing ways that people should be treated equally. The Belmont Report mentions five, though others exist: (1) to each person an equal share, (2) to each person according to individual need, (3) to each person according to individual effort, (4) to each person according to societal contribution, and (5) to each person according to merit (National Commission, 1979, B.1).

While different ideologies tend to embrace a particular material principle over others (e.g., communism focuses far more on achieving equal shares than capitalism, which focuses more on contribution or ability to pay), most societies are highly eclectic and distribute different kinds of goods using different principles. For example, a society may ration staple foods according to need (e.g., through the USDA Food Stamp Program) while rationing luxury items such as Champagne strictly according to ability to pay. Other goods involve very complex rationing systems. For example, in admitting students, universities may consider merit (for example, grades and test scores), ability to pay, financial need, and the value of diversity.

Different theories of justice—for example, utilitarian, libertarian, communitarian, and egalitarian theories—provide rationales for various material principles (Pojman & McLeod, 1998). These theories rest upon different visions of human freedom and responsibility, of the individual's relationship to society and the common good, of the origins of property, and of general human flourishing. Resolving such disputes extends far beyond the scope of a book on research ethics.[1]

Rather than attempt to develop a universal theory of justice that can be applied to research, this chapter will focus upon the concrete challenges to justice presented by human research. While the Belmont Report and most commentators focus almost exclusively upon issues of distributive justice in research, we will additionally examine briefly issues of restorative and procedural justice.

In what follows, we will try to avoid two forms of naïveté. On the one hand, it is naïve to assume that all inequalities are unjust or unethical. We cannot, and many would argue, should not, eliminate all inequities. (For example, a participant who drops out of a study cannot expect the same benefits from participation as an individual who remains in a study.) The just distribution of benefits and burdens is not a simple matter of intuition. It is often very difficult to achieve, there is rarely if ever "one right" allocation system, and achieving a satisfactory system often requires inclusion of multiple stakeholders in transparent processes that involve compromise. Anyone who has engaged in so-called participatory research will know this already. On the other hand, as the opening epigraph suggests, it is also naïve to assume that matters of justice are so complex that all views are equally valid and we can never really know a situation is unjust. The history of research contains many examples of unjust research. For example, the Tuskegee Syphilis study did not involve an honest attempt to ensure just distribution of the benefits and burdens of research; it was an ethical failure, presumably involving a failure to acknowledge the basic equal worth of all human beings.

EQUAL ABILITY TO SAY "NO": THE ORIGINAL EMPHASIS

As noted in chapter 1, when the whistle was blown on the Tuskegee syphilis study, the U.S. government formed the National Commission for the Protection of Human Subjects of Biomedical and Behavioral Research. Across a 5-year

---

1. Useful overviews to the theory of justice include Beauchamp & Childress (2001) and Rawls (1999).

period, the National Commission issued nine reports, many of which formed the basis of our current research regulatory system. One of these reports addressed "research involving those institutionalized as mentally infirm" (National Commission for the Protection of Human Subjects of Biomedical and Behavioral Research, 1978). In preparation for its work, the Commission conducted a survey of 151 researchers who engaged in research involving people with mental disorders. The survey found that over 60% of subjects were recruited from institutional populations through professional access (Appendix, 1–46). Less than 1% were drawn from the general population, and accordingly less than 3% involved recruitment using advertisements or notices. In her presentation to the National Commission on minority perspectives, Mary Harper also observed that a significant majority of patients in psychiatric hospitals and in prisons are nonwhite (Harper, 1978). Thus, a picture of participant recruitment emerged that was quite troubling: the majority of participants in mental health research studies were minority members with mental health disorders recruited by physicians while living in institutions.

It is important to note that by the time the National Commission had convened, the ethics of research had already evolved somewhat. But this does not erase the fact that the United States had a spotty record of research with institutionalized subjects. In her book *Subjected to Science*, Susan Lederer (1995) describes research at San Quentin and generalizes to the climate of medical research in institutions, including so-called mental hospitals:

> In 1920 physician L. L. Stanley described the implantation of human testes from recently executed convicts into eleven male prisoners. In addition to the human implants, the doctor transplanted ram testicles into 23 prison inmates suffering from various complaints. To antivivisectionists, the testicular implants illustrated how prisoners, like children in orphanages, soldiers, and the patients in mental hospitals, "furnished ample material for scientific curiosity." (p. 112)

As we saw in the previous chapter, being institutionalized is a source of vulnerability. Like most sources of vulnerability, it compromises the participants' ability to say "no" to research given the uneven distribution of power and tacit or overt forms of coercion that may exist in institutional settings.

How does the ability to grant informed consent relate to the principle of justice? In large part, because threats to consent may create an *unequal ability* to say "no." As the Belmont Report observes,

> An agreement to participate in research constitutes a valid consent only if voluntarily given. This element of informed consent requires conditions free of coercion and undue influence. Coercion occurs when an overt threat of harm is intentionally presented by one person to another in order to obtain compliance. Undue influence, by contrast, occurs through an offer of an excessive, unwarranted, inappropriate or improper reward or other overture in order to obtain compliance. Also, inducements that would ordinarily be acceptable may become undue influences if the subject is especially vulnerable. (C1)

In chapter 6, we examined the various kinds of vulnerability that the National Bioethics Advisory Commission identified: cognitive or communicative; institutional; deferential; medical; economic; social. DuBois (2005) observes that in the context of research, vulnerability refers to a diminished capacity to protect oneself. The informed consent process is the primary forum for self-protection insofar as it enables the individual to consider risks and benefits in the light of his or her own values and then make a free choice whether or not to participate. Thus, it is not surprising that most of the forms of vulnerability turn out to present a threat to the individual's ability to grant informed consent, or perhaps more apropos, to decline participation. In other words, vulnerabilities introduce factors that generally create inequities in participants' ability to say "no" to research participation.

At the time when the National Commission began its work, research participation was widely perceived to be burdensome and risky. Accordingly, the National Commission's prevailing justice concern was with protecting those who are less able to protect themselves.[2] This tendency was wedded to a desire to avoid significant risk, both on the part of participants and investigators who feared legal liability. Charles McCarthy, who spent much of his career at the Public Health Services, offers a partial explanation of how these views evolved and eventually led to the routine exclusion of half of our population:

> Influenced by the thalidomide tragedy [in which babies were born with devastating physical deformities], pregnant women feared that their offspring could be adversely affected by their participation in research. Investigators and research sponsors feared litigation if women of childbearing potential were involved in drug studies. Research was widely considered to be a risky burden rather than an opportunity to receive state-of-the-art medical care at reduced cost. (McCarthy, 1998, p. 24)

Thus, a combination of a protectionist notion of justice with a risk aversion derived from well-publicized instances of significant research-related harms led IRBs to routinely question the inclusion of vulnerable populations in research.

A second justice concern that occupied the National Commission was that vulnerable individuals were disproportionately bearing the burdens of research. While justice concerns about consent may derive simply from an unequal ability to say "no," they become even more salient when they result in an unequal or disproportionate representation of vulnerable participants in risky research. Thus, the National Commission urged that "the selection of research subjects needs to be scrutinized in order to determine whether some classes (e.g., welfare patients, particular racial and ethnic minorities, or persons confined to institutions) are being systematically selected simply because of their easy availability, their compromised position, or their manipulability, rather than for reasons directly related to the problem being studied" (National Commission, B3).

---

2. While this chapter documents a shift in the prevailing interpretation of justice, there are some who believe that protection should remain the dominant concern in the review of research involving vulnerable research participants (Moreno, 2001).

EQUAL ACCESS TO RESEARCH STUDIES

The preceding section described the prevailing concerns IRBs and policymakers had regarding justice in research during the 1970s. However, in less than a decade, several groups—but especially women and patients with HIV/AIDS—challenged the prevailing interpretation of what the principle of justice implies for the conduct of human research.

When AIDS was first identified, it was understood to be fatal. No treatments existed, and it appeared that all patients who developed AIDS died within a few years. Levine observes that when therapeutic experiments for AIDS first began, patients were desperate. They were willing to trade unknown risks for the prospect of any sort of effective treatment. "Some patients, with the complicity of their physicians, managed to enroll by fudging data or lying outright, a practice well known in cancer trials" (C. Levine, 1996, p. 108). Nevertheless, the battle for increased access to studies soon was fought not just in the name of gaining immediate access to potentially beneficial therapies, but also in the name of social justice.

> Groups disproportionately affected by HIV/AIDS—prisoners, drug users, and women (including many members of ethnic minorities)—were excluded from trials, either because of strict protocol entry criteria or because of lack of access to the physicians and healthcare institutions that control research. Interestingly, the initial calls for broadened access often came from those who were included—gay white men—and not just, or possibly not even primarily, from those who were excluded. (C. Levine, 1996, p. 109)

At the same time, "along with concerns for women's rights came the awareness that many drugs administered to women had never been tested in women" (McCarthy, 1998, p. 26). McCarthy summarizes the change of tide brought on by both women's groups and AIDS activists:

> Thus, over a couple of decades attitudes had come full circle. Clinical studies once viewed as onerous, dangerous, and burdensome were now regarded as highly desirable because they offered low-cost, state-of-the-art medical treatment. On this view, exclusion from research for any reason could lead to charges of discrimination and violations of the principle of distributive justice. (McCarthy, 1998, p. 27)

The Belmont Report had tangentially acknowledged that research could be beneficial and that this, too, must be considered in making judgments about research, noting that researchers should "not offer potentially beneficial research only to some patients who are in their favor" (National Commission, 1979, C.3). However, in the process of encouraging heightened protections for vulnerable participants, barriers to inclusion were erected. Nevertheless, by the 1990s, the field of research ethics had broadly embraced what Brody calls a "new balancing conception" of justice in research, which emerged in response to the tension described in this chapter. Given our imperfect knowledge of the outcomes of any given study and the tension between competing justice concerns—to protect and to ensure fair access—it is clear that IRBs, communities, and researchers need to engage in balancing activities of the sort described in chapter 3. That is, to the extent that we weaken protections to ensure access, we should strive to ensure that the compromise is necessary, is likely to be effective in achieving its beneficent aims, the infringement is the least possible, and the anticipated benefits are proportionate to the risks. Below, in the section on procedural justice, we will consider processes that may assist us in this delicate balancing act.

One result of society's embracing of the balancing approach just described is that even while IRBs maintain a responsibility to consider heightened protections for vulnerable participants, federal policies have been developed that require the inclusion of minority members, women, and children as appropriate. The primary purpose of these policies is to ensure that the products of research serve all members of society appropriately, for example, by ensuring that FDA-approved drugs may be safely used by women, children, and minority members and that research is conducted that addresses problems unique or disproportionately experienced by members of these groups.

Access to Participation as an Exercise of Autonomy

While individuals belonging to certain groups—for instance, women with breast cancer, patients with HIV/AIDS, and parents of children using drugs that were not tested for safety with children—argued for inclusion to ensure a socially just distribution of the benefits of research, mental health consumers often put forth a different argument for equal access to research studies. Protectionism functions by labeling individuals as vulnerable and less able to exercise self-determination. Mental health consumers have frequently been labeled vulnerable when institutionalized, when suffering economic hardship, when cognitive deficits might interfere with comprehension or reasoning, or when socially stigmatized (National Bioethics Advisory Commission, 1999). Although protectionist policies are well meaning, some consumers and consumer advocates have insisted upon their equal right to consent to participation. In his paper to the National Commission, Joseph Goldstein argued that

> To empower a group of self-appointed (or politically appointed) wisemen to determine . . . whether an adult individual has the competence to judge what is best for himself or herself is a total affront to his or her human dignity . . . . The goal is not to protect a subject from himself but is to protect his or her person and autonomy from the exploitative potential of authority to coerce, cajole, entice or deceive anyone, but particularly disadvantaged persons into "consenting" to be and remain research subjects without regard to their wishes. (Goldstein, 1978, pp. 2/13–2/14)

While one could argue that assessing competence is in fact a form of ensuring that an individual is capable of exercising autonomy and protecting him or herself from exploitation, Goldstein and others are also correct that protectionist concerns can stigmatize and can unfairly lead to exclusion from participation in research. A balancing approach requires that we not infringe on a value more than necessary to achieve our goal. In this context, it may require us to try to foster, restore, or supplement (through the activity of a surrogate or advocate) a potential participant's ability to grant consent rather than to exclude a willing individual from participation.

EQUAL ACCESS TO THE FRUITS OF RESEARCH

Building upon the Belmont Report, chapter 2 developed a "humanized" set of ethical principles. It was proposed that the overarching principle is "respect for human beings," and each of the specific principles articulates a specific dimension of human nature that should be respected. Above we saw that at least one advisor to the National Commission (Goldstein, 1978) suggested that our primary concern with research participants who have mental disorders should be avoiding exploitation. While there are many forms of exploitation—for example, in relation to work, trade, or sexuality—they all share in common an ethical failure of the most basic sort, a failure to respect the humanity of an individual or a class of people. We always see the dynamic of "dehumanizing" the other. Rob Helms, editor of *Guinea Pig Zero*, writes of his efforts to share the experiences of "professional" human research participants with potential participants, "This journal keeps in mind that we volunteers can and should maintain an awareness and a will, because if we do not, we will fall victim to the evil uses devised for us by scientists who forget that we and they are of the same species" (www.guineapigzero.com, unpaginated).

Lederer reminds us that "some physicians preferred to purchase slaves who were afflicted with the medical conditions they hoped to study" (Lederer, 1995, p. 116).[3] Why would this be the case? Precisely because by enslaving people, we consign them a species status different from other human beings, and individuals feel more justified denying their human rights.

Whenever we see forgetfulness or outright denial of a participant's humanity, we find that matters of justice, which can appear gray when analyzed theoretically, suddenly become black and white.

Kant's ethical theory was an ethic of respect. Kant wrote that we should "act in such a way that you treat humanity, whether in your own person or in the person of another, always at the same time as an end and never simply as a means" (Kant, 1785/1993, p. 36). This principle allows us to develop a very appropriate definition of *exploitation* in research. Exploitation involves treating a human subject merely as a means to someone else's end, whether it be the end of an investigator, sponsor of research, or society. The other's end may be selfish or unselfish; it may be to pursue a potentially lucrative patent or to gain new knowledge that will benefit a group of people. But however noble the end, if the human subjects' self-determination, well-being, vulnerability to harm, and basic worth as human beings are ignored, then it is exploitive.

One common form of exploitation in research—whether intentional or due to the social context of research—occurs when research participants assume the risks involved in developing new therapies without any prospect of having access to the resulting therapies. The Belmont Report categorically states that

---

3. Lederer (1995) cites Savitt (1982) to support this claim.

whenever research supported by public funds leads to the development of therapeutic devices and procedures, justice demands both that these not provide advantages only to those who can afford them and that such research should not unduly involve persons from groups unlikely to be among the beneficiaries of subsequent applications of the research. (National Commission, 1979, B3)

Perhaps the most egregious violations of this moral rule occurred as pharmaceutical companies conducted research (some of which might not be approved by US IRBs) in developing nations, whose citizens lacked the financial means to purchase the medications that eventually reached the market (Wilmshurst, 1997; National Bioethics Advisory Commission, 2001). Nevertheless, this sort of thing occurs in the United States as well under very normal circumstances. Emily Elliot describes her experience as a subject in a study of Celexa, a medication that is meant to reduce the frequency and intensity of panic attacks. She received no payments for being in the study. She experienced some side effects while in the study—particularly as she adjusted to the medication—but in the end decided that she preferred the study medication to the medication she had been using. After the study was complete, the principal investigator gave her a five-week supply of the drug for free. Discussing her future treatment plans, she writes:

> I've often wondered if it's better to take a proactive drug like Celexa and not be able to come, or to take a reactive drug like Xanax and be a total horndog. The answer I've reached is yes, I'll go with the proactive, as long as the drugs are free. Once my supply runs out I'll reverse that statement. (p. 32)

In *Ethical Dialogues on Behavioral Health Research*, several mental health consumers who had participated in clinical trials expressed their disappointment upon learning they would not receive study drugs after the study had ended (DuBois & Campbell, 2006). While admitting that the consent form may have disclosed this, they were nevertheless surprised when they did not receive the medications for free—perhaps because they found such a state of affairs strongly ethically unintuitive. Because they could not afford the medications, they lacked access to the drugs they helped to develop. Admittedly, in determining whether participants might have a justice claim to receive a drug, one might consider what sort of clinical trial they participated in. Those who participate in a phase I trial, aimed primarily at establishing product safety and dosage rather than efficacy would seem to have a greater claim than those who participate in phase IV trials that track outcomes of already approved medications.

Other forms of distributive justice concerns in research do not necessarily involve exploitation but nevertheless involve inequities. Referring to early studies using AZT to treat AIDS, Macklin and Friedland (1986) note that studies were conducted almost entirely with homosexual male patients. They note that although intravenous drug abusers "were excluded according to a 'medical' rationale—this group tends to be 'unreliable' and 'noncompliant,' and hence not a good study population—the resulting distribution of benefits was nonetheless unjust" (p. 275). That is to say, prior to being approved by the FDA, the only patients to benefit from AZT were those enrolled in clinical trials, and patients who used intravenous drugs were systematically excluded from receiving these benefits by being excluding from participation in clinical trials. While good scientific practices may require one to exclude some individuals from participation, exclusion is rarely justified when it merely increases convenience and may reduce the generalizability of results or the justice of recruitment methods. Frequently creativity and hard work can overcome obstacles to participation. For example, Cottler et al. (1996) report on techniques used by a group of community-based researchers to maintain a 96.6% participation rate in a longitudinal study of drug abusers.

RESTORATIVE JUSTICE

Simultaneous with the work of the National Commission following the Tuskegee syphilis study, the Department of Health, Education, and Welfare created a task force to consider whether DHEW had an obligation to compensate injured research subjects.

> The Task Force likened research volunteers to military personnel who undertake risky missions on behalf of society. It argued that just as military personnel are entitled to receive compensation for service-related injuries, so research subjects should be compensated for that amount of injury that is in excess of that which is reasonably associated with the illness from which the subject may be suffering. (McCarthy, 1998, p. 25)

In part due to turnover in DHEW leadership and the dissolution of DHEW's ethics advisory board, DHEW took no action on the recommendations. The task force's report was eventually forwarded to the newly formed President's Commission in 1980. McCarthy (1998) summarizes the Commission's somewhat ambivalent recommendations:

> The President's Commission concluded that compensation for research is probably ethically justified, but called for an experiment to test the feasibility and cost of such a compensation system. However, no legal basis on which to initiate such an experiment could be discovered, and the experiment was never devised or conducted. (p. 25)

The issue of compensation for injury arises not only in clinical research with patients enrolled in therapeutic trials; it also arises in studies involving healthy, paid volunteers. Robert Helms, the most visible such subject, writes that

> when some irregularity occurs in a guinea pig's [i.e., human subject's] body and the CPU [clinical pharmacology unit] sends him to the local hospital for a look, a bill will later appear in his mail slot. . . . As if there were even the flimsiest conceivable argument for a volunteer being responsible for costs. It happens . . . all over the place. We recommend calling the billing department and teasing the shit out of them. I've never met a guinea pig who for a single moment would consider paying for a medical procedure which had any connection to a drug study. (Helms, p. 17)

While Helms may be savvy about dealing with bills, others may not be. More-over, one wonders whether billing departments routinely let slide bills that are particularly large, and when they are written off, whether the billing process adversely affects the credit of participants who do not pay bills (Daly, Oblak, Siefert, & Shellenberg, 2002; Iltis, 2004).

Restoration arguably presents one of the clearest examples of ethical duties extending beyond the scope of legal duties. At present, our research regulations require that, in greater than minimal risk research, informed consent forms must provide "an explanation as to whether any compensation . . . [or] medical treat-ments are available if injury occurs and, if so, what they consist of, or where fur-ther information may be obtained" (45CFR46.116[a][6]). No regulation requires that compensation for research-related injury be provided (including even free treatment for the problem caused), only that one disclose whether and how it will be provided. Nevertheless, research regulations also state that

> No informed consent, whether oral or written, may include any exculpatory language through which the subject or the representative is made to waive or appear to waive any of the subject's legal rights, or releases or appears to release the investigator, the sponsor, the institution or its agents from liability for negligence. (45CFR46.116)

That is, if research-related harm is incurred through negligence, then partici-pants retain their full rights to seek restitution through the courts (i.e., to seek tort remedies). This of course requires that participants or their survivors have the knowledge and means to use the tort legal system.

While the government funds a large number of human research studies each year, the only instances of government-funded restitution for research-related injury have been in connection with very high profile cases of harm due to the conduct of blatantly unethical research without or with only inadequate informed consent, for example, in the Tuskegee syphilis studies and various radiation studies (Moreno, 2000).

PROCEDURAL JUSTICE

Proper inclusion of groups in research is no easy task. Partly due to mistrust or fear, it can be difficult to recruit members of some groups. Moreover, there are fundamentally different reasons that one may seek to include members of groups: (1) to test hypotheses about differences across races and ethnicities; (2) to generate hypotheses about differences across races and ethnicities; and (3) to ensure equitable distribution of risks and benefits of participation in research (Corbie-Smith et al., 2004; Garber & Arnold, 2006). Indeed, ensur-ing that research benefits all people, regardless of their group memberships, requires the conduct of research with diverse groups. Yet given this planet's history of racism and abuse of minority groups, we face a dilemma that is well described by Patricia King (2005):

> Targeting a group . . . may be necessary to obtain important information or to increase resources that might improve the health status of the group. On the other hand, there is danger that conscious attention to the health needs of

groups risks feeding and nourishing the stereotypes and prejudices that have historically oppressed and stigmatized groups, making them vulnerable in the first place. (p. 143)

King proposes at least two mechanisms to assist in balancing that are consistent with the substantive and procedural ethical framework presented in this book. The first we can call becoming culturally competent. She emphasizes the need to investigate and understand the particularities of the group's experiences in order to better meet their needs. For example, the "historical experience of African Americans with research and medicine explains their reluctance to participate in research" (King, 2005, p. 143), and African Americans cannot be adequately served by researchers until this underlying reluctance is addressed. Similarly, groups of mental health consumers may share experiences, attitudes, or stories that should be investigated and understood. The second is what we have called the principle of "voice" or "participation."[4] She writes, "attention should be paid to the experiences of group members, because their insights might be helpful in constructing fair institutional and public policies" (King, 2005, p. 143).

In chapter 2, we saw that ethical considerations may either be substantive or procedural. Of all the ethical principles commonly invoked, justice is the principle most commonly seen to have a strong procedural dimension. Empirical studies have shown that people seek not only outcomes that are just, but also procedures for determining outcomes that are seen to be fair by those who are affected by outcomes (Lind & Tyler, 1988; Tyler & Rasinski, 1991).

The common denominator to many, if not most, embodiments of procedural justice is providing people with a voice in what happens. While earlier chapters explored some common ways of giving people a voice in research (e.g., through the consent process, participatory research methods, and town hall meetings), the use of empirical research methods may be one of the most effective. For example, in 1995, Aman and Wolford published an article, "Consumer satisfaction with involvement in drug research: A social validity study." By "social validity" they referred to society's or participants' judgments about three things: (1) the significance of the research goals (e.g., the symptoms chosen for study); (2) the appropriateness of the study procedures; and (3) the importance of the outcomes or effects of the study. When Aman and Wolford conducted such research with the parents of their child participants (who were diagnosed with mental retardation), they found that—in 1995—theirs was the first such study with participants enrolled in a drug trial. This is simply amazing if one considers that the Belmont Report and the Common Rule consistently discuss the importance of benefits as well as risks. It is not that the matter of benefits is completely ignored by IRBs. It is rather that the benefits considered are typically only those *identified by re-*

---

4. I view this principle as procedural rather than substantive. It refers to participation as a means of fostering all the other substantive principles, such as autonomy, beneficence, nonmaleficence, etc. Although it has not been called such, this principle has been emphasized in the writings of Joan Sieber and in the 1998 interagency government report on community research. And it captures part of the ideal originally articulated in Jonas's seminal piece. It clearly lies behind APA's very early advocacy for the use of the term "participant" rather than "subject."

searchers, which in turn may reflect the priorities of an industry sponsor of research rather than consumers. Aman and Wolford's (1995) study and those like it provide participants with a voice in shaping research agendas so that research provides benefits most urgently sought by participants and advocates. (In chapter 10, "Identifying and Managing Conflicts of Interest," some of the challenges of giving communities or advocates a voice are explored.)

While such research is not yet common, it is worth noting that a new journal was recently founded, the *Journal of Empirical Research on Human Research Ethics* (JERHRE, pronounced "Jerry"), which is entirely dedicated to fostering research that will provide an evidence base for research ethics and offer both researchers and participants a voice in research oversight.

PARTICIPANT RESPONSIBILITIES

Thus far we have considered only the duties that researchers have in the research enterprise. It is easy to understand why research regulations and most ethical discussions focus only on the behavior of researchers; they developed as a reaction to abuses. Nevertheless, insofar as research involves relationships and interactions between human beings (with sponsors, participants, institutions, IRBs, and society), all parties involved have ethical responsibilities.

Is There a Duty to Participate in Research?

When the National Commission examined research with institutionalized individuals with mental disorders, it observed that the American Bar Association's Commission on the Mentally Disabled stated that research with mentally disabled persons should relate directly to "the etiology, pathogenesis, prevention, diagnosis, or treatment of mental disability, and should seek only such information as cannot be obtained from other types of subjects" (1978, p. 60). On the other hand, the Commission noted that some theorists (they named Engelhardt, Veatch, and McCormick) would offer the following argument:

> All persons, insofar as they are members of a social community, have a duty to help others in that community. As an expression of common humanity, every person ought to benefit others and ought to be benefited by others . . . . Thus persons who are mentally infirm share to an equal degree with other persons this duty of beneficence; and it might even be argued that it would be a violation of their right to pursue their moral obligations if this class of individuals were categorically excluded from such participation. (1978, p. 61)

Along these lines, we may also ask whether there is a duty to participate well, if one agrees to participate in a study.

Participating Well

Just as the Joint Commission on the Accreditation of Healthcare Organizations (JCAHO) speaks of patient rights and responsibilities, should we also speak of participant rights *and responsibilities*?

What follows is meant to initiate a discussion rather than provide a comprehensive answer to the question rhetorically proposed. But one could argue that the following are at least prima facie duties of research participants:

- Provide honest information in establishing eligibility for a study. Failure to do so may yield publication of inaccurate information or could lead to harm if a participant's condition prohibits safe inclusion.
- Participate fully in the informed consent process. Consent cannot be informed if participants do not seek to understand a study; researchers may communicate information but cannot unilaterally cause understanding or retention of information.
- Decline participation if you are not willing to accept the risks or do not wish to participate.
- Report adverse events in a timely fashion. Reporting adverse events or reactions is essential to ensuring the safety of a study for participants, both the one experiencing an adverse event and others enrolled in a study. Simply dropping out of a study and discontinuing an intervention may be harmful both to oneself and to others, including future patients who might receive the intervention if approved.
- Follow the protocol or follow proper procedures for withdrawing from a study. Participants should be free to leave a study at any time, but they should not use their freedom to undermine a study's reliability or to waste the time and resources of researchers and sponsors.

Of course, there are times when doing some of these things may be very difficult. Participants who live in poverty may genuinely understand risks and seek to avoid them, yet believe that they are outweighed by the prospect to earn a few dollars or to receive free medical care. Participants who are imprisoned or who are subordinates may feel that declining participation is not merely awkward but could lead to negative consequences. Here we see the need to empower participants to whatever extent is possible. This may require creativity and input from participant populations prior to beginning recruitment.

Case Study: Reimbursing Participants for Their Time in a Psychotherapy Trial

Dr. Johnson is a clinical psychologist and researcher at an outpatient behavioral health facility affiliated with a large medical school. Her main research interest is contrasting psychotherapeutic to pharmacological treatments of bipolar disorder. She believes that psychotherapy can be more effective than is commonly believed, and in her practice she finds that many patients seek an alternative to drug therapies that often have unwanted side effects. In her current study, all participants will have weekly visits for assessment. Those randomized to drug therapy would additionally have a blood draw; those randomized to psychotherapy will additionally have a 45-minute cognitive-behavioral counseling session. All participants will be required to be free of medications prior to being randomized. Her protocol makes adequate provisions for safety monitoring and provides for a "rescue arm" for those who do very poorly off their medications.

Dr. Johnson has typically recruited participants for her studies through the local chapter of a national support group for people with mental disorders and their families. However, in her most recent study, almost no one responded to her recruitment poster. So she decided to make a few inquiries to find out why. She was told by several people that the group had been talking about the level of compensation studies offer. They decided that if researchers get paid for their time, participants should get paid for their time as well. They felt offended by offers to cover just their "travel expenses," because it implies that their time is worth nothing. One person who is very active in the group said, "Look, you know many of us have trouble finding and keeping good jobs. We need the money. But that's not the point. It's a matter of fairness, a matter of our dignity."

Following that meeting, Dr. Johnson went to her sponsor and her IRB and eventually got permission to offer $15 per visit for their time plus $5 for travel. Within two weeks, she nearly met her enrollment goal. At first she felt good about this approach and agreed with her participants that it was only fair that they get compensation for their time. However, she started to have second thoughts when she was explaining randomization during the informed consent process and a participant said to her, "Look, boss, you put me in whatever group you think is best." That same day she tried to obtain informed consent from another participant. But this person clearly showed no interest in learning the details of the study. Instead he asked several times when they would get paid and whether he could get an advance because he's late on his rent. Dr. Johnson is now considering whether she should go back to her IRB to change the protocol again to cover just participants' expenses.

What should she do?

CASE COMMENTARY

As this case illustrates, participants are not the only stakeholders as protocols are reviewed. The details of a protocol may also affect researchers (e.g., their ability to recruit and meet their scientific goals) and the sponsors of research (e.g., their ability to get reasonable results from the research they have funded, often with public money). In what follows, we will assume that the interests of participants will generally take precedence over the interests of others; however, the interests of researchers, sponsors, and society should not be thwarted arbitrarily.

We will begin with some very general reflections on the use of financial incentives in research before considering the specifics of the case at hand.

Why Do Researchers Offer Payments?

Researchers may offer payments to participants for several reasons:

1. To provide *compensation* . . .
    a. *for expenses*. For example, a protocol may provide payments to cover costs of transportation or child care

b. *for time*. For example, a protocol may offer participants payment by the hour or per visit to compensate for time spent participating

c. *for risks or harms*. Limited empirical data suggests researchers do consider the levels of risk and discomfort when determining amounts of payments for participation (Iltis, DeVader, & Matsuo, 2006). While increased payments for increased risks causes some concern about compromising the voluntariness of participation, there is certainly precedent in the realm of employment for "hazard pay"

While the particular thing compensated may vary, in each case compensation is a form of fostering fairness in the sense of *quid pro quo* ("this for that").

2. To convey *respect or gratitude*. Payments can also serve as tokens or symbols of respect or gratitude. If a participant is provided with a $25 gift card for spending a full day at a research site, this cannot be considered fair compensation for time (at present in the United States). However, it may nevertheless serve to communicate a sense of appreciation for participation

3. To *motivate participation*. Extra pay may be offered to participants for extra risks or burdens not merely out of a sense of fairness or to convey gratitude, but simply so that a researcher may motivate a sufficient number of individuals to enroll in a study

Each of these reasons for providing payments can be legitimate. However, ethical concerns tend to arise particularly when they are intended to influence a potential participant's decision whether or not to participate.[5]

Do Participant Motives Matter?

While empirical studies often discover a different hierarchy of motives (depending on the kinds of participants interviewed or the kinds of studies in question), the basic kinds of motives for research participation are fairly consistent. These include the following motives, which are divided into two broad categories:

- Primarily self-regarding:
  - Financial reward
  - To receive treatments or medical care at little or no cost
  - To receive new treatments that may be more beneficial than standard-of-care treatments
  - To satisfy curiosity or for the experience
  - Personal sense of satisfaction

---

5. While regulations do not prohibit participation in research for financial consideration, the *IRB Guidebook*, which provides OHRP-sanctioned interpretations of the regulations, states that IRBs should not consider financial payments to be a benefit as they conduct the required risk-benefit analysis (chapter 3, section A).

- Primarily altruistic or other-regarding:
  - To benefit society through the development of new medications, treatments, or programs
  - To benefit a particular group to which they belong, for instance, drug users or patients with a disorder
  - To advance scientific knowledge

A review of empirical studies of the motivations of normal, healthy volunteers found that the vast majority of participants, often 90% or more, are primarily motivated by financial gain (Tishler & Bartholomae, 2002). The few studies of individuals with substance abuse or mental health disorders have found mixed motivations—to help others like themselves, financial gain, and the prospect of free therapeutic benefit (Fry & Dwyer, 2001; Kaminsky et al., 2003)—which is also consistent with the *Dialogues DVD* discussion groups with mental health consumers and with research with patients with medical disorders such as cancer and heart disease (Getz & Borfitz, 2002).[6]

To what extent should IRBs concern themselves with the reasons that people choose to enroll in a study? On the one hand, it seems inappropriate to ask IRBs to serve as "motive police" who try to exclude participation for reasons they deem ignoble. Certainly, it would be wrong to approve only participation motivated exclusively by the altruism of well-to-do individuals or by patients in need who hold reasonable expectations of benefits. Both policies would, among other things, restrict many individuals' liberty to act to benefit others, even when research poses minimal risk. On the other hand, it is not clear that those responsible for oversight should entirely ignore the reasons that individuals choose to participate in research. Sam Adams, writing in the pages of *Guinea Pig Zero*, recounts his painful experience of donating bone marrow for $50:

> [The physician-investigator] asked if I was a student, and I told him I was a medical transcriptionist. He seemed puzzled by this. . . . Since I wasn't a starving student and was actually an "office professional," he probably thought I had a decent income, health insurance, a car and a home in the suburbs like most of the clean-cut young white males he encountered. The fact that I was here doing this for cash meant I was at least a rather strange person. Instead of challenging him, I just waited for him to do his job so I could pull my pants up and leave. (p. 42)

This story suggests that in at least some studies—for example, painful studies with no prospect of direct benefit—researchers expect that only individuals who are hard up for cash would reasonably enroll.

So when do motives matter? One answer is, when they significantly conflict with participant autonomy, which in chapter 2 was presented as respect for individuals as rational and self-determining.

---

6. Here we consider the main things that motivate participation. Among the main obstacles to participation are desires to avoid placebo, fear of side effects, fear of losing access to a drug after a trial stops, and inconvenience (Getz & Borfitz, 2002).

The Continuum of Autonomy

Why do we ever choose one course of action rather than another? What makes an action free or voluntary? Is it that one could have done otherwise or simply that the action was the result of the acting person rather than environmental or biological factors alone (Chisholm, 1989)? If one believes that free choice is just an illusion, then are debates about undue influence silly? Basic questions about free choice have been disputed as long as human beings have engaged in philosophical reflection, and consensus remains elusive even as knowledge of neuropsychology increases.

From the Nuremberg Code through current U.S. research regulations, we find that research participation is supposed to be *voluntary* or freely chosen by the participant. Let us consider briefly how voluntariness exists on a continuum. The following is a description of "participation" ranging from absolutely no voluntariness to "ideal" voluntariness.

1. Being *subjected to* research without any choice made by the subject. Examples include research on infants, subjects with profound mental retardation, or patients in a coma
2. *Forced* participation, that is, instances when the subject chooses to participate only because he or she is under the threat of force. Examples would include participation by concentration camp prisoners under threat of death or participation by laboratory employees under the threat (even tacit) of losing employment or participation by students under threat of failing a course
3. *Unduly influenced* choices, for example, a choice so strongly motivated by a need for money that an individual ignores the risks of participation
4. *Reasonably motivated* choices, whether for altruistic reasons (e.g., donating 15 minutes of time to complete a survey for a graduate student) or self-regarding reasons (e.g., to foster knowledge of a disorder an individual suffers from)

It is important to observe that the vast majority of ethical debate about the use of financial incentives surrounds the first and third categories. Few people would defend "forced" participation, and few people would object to research participation that appears reasonably motivated. Category 1 participation was discussed briefly in chapters 4 and 5; such research may be permitted under very specific circumstances, for instance, when the risk-benefit ratio is reasonable and permission is granted by a surrogate or community. However, there are times when financial incentives also create concerns about category 1 participation; for example, if an incentive might unduly influence a parent's decision to enroll a newborn in a study.

As we consider the issue of undue influence, it is useful to observe that it arises only from a combination of the incentive with participant characteristics. To provide just a few examples, the prospect of earning $15/hour to participate in research is unlikely to unduly influence those who have jobs earning more than $15/hour; the prospect of receiving free medications is unlikely to influence those who have excellent health insurance; the possibility that research participation will make us appear prosocial in the eyes of others is more likely to influence the decision of someone who is imprisoned and coming up for parole than someone who is not imprisoned. Therefore, consideration of undue influence always requires consideration not only of the incentive, but of the interaction between the incentive and participant characteristics.

Nevertheless, in each of the examples just offered, the vulnerable individual is motivated by something that may appear "rational": to earn money, to obtain health care, or to get parole. To what extent can and should IRBs try to ensure that their decisions are not "unduly influenced"? Policing freedom of choice is a difficult and perhaps overly ambitious activity. It requires one to get inside another person's head to understand his or her motives and decisions, and it is not clear that we always have the moral authority to scrutinize such decisions (Goldstein, 1978).

A weaker goal of research review would be to consider whether an allegedly unduly influenced choice goes against the best interests of the participant. This criterion, too, may be difficult to enforce, and one could again question the authority of those who provide oversight. After all, whose standard of best interests should be used, those of an IRB member or those of a participant, one who perhaps seeks to buy his next drink? Nevertheless, when it appears that a decision is against the best interests of a participant, and that participation is due solely to financial incentives, one fears that the research is exploitive, that the participant is actually being used merely as a means to someone else's ends. In general, U.S. research regulations and review have tended to err on the side of protecting participant well-being over protecting individuals' liberty to enroll in a study (Moreno, 2001).

Risks and Vulnerability

One problem with "balancing" solutions to ethical problems in research is that solutions typically must be generic. Protocols are usually tailored to populations, not individuals. For example, when IRB members consider whether to allow a payment of $15/hour for the time of participants, they must grapple with the fact that some potential participants may be homeless and addicted to alcohol while others may be gainfully employed and addiction free. Yet, for reasons of scientific standardization, fairness, and oversight, IRBs may be reluctant to allow researchers to determine the appropriate amount of payment on a case-by-case basis. This certainly interferes with an IRB's ability to respect the principle of least infringement. Perhaps in an ideal world, we would reduce or eliminate payments only for those individuals whose autonomy would be significantly impaired by a payment; yet this is rarely possible.

Accordingly, one may ask the question: is it ever okay to accept diminished autonomy? Or, if we must err on one side or the other, is it ever okay to err on the side of offering payments that provide fair compensation for time and allow researchers to meet their enrollment goals, rather than erring on the side of protecting voluntariness?

One approach would be to allow fair compensation and disregard the influence on voluntariness whenever a group of reviewers—including members of the participant community—consider participation to be consistent with one's best interests. Thus, for example, if a study involves minimal risks—say, just the risk of boredom or lost time while completing a survey—it seems unproblematic if an individual is motivated primarily by money and is otherwise not expected to benefit from participation. However, things change as risks increase. When reviewers find that participation appears contrary to an individual's best interests—except for the prospect of earning money—then concerns about voluntariness become increasingly relevant. As noted above, this means being concerned not merely with the incentives offered, but the interaction of the incentives with participant characteristics (or vulnerabilities).

The Case at Hand

It is clear in the case at hand that there is no magic dollar amount that will enable Dr. Johnson to meet all of her ethical goals: to provide fair compensation for time, to avoid unduly influencing decisions, and to meet her enrollment goals in a study she believes will yield important knowledge about the treatment of bipolar disorder. If the amount is too low, participants will consider it disrespectful and unfair,[7] and they will refuse to enroll. If the amount is high enough to be perceived as fair and motivating, it is likely to lead some participants to disregard the risks of participation.

Thus, once again, we find values in conflict and need to seek a solution that allows us to balance competing interests.

A good starting point in such situations is to discuss the competing values and goals with key stakeholders. Dr. Johnson has done this in at least an informal manner with potential participants and formally with her sponsor and IRB. The informal discussion with potential participants sufficed to raise awareness of concerns about fairness and dignity. However, more formal discussion—perhaps in a meeting at the peer-support center—would enable her to express her concerns about the quality of informed consent, especially comprehension of risks. This would also allow her to demonstrate a commitment to nonexploitation and to explore whether a lesser dollar amount might be viewed as respectful and less problematic. She might even explore whether participants fully understand the difference between therapeutic and nontherapeutic studies. While a "therapeutic" study cannot guarantee benefits to participants, many participants in therapeutic

7. Indeed, not only participants but also some ethicists have raised concerns about the fairness of withholding payment from participants for their time, particularly when—unlike the case at hand—research is nontherapeutic. See, for example, Brody (2001): "Many have expressed the concern that substantial payments to research subjects in nontherapeutic projects will impair the voluntariness of their choice to participate and have therefore urged that these payments be minimized, if not altogether eliminated. [He refers to the IRB Handbook, pp. 3–45] . . . I have been troubled by this view because (a) it promotes the exploitation of subjects who are paid too little in light of the burdens imposed by the research and (b) it fails to explain why research subjects should be treated differently from others (e.g., workers) who can get ample pay for their efforts . . . .Why in this setting only is it thought to be inappropriate to pay people sufficiently to make them want to undergo the burdens in question? It cannot be the risk issues, because in other settings people are appropriately paid more to undergo risks. . . . Here is a cynical explanation . . . : it serves the interests of the research community, which does not have to bear this extra cost of properly paying subjects" (p. 3).

studies find the prospect of benefit—either to themselves or their community—sufficient to motivate participation.

Nevertheless, such conversations are unlikely to eliminate concerns about fair payment with this participant group and are unlikely to eliminate all undue influence when some participants are clearly in need of money and motivated solely by the payments.

It may be helpful to consider what precisely the problem is with the current level of payment. The IRB has decided that the risk-benefit ratio is sufficiently acceptable to approve the study, and nobody is forcing participation. Nevertheless, problems remain. In chapter 5, we saw that decision-making capacity requires participants to understand information about a study, to appreciate how it pertains to them, to be able to reason with the information (e.g., weigh risks and benefits), and to express a clear decision. One way of conceiving the problem in this study is to say that the payment is interfering with participants' ability to appreciate the nature of randomization and the risks of the study. Because some participants are interested only in getting paid, they are uninterested in learning information that is essential to understanding the study and granting informed consent. Accordingly, the problem may be addressed by addressing decision-making capacity. As part of the consent process, Dr. Johnson could quiz participants about information shared in the consent form. (See, e.g., the Friends of Research "Informed Consent Evaluation Tool," available at http://www.friendsresearch.org/Investigators_IRB.htm.) By discussing responses with participants, Dr. Johnson might be able to foster understanding of the protocol and reasoning about risks and benefits. If she encounters participants who remain interested only in the payment, then she could declare them ineligible for participation.

Case Study: Biological Studies of Aggressive Behavior in Preteens

From 1992 to 1995, researchers at the New York State Psychiatric Institute and the College of Physicians and Surgeons of Columbia University conducted studies to understand factors that contribute to aggressiveness in children (Pine et al., 1997; Pine et al., 1996). This research was considered socially important because children who display risk factors are more prone to antisocial personality disorders, criminal activity, and substance abuse in adolescence and adulthood. Previous nonhuman primate and human data suggested that genetic factors, biological factors—especially serotonergic function—and environmental factors contribute to the development of aggressive behavior. These studies were approved by Institutional Review Boards. Consent was obtained from parents.

In one of the studies (Pine et al., 1996), researchers gained access to sealed court records (without a court order) to identify younger brothers of young male offenders in New York. Families of 126 boys were contacted. Parents were offered financial incentives (from $125 to $175 in various legs of the studies) for their child's participation. Researchers aimed to examine associations among rearing factors, children's behavior, and platelet 5-HT2a receptor characteristics of 34 boys. Fourteen to 24 months later, 109 boys from the original 126 underwent psychiatric reexaminations; 56 of these boys were considered eligible to participate in a follow-up study (Pine et al., 1997). Exclusion criteria included: any physical illness, abnormal blood chemistry values, current use of any medication or illicit substance, and needle phobia.

The 56 eligible boys were approached to participate in a "challenge study" that involved administering fenfluramine to provide a serotonergic response measured by prolactin levels. The boys received a four-hour home visit during which time interviewers completed the Home Observation and Measurement of the Environment Inventory. The boys also underwent psychiatric evaluations aimed above all at establishing the presence or absence of oppositional defiant disorder, conduct disorder, and attention deficit hyperactivity disorder (ADHD). Researchers hypothesized that levels of prolactin would correlate with adverse rearing conditions and assessments of aggressive child behavior. Thirty-six boys were eligible, and 34 complied with the prechallenge protocol. Of the 34 who participated in the challenge study, 44% were African American and 56% were Hispanic. The researchers described all of the boys as from impoverished families. In commentaries on the study, an institutional representative said that "the subjects ended up being African American and Hispanic because of the composition of the neighborhood in which they were selected" (Grinfeld, 1998, unpaginated).

During the fenfluramine challenge leg of the study, the boys followed low-monoamine diets for four days. They fasted the night before the challenge and received no food or liquids during the challenge. An intravenous catheter was inserted at 8:30 a.m. and blood was sampled hourly until 2 p.m. At 10 a.m. oral fenfluramine hydrochloride was administered.

Researchers found higher prolactin responses correlated both with adverse rearing conditions and child aggression. Given the correlational nature of the study, the researchers noted that they could not determine how serotonin, rearing conditions, and child aggression might be causally related.

Assume the role of an IRB member at a sponsoring institution. What modifications, if any, would you require before approving future studies of this nature?

CASE COMMENTARY

This historical case generated a good deal of controversy (Grinfeld, 1998; Hilts, 1998) and prompted an investigation by the federal Office of Protection from Research Risks (OPRR, now OHRP). The deputy director of the New York State Psychiatric Institute (NYSPI), one of the study sites, offered the following reply to the controversy:

Assaults like this on properly conducted research will certainly have the effect of putting barriers to further scientific work in this area. This will only mean that people suffering from significant psychiatric problems will be denied access to all the benefits of current biomedical technology, and therefore, will continue to be second class citizens when compared to people suffering from other illnesses. (Grinfeld, 1998, unpaginated)

OPRR's investigation actually concurred that the IRB review and approval of the study were consistent with federal regulations, and they did not cite the investigators or institutions with any ethical misconduct.

Others disagree with this finding (Shamoo & Tauer, 2002). It appears that OPRR focused above all on the content of the consent forms and the interpretation of allowable risks in research with children. OPRR did not examine issues related to privacy and confidentiality. As Koocher (2005) and Shamoo and Tauer (2002) note, the recruitment of participants involved a breach of confidentiality by probation authorities at the request of the researchers (by sharing sealed records without a court order). OPRR also did not examine whether the study entailed a breach of the Belmont Report's principle of justice and the corresponding requirement of the Common Rule (45CFR46.11[a][3]) that IRB's only approve studies after determining that the "selection of subjects is equitable." The same paragraph of the Common Rule states that IRBs "should be particularly cognizant of the special problems of research involving vulnerable populations, such as *children*, prisoners, pregnant women, mentally disabled persons, or *economically or educationally disadvantaged persons*" (emphasis added). While Shamoo and Tauer (2002), who have published the most thorough ethical review of this case, focused on whether the study satisfied the regulatory risk-benefit ratio required to permit research with children, given the focus of this chapter, I will analyze the case through the lens of justice. In particular, I will focus upon two aspects of justice in research: equal ability to say "no," and equal distribution of benefits and burdens.

Unequal Ability to Say "No"?

As noted above and in chapter 6, vulnerability refers to a reduced ability to protect oneself. Because the informed consent process provides the primary opportunity for self-protection, most forms of vulnerability turn out to involve something that weakens one's ability to participate fully in the consent process, or more precisely, one's ability to decline participation in a study. There were several reasons that participants in the fenfluramine studies might find it more difficult than your average participant to decline participation. First, they were children. Given their age, their cognitive capacity to understand risks and to weigh them against anticipated benefits is not fully developed. Moreover, children are frequently inclined or pressured to defer to the authority of their parents. Second, they and their parents were poor. Koocher (2005) cites IRB forms that indicate the compensation included "a $25 gift certificate for the child [to Toys R Us], $100 paid to the parents 'for your child,' and $25 to cover transportation costs" (p. 182).

Given their poverty, the financial incentives may have been far more enticing to them than to others. This does not mean that the study would have been more ethical had the participants received less compensation for their time, but it does merit consideration. Third, as Koocher observes:

> The fact that the child participants' parents knew the probation department had cooperated in making their names available constitutes a de facto coercive pressure of significant proportions. The mother who reported hoping that her incarcerated son might benefit because of his younger

brother's cooperation in the drug study (Guart, 1999) clearly illustrates this point. (Koocher, 2005, p. 185)

The study was not coercive in the sense that the investigators forced participation. The fact that 36% of parents approached for permission refused to allow their children to participate suggests that they, at least, felt free to decline participation. It does not, however, mean that there was no undue influence upon the 64% who did grant permission for their children's participation. The three considerations presented here indicate that the participants in this study were vulnerable, and they did not have an ability to decline participation that was equal to your average, economically stable adult living in society. Was this inequality unjust? In any case, at least some of the threats to their ability to decline participation could have been mitigated. For example, the investigators could have gone to greater lengths to dispel any illusions that parents might have had that participation in the study could assist their incarcerated sons. To reduce the conflict of interest that an impoverished parent might have when offered cash for their child's participation, investigators might have offered larger children's gift certificates and money for transportation costs alone. (Ironically, one of the variables the investigators were investigating was precisely abuse and neglect by parents—so there is no room here for naïvely assuming that all parents put their child's interests first.) More important, as we will see below, there were no scientific reasons that the population in the study needed to share uniformly these traits of vulnerability.

As noted before, the significance of questions pertaining to undue influence increases as the risks or burdens associated with a study increase. It is partly in light of the level of risk and the unjust distribution of risks and benefits that concerns about the quality of informed consent linger.

Unequal Distribution of Risks and Benefits?

Shamoo and Tauer point to two regulatory criteria that had to be met before an IRB could approve these studies. First, the procedure needed to present experiences to subjects that were "reasonably commensurate with those inherent in their actual or expected . . . situations" (45CFR46.406[b]). Second, the procedure needed to be likely to yield generalizable knowledge about the subjects' condition, which is of vital importance for the understanding or amelioration of the subjects' condition (45CFR46.406[c]). These conditions would be satisfied, for example, in a clinical trial of medications intended to treat ADHD when the study sample included only children diagnosed with ADHD. In order to justify the fenfluramine challenge studies, the researchers needed to argue that the children did have a "condition," namely, the children showed "clinically significant aggressive behavior" or were "raised in a social environment that is conductive to the development of chronic aggression," though the published article on the study more frequently describes them simply as "younger brothers of convicted delinquents" (Pine et al., 1997).[8] Furthermore, even if the subjects were "at risk" of developing chronic or clinically significant

8. In discussing this case with classes, participants repeatedly pointed out that in some environments it is very difficult to tell when aggression is "clinically significant" versus adaptive or a form of self-preservation.

aggression, issues of justice in the distribution of risks and benefits remain. For example, Koocher 2005 cites evidence that "applying an 'at risk' label to a child may lead to significant adverse future consequences" (p. 187). We cannot know what effect such labeling had on how the boys, their parents, and the local authorities came to view the boys. Moreover, the biased sampling combined with the labels could only contribute to undesirable social stereotyping of African American and Hispanic boys.

Recall that the explanation offered for the racial distribution of the sample (100% African American or Hispanic) was that it was representative of the community surrounding the research institution. This certainly makes it sound like the researchers decided to use a convenience sample. There is nothing wrong with convenience sampling in the initial phases of some kinds of research, particularly when risks are minimal. However, apart from concerns about the generalizability of their results, the very last paragraph of the Belmont Report states:

> One special instance of injustice results from the involvement of *vulnerable subjects*. Certain groups, such as *racial minorities, the economically disadvantaged*, the very sick, and the institutionalized may continually be sought as research subjects, owing to their ready availability in settings where research is conducted. Given their dependent status and their frequently compromised capacity for free consent, they should be protected against the danger of being involved in research *solely for administrative convenience*, or because they are *easy to manipulate as a result of their* illness or *socioeconomic condition*. (National Commission, 1979, C3) [Emphasis added.]

That is to say, whatever the merits of a convenience sample, they are outweighed when participants are vulnerable, especially when risks are greater than minimal, the inclusion criteria and publication of results risk stigmatizing participants, and there are no expected direct benefits to the participants.

It is useful to note that some studies with vulnerable children using the same exact drug failed to raise the ethical concerns that these studies raised. In the case compendium edited by Hoagwood, Jensen, and Fisher (1996), one of the cases they hold up as illustrating good ethical problem-solving involved the administration of fenfluramine to children with mental retardation and ADHD (Aman et al., 1993). Given the children's mental retardation, one might assume that this study was more problematic, not less so—so why did it illustrate good ethical practices? First, the study was meant to investigate a drug treatment that would directly benefit either the participants or children just like them. Fenfluramine (Pondamin) was being studied as an alternative to metylphenidate (Ritalin) in treating hyperactivity and inattention because previous research indicated it was promising. Risks of the study were fully disclosed, but many parents enrolled their children because they did not respond well to existing treatments. The researchers provided parents with excellent information on common side effects, provided multiple contact numbers, had provisions for quickly identifying blind assignments to experimental conditions, and had rescue arms in place. In order to maximize benefits to the children, with permission of the parents, each child's physician was sent a letter detailing the child's responses to the various arms of the study and providing suggestions pertaining to treatment. Finally, they followed up participation in the study with a "consumer satisfaction" survey of parents to determine their level of satisfaction with the staff, the conclusions reached, and the information provided (Aman & Wolford, 1995). Eighty-eight percent of parents said they would join the study again if faced with the same choices. This latter study provides a sharp contrast to the fenfluramine challenge studies.

Conclusion

It is worth reviewing the ethical criteria commonly used to justify a decision when values clash: necessity, efficacy, least infringement, proportionality, and proper process. In this particular analysis of the fenfluramine challenge studies, the clash ing values are the principle of justice (pertaining to the consent process and the distribution of risks and benefits) and the principle of beneficence (the knowledge to be gained about the relationship between childhood aggression, genetics, and environment).

Was it necessary to tolerate the inequities found in this study in order to gain the knowledge sought? We have already seen that it was not. In contrast to the study of fenfluramine's therapeutic effects with children with mental retardation and ADHD, the challenge study's hypotheses did not require a population consisting only of African American and Hispanic children. Moreover, the challenge study researchers did not respect the principle of least infringement (i.e., they did not reduce inequities to what was minimally required). As multiple commentators have noted, the same knowledge could have been gained by recruiting in more racially and economically diverse neighborhoods; the incentives could have re-duced the amount of cash offered to parents; and greater efforts could have been made to assure parents that the courts would not know whose children partici-pated or did not participate.

Did the inequities in this study effectively achieve the investigators' aims? In-centives aside, the inequities had precisely the opposite effect. As the institutional spokesperson observed, the controversy surrounding the fenfluramine studies ac-tually thwarted potentially beneficial research on aggression in youth. Accord-ingly, it is very hard to argue that the good to come of the study was proportionate to the inequities involved and the resulting stigma to the children. Again, by way of contrast, the ADHD fenfluramine study also involved a highly vulnerable pop-ulation of individuals who could not consent for themselves, which always gives one pause. But it was designed to yield "proportionate" information: important information about which of three arms best treated symptoms the participants actually had.

In conclusion, the fenfluramine studies rightly generated ethical controversy, much of which could have been avoided through changes in the study design.

Further EMHR Resources

- Unit five of the *Dialogues* DVD contains an interview with Diane Scott-Jones and excerpts of a focus group with mental health consumers on recruitment in research
- Unit six of the *Dialogues* DVD contains an interview with Vetta Sanders Thompson and excerpts of a focus group with mental health consumers on cultural competence in research
- www.emhr.net contains a bibliography and further case studies on recruitment and justice concerns

REFERENCES

Aman, M. G., Kern, R. A., McGhee, D. E., & Arnold, L. E. (1993). Fenfluramine and methylphenidate in children with mental retardation and ADHD: Clinical and side effects. *Journal of the American Academy of Child and Adolescent Psychiatry, 32*(4), 851–859.

Aman, M. G., & Wolford, P. L. (1995). Consumer satisfaction with involvement in drug research: A social validity study. *Journal of the American Academy of Child and Adolescent Psychiatry, 34*(7), 940–945.

Beauchamp, T. L., & Childress, J. F. (2001). *Principles of biomedical ethics* (5th ed.). New York: Oxford University Press.

Brody, B. A. (2001). Making informed consent meaningful. *IRB: Ethics & Human Research, 23*(5), 1–5.

Centers for Disease Control and Prevention, Department of Health and Human Services, National Institutes of Health, Food and Drug Administration, Human Resources and Services Administration, Substance Abuse and Mental Health Services Administration, et al. (1998). *Building community partnerships in research: Recommendations and strategies.* Accessed May 6, 2007, at http://www.minority.unc.edu/reports/cdc1998/CttyPartInResCDC1998.pdf.

Chisholm, R. (1989). *On metaphysics.* Minneapolis: University of Minnesota Press.

Corbie-Smith, G., Miller, W. C., & Ransohoff, D. F. (2004). Interpretations of "appropriate" minority inclusion in clinical research. *American Journal of Medicine, 116*, 249–252.

Cottler, L. B., Compton, W. M., Ben-Abdallah, A., Horne, M., & Claverie, D. (1996). Achieving a 96.6 percent follow-up rate in a longitudinal study of drug abusers. *Drug and Alcohol Dependence, 41*, 209–217.

Daly III, H. F. T., Oblak, L. M., Siefert, R. W., & Shellenberger, K. (2002). Symposium: Barriers to access to health care: Into the red to stay in the pink: The hidden cost of being uninsured. *Health Matrix: Journal of Law-Medicine, 12*, 39–61.

DuBois, J. M. (2005). Vulnerability in research. In E. A. Bankert & R. J. Amdur (Eds.), *Institutional review boards: Management and function* (2nd ed., pp. 337–340). Boston: Jones & Bartlett.

DuBois, J. M., & Campbell, J. (2006). *Ethical dialogues in behavioral health research.* St. Louis: Missouri Institute of Mental Health (www.amazon.com).

Engelhardt, H. T. (1996). *The foundations of bioethics* (2nd ed.). New York: Oxford University Press.

Fry, C., & Dwyer, R. (2001). For love or money? An exploratory study of why injecting drug users participate in research. *Addiction, 96*, 1319–1325.

Garber, M., & Arnold, R. M. (2006). Promoting the participation of minorities in research. *American Journal of Bioethics, 6*(3), W14-W20.

Getz, K., & Borfitz, D. (2002). *Informed consent: A guide to the risks and benefits of volunteering for clinical trials.* Boston: CenterWatch.

Goldstein, J. (1978). On the right of the "institutionalized mentally infirm" to consent to or refuse to participate as subjects in biomedical and behavioral research. In National Commission (Ed.), *Appendix to "Research involving those institutionalized as mentally infirm"* (pp. 2/1–2/39). Washington, DC: Department of Health, Education, and Welfare.

Grinfeld, M. J. (1998). Researchers under fire: Feds to probe studies on kids, dueling agencies yield to confusion. *Psychiatric Times, 15*(6), retrieved on January 13, 2007, from http://www.psychiatrictimes.com/p980601a.html.

Guart, A. (1999, May 30). Mom: I was duped when son became "drug guinea pig." *New York Post. Online edition,* p. 6.

Harper, M. (1978). Ethical issues on mental health research from a minority perspective. In National Commission (Ed.), *Appendix to "Research involving those institutionalized as mentally infirm"* (pp. 6/1–6/41). Washington, DC: Department of Health, Education, and Welfare.

Hilts, P. (1998, April 15). Experiments on children are reviewed. *New York Times,* p. 3.

Iltis, A. S. (2004). Costs to subjects for research participation and the informed consent process: Regulatory and ethical considerations. *IRB: Ethics & Human Subjects, 26*(6), 9–13.

Iltis, A. S., DeVader, S., & Matsuo, H. (2006). Payments to children and adolescents enrolled in research: A pilot study. *Pediatrics, 118*(4), 1546–1552.

Kaminsky, A., Roberts, L. W., & Brody, J. L. (2003). Influences upon willingness to participate in schizophrenia research: An analysis of narrative data from 63 people with schizophrenia. *Ethics and Behavior, 13*(2), 153–172.

Kant, I. (1785/1993). *Grounding for the metaphysics of morals* (J. W. Ellington, Trans., 2nd ed.). Indianapolis, IN: Hackett.

King, P. A. (1998). Race, justice, and research. In J. P. Kahn, A. C. Mastroianni, & J. Sugarman (Eds.), *Beyond consent: Seeking justice in research* (pp. 88–110). New York: Oxford University Press.

King, P. A. (2005). Justice beyond Belmont. In J. F. Childress, E. M. Meslin, & H. T. Shapiro (Eds.), *Belmont revisited: Ethical principles for research with human subjects* (pp. 136–147). Washington, DC: Georgetown University Press.

Koocher, G. P. (2005). Behavioral research with children: The fenfluramine challenge. In E. Kodish (Ed.), *Ethics and research with children* (pp. 179–193). New York: Oxford University Press.

Lederer, S. E. (1995). *Subjected to science: Human experimentation in America before the second world war.* Baltimore: Johns Hopkins University Press.

Levine, C. (1996). Changing views of justice after Belmont: AIDS and the inclusion of "vulnerable" subjects. In H. Y. Vanderpool (Ed.), *The ethics of research involving human subjects* (pp. 105–126). Frederick, MD: University Publishing Group.

Lind, E. A., & Tyler, T. R. (1988). *The social psychology of procedural justice.* New York: Plenum Press.

Macklin, R., & Friedland, G. (1986). AIDS research: The ethics of clinical trials. *Law, Medicine, and Healthcare, 14,* 273–280.

McCarthy, C. R. (1998). The evolving story of justice in federal research policy. In J. P. Kahn, A. C. Mastroianni, & J. Sugarman (Eds.), *Beyond consent: Seeking justice in research* (pp. 11–31). New York: Oxford University Press.

Moreno, J. D. (2000). *Undue risk: Secret state experiments on humans*. New York: W. H. Freeman and Company.

Moreno, J. D. (2001). Goodbye to all that: The end of moderate protectionism in human subjects research. *Hastings Center Report, 31*(3), 9–17.

National Bioethics Advisory Commission. (1999). *Research involving persons with mental disorders that may affect decisionmaking capacity: Vol. 2. Commission papers*. Bethesda, MD: National Bioethics Advisory Commission.

National Bioethics Advisory Commission. (2001). *Ethical and policy issues in international research: Clinical trials in developing countries*. Bethesda, MD: National Bioethics Advisory Commission.

National Commission. (1979). *The Belmont report: Ethical principles and guidelines for the protection of human subjects of research*. Washington, DC: Department of Health, Education, and Welfare.

National Commission for the Protection of Human Subjects of Biomedical and Behavioral Research. (1978). *Research involving those institutionalized as mentally infirm: Report and recommendations*. Washington, DC: Department of Health, Education, and Welfare.

Pine, D. S., Coplan, J. D., Wasserman, G. A., Miller, L. S., Fried, J. E., Davies, M., et al. (1997). Neuroendocrine response to fenfluramine challenge in boys: Associations with aggressive behavior and adverse rearing. *Archives of General Psychiatry, 54*(9), 839–846.

Pine, D. S., Wasserman, G. A., Coplan, J. D., Fried, J. E., Huang, Y.-Y., Kassir, S., et al. (1996). Platelet serotonin 2a (5-ht sub 2a) receptor characteristics and parenting factors for boys at risk for delinquency: A preliminary report. *American Journal of Psychiatry, 153*(4), 538–544.

Pojman, L. P., & McLeod, O. (Eds.). (1998). *What do we deserve? A reader on justice and desert*. New York: Oxford University Press.

Rawls, J. (1999). *A theory of justice* (Rev. ed.). Cambridge, MA: Belknap Press of Harvard University Press.

Savitt, T. L. (1982). The use of blacks for medical experimentation and demonstration in the old south. *Journal of Southern History, 48*, 331–348.

Shamoo, A. E., & Tauer, C. A. (2002). Ethically questionable research with children: The fenfluramine study. *Accountability in Research, 9*, 143–166.

Tishler, C. L., & Bartholomae, S. (2002). The recruitment of normal healthy volunteers: A review of the literature on the use of financial incentives. *Journal of Clinical Pharmacology, 42*, 365–375.

Tyler, T. R., & Rasinski, K. (1991). Procedural justice, institutional legitimacy, and the acceptance of unpopular U.S. Supreme Court decisions: A reply to Gibson. *Law and Society Review, 25*(3), 621–630.

Wilmshurst, P. (1997). Scientific imperialism: If they won't benefit from the findings, poor people in the developing world should not be used in research. *British Medical Journal, 314*, 840.

8

Research Questions and Study Design

The ethics of research is not about etiquette; nor is it about considering the poor hapless subject at the expense of science or society. Rather, we study ethics to learn how to make research "work" for all concerned. The ethical researcher creates a mutually respectful, win-win relationship with the research population; this is a relationship in which subjects are pleased to participate candidly, and the community at large regards the conclusions as constructive.
—J. E. Sieber, *Planning Ethically Responsible Research*

Research is a human activity that yields products such as new knowledge, new medications, or improved educational practices. Contrary to contemporary practice, the ancient Greek philosopher Aristotle spoke of four different kinds of causes of human products. The end result of an action—say, the new knowledge gained from research activities—he called the "final cause," not primarily because it comes last in time, but because it is the end toward which we act. The final cause provides our motivation; in other words, it "causes" us to cause things.

Research questions or hypotheses state an end product that we seek; they state what we want to learn from a study, what motivates our research endeavor. Until now, we have examined how research questions can be investigated ethically, and we have assumed that research should not be conducted using illicit means. For example, Nazi experiments yielded knowledge about bodily reactions to extreme stresses, and the Tuskegee syphilis trial produced most of the scientific publications that exist on the natural course of syphilis. Nevertheless, because the research questions these studies posed could only be answered by subjecting human beings to inhumane treatment, it would have been best had they never been investigated. Most of this chapter continues along these lines, exploring ethical means of conducting research.

However, a more fundamental question deserves brief examination: are some research questions ethically problematic? Are there some ends we should not seek regardless of means?

The Bible story of creation tells us that God forbade humans to seek certain kinds of knowledge, and Adam and Eve became mortal and were driven from the Garden of Eden only when they ate fruit from the tree of knowledge of good and evil (Genesis 2:15). Johnson (1996) has observed that some contemporary philosophers question whether knowledge of genetics, which may tell us of our future health or how to manipulate our biological nature for our own purposes, should be avoided, as it may similarly transform not only our self-perceptions but perhaps even our very nature. However, she also observes that such arguments are difficult to sustain apart from appeals to the authority of God, which are not likely to find broad support in a pluralistic, secular society.

Other arguments against asking certain research questions revolve around the consequences of the new knowledge. Knowledge of how to split atoms and nuclei, for example, not only satisfied human curiosity and provided an economical source of energy but also contributed to the use of horrific weapons and ongoing fears that such weapons could be used again on a much larger scale (Singer, 1996).

Less dramatic, but nevertheless significant, examples of knowledge with undesirable consequences exist in mental health research. For example, gathering data on the influence of race, ethnicity, and culture on variables such as depression, substance abuse, and suicide may be important in designing culturally competent interventions (Cuellar & Paniagua, 2000; Lynch & Hanson, 1992; Philleo & Brisbane, 1997). At the same time, research that discovers higher prevalence of disorders among minority groups than among the dominant population can be stigmatizing and negatively influence the lives of members (Fisher et al., 2002; Weijer, 1999).

Mental health consumers have also criticized some research questions for failing to reflect the priorities of consumers. For example, consumers may seek greater knowledge of recovery or of support systems that assist consumers in living with mental illnesses, but these topics will not generate profits for pharmaceutical companies, which now sponsor more research than the U.S. federal government (Griffiths, Jorm, Christensen, Medway, & Dear, 2002; Scott, 1993; Whitaker, 2002). While research questions that are motivated by profit may not be unethical per se, beneficence requires society to take an interest in the needs of people with mental health disorders.

Finally, some research questions are unethical precisely because they will not generate knowledge. Rather, they are likely only to reinforce the assumptions upon which they rest. For example, Koocher and Keith-Spiegel (1990) describe a study of mothers of daughters who were abused by their fathers that only asked questions that could confirm a mother's pivotal role in contributing to abuse but not disconfirm it.

What follows from these reflections? Should certain questions be avoided, and if so, should IRBs or other oversight bodies enforce research prohibitions? On the one hand, Johnson (1996) offers reflections that seemingly support avoiding certain kinds of research, if only through the internal sanctions of researchers themselves:

> if we think of science as a profession and part of society, science comes into view as a collective enterprise that must be accountable to the society of which it is a part. The society (a country or the world at large) is only justified in recognizing the profession and granting it resources and privileges when it is convinced that doing so will bring about the end which the society hopes to achieve with science. (p. 217)

On the other hand, Singer (1996) suggests that if research is perceived to benefit any particular group, it will be very difficult to stop it from being pursued.

Moreover, prohibiting certain kinds of research, for example, research on race and IQ, often backfires; it produces an air of suspicion and a sense that there is a conspiracy to cover something up. Finally, eschewing knowledge may ultimately handicap us in solving problems, and often controversial problems are among the most difficult to solve.

Perhaps wisdom lies between naïvely assuming that knowledge should always be sought and dismissively prohibiting the pursuit of any knowledge that may be controversial or potentially harmful. At least in many contexts, following the principle of "least infringement" may be appropriate. For example, research on the prevalence of substance abuse disorders among a specific racial or ethnic group may be less stigmatizing if conducted without a comparison group from the general population (Fisher et al., 2002).

Sieber (1992) also observes that following good habits of engaging the larger scientific community may provide correction and balance that individual studies cannot provide. Presenting assumptions and the limitations of data in publications; consulting with or citing scientists who support alternative hypotheses; sharing data with scientists who want to verify or test alternative hypotheses—all of these standard scientific practices can add balance to our research questions and the data they shape.

The remainder of this chapter explores the major study designs used to investigate a wide variety of research questions.

BEHAVIORAL AND SOCIAL SCIENCE (BSS) RESEARCH

BSS research involves a vast array of methodologies, including surveys, interviews, natural behavioral observation, laboratory experiments, and field research (Citro, Ilgen, & Marrett, 2003). Just as the Tuskegee syphilis study and the Willowbrook experiments provide common starting points for the discussion of ethics in biomedical research, so, too, Milgram's obedience studies and Humphrey's studies of men who have sex with men (MSM) loom large in discussions of ethics in BSS research.[1]

Stanley Milgram (1974) conducted a series of studies on obedience to authority during the 1960s. Participants were led to believe that the studies concerned the effect of punishment on learning. After a rigged drawing of slips of paper from a hat, participants were assigned the role of "the teacher," who was supposed to administer a shock to a learner (an actor trained by the investigator) every time the learner made an error in learning paired words. With each new error, the participant was instructed to give a stronger shock. In fact, no shocks were actually administered to the learner. However, participants could see the learner sitting, attached to wires, in an adjoining room—and he acted convincingly as though he were receiving shocks. When participants objected to administering shocks, the experimenter urged them to do so using a series of prompts ranging from "please continue" to "you have no other choice, you must go on." Of the 40 participants,

---

1. The Milgram study is described in more detail in chapter 10 and the Humphreys studies are described in more detail in the cases compendium published at www.emhr.net.

26 obeyed orders to the end, administering shocks labeled as "danger—severe shock" and "XXX—450 volts," even though this caused the "learner" to pound on the wall, apparently in excruciating pain, and eventually to become unresponsive. These studies have been hailed by many as brilliant and ethically legitimate and by others as ethically problematic for deceiving participants and causing them distress (Baumrind, 1964; Blass, 1991; Korn, 1997).

From 1965 to 1968, Laud Humphreys conducted dissertation research on men who have impersonal sex with men (Humphreys, 1970). Without disclosing his role as a sociology researcher, Humphreys played the role of "watch queen," that is, he looked out for intruders while men performed sex acts in the public rest-rooms of parks in major metropolitan areas. He later disclosed his role to some men he had observed and interviewed them on their daily lives. In other cases, he recorded his subjects' license plate numbers to track where they lived. A year later, after changing his hair and attire, he interviewed these same men in their homes under the guise of conducting an anonymous public health survey. Many in the gay and MSM communities welcomed Humphreys' research, and Hum-phreys received the C. Wright Mills Award of the Society for the Study of Social Problems for his tearoom trade study (Humphreys, 1975). Yet it has also been criticized for failing to obtain informed consent, for using deception, for invad-ing privacy, and for subjecting people to significant risks should confidentiality have been breached (Beauchamp, Faden, Wallace, & Walters, 1982); Humphreys himself had some misgivings about the study years later (Humphreys, 1975).

A "Panel on Institutional Review Boards, Surveys, and Social Science Re-search" convened by the National Research Council concluded that the ethical issues in BSS research typically fall under two categories: informed consent and confidentiality/privacy. Because these issues are discussed systematically in chap-ters 4 and 9 respectively, the following discussions are brief and aim at raising awareness rather than resolving the issues.

Privacy and Confidentiality Issues

Whereas the term "confidentiality" refers to the interest people have in controlling access to *information or data* about them, "privacy" refers to the interest people have in restricting the access of others to themselves. Determining what constitutes a pri-vacy violation can be difficult because views may vary across cultures, developmen-tal stages, and contexts (DuBois, 2004b; Laufer & Wolfe, 1977). For example, going to the bathroom is ordinarily considered a private behavior in the United States, but few would consider it a privacy violation if someone were observed urinating in a public outdoor space. Similarly, had Humphreys installed cameras in individuals' bedrooms without their knowledge and consent, his observations would clearly have violated rights to privacy. However, because his observations were made in public bathrooms, where stalls lacked doors and "watch queens" were allowed to observe, he claimed that he did not violate subjects' rights to privacy (Humphreys, 1975).

However, matters of privacy are not adequately understood only in terms of rights. Even when participants grant permission to be observed in ethnographic or field research, they may experience discomfort and a sense that their privacy is being invaded (Parrot, 2002).

While Humphreys defended his observation of sexual behaviors in public spaces, he recognized a strict obligation to protect the confidentiality of the data he gathered. Most of the actual harms that can occur in BSS research result from breaches of confidentiality. Humphreys's study provides a powerful example of such risks (though there were no breaches of confidentiality in his study, but rather invasions of privacy). For example, one could imagine that if his data were discovered, some of the men might have been at legal risk (sodomy was illegal and tearooms were raided by police in the 1970s). Moreover, most of the men observed, contrary to prevailing stereotypes, were married and employed: they would have risked divorce, social embarrassment, and loss of employment. The harms that can ensue from a breach of confidentiality are essentially the same regardless of whether data is gathered through observation, mail surveys, or interviews; thus, breaches of confidentiality can present a significant source of risk even when seemingly innocuous procedures are used (Warwick, 1982).

Chapter 9 explores the use of "certificates of confidentiality" as a way of protecting confidential data from subpoena (Hoagwood, 1994; Marshall, 1992), particularly in research that could place participants at legal risk. It additionally presents techniques for safeguarding confidential data throughout the various stages of a study.

As we will see, one of the best ways of protecting data is to gather it anonymously or else to completely de-identify data. However, doing so may generate new risks or ethical challenges. For example, it may restrict investigators' ability to intervene appropriately or to share individual results with participants (Shaw, 2003). Research by Fisher (2003) found that participants do not always wish to have confidentiality placed above other benefits; many would prefer to know that they will receive the help they need even when this means that data will not be de-identified and others may be contacted to provide assistance.

Different methodologies may also give rise to unique threats to confidentiality. For example, researchers frequently record qualitative interviews, enabling people to identify participants by voice or image. Participants often provide high levels of biographical detail about themselves making them identifiable even when names are removed or changed. Moreover, because participants share not just discrete information but their life stories, questions arise regarding ownership of data and ensuing rights to control its presentation and interpretation (Smythe & Murray, 2000). Participants may also introduce private information about third parties, for example, parents, spouses, or employers (M. W. Smith, 1995). When detailed information is given about third parties, this may constitute an infringement on their privacy without consent (Hadjistavropoulos & Smythe, 2001).

Focus groups additionally raise concerns that confidentiality may be lost due to disclosure in group settings (M. W. Smith, 1995). When sensitive issues are discussed, the importance of confidentiality must be discussed with participants and the risk of a breach should be disclosed (Gallant, 2002; M. W. Smith, 1995).

Consent Issues

Informed consent is frequently modified or waived in BSS research. This may not present a problem in certain contexts. For example, many speak of "implied consent" when it is clear to an adult participant that he or she may choose not to complete a survey and return it by mail; the act of completing and returning a survey implies agreement to participate (Capron, 1982). While research regulations do not mention implied consent, it is allowable whenever research is exempt from the regulations or an IRB grants a waiver of consent. Ethicists and policy bodies have endorsed its prudent use (Capron, 1982; Citro, Ilgen, & Marrett, 2003). In general, even when consent is waived, investigators should still inform participants (e.g., in a cover letter) that participation is voluntary, how data will be used, and how confidentiality will be protected (DuBois, 2002).

In other contexts, foregoing or modifying informed consent can be controversial. Most studies that involve the use of deception or the withholding of key information such as a study's purpose must meet the standards for a waiver of informed consent (discussed in chapter 4); but even when they meet these standards, concerns remain about eroding trust in researchers or causing embarrassment during debriefing (Warwick, 1982).

In school-based research, BSS researchers sometimes use so-called "passive consent" procedures. Passive consent involves only informing a parent or participant about a study and providing information on how to opt out; by default, the child or individual becomes a participant. However, passive consent runs the risk of being no consent whatsoever: from the absence of a response, one cannot infer that a parent has received, read, and understood information mailed to an address, nor that they agree to their child's participation (Hoagwood, Jensen, & Fisher, 1996). Thus, it should not really be called a form of consent and should be reserved only for studies that are ethically deemed to meet the criteria for a waiver of consent.

Even when informed consent is pursued, BSS methods can make consent challenging. For example, unstructured interviews may hamper accurate disclosure of what information might be gained or the risks the information might pose if made public (Smythe & Murray, 2000).

Moreover, the consent process itself can introduce risks. In some studies, the only threat to the confidentiality of data arises from a written, signed informed consent form. When this is the case, IRBs should consider using their discretion to waive or modify written informed consent (Citro, Ilgen, & Marrett, 2003; Sieber, 1992).

Justice, Relationality, and Sanctioning

While the National Research Council is likely correct in viewing informed consent, privacy, and confidentiality as the main ethical issues in BSS research, other concerns exist. Justice concerns arise when surveys are written at a level that excludes people with low levels of literacy from full participation or excludes entirely people who do not speak the native language. Telephone surveys necessarily exclude people who do not, or cannot afford to, have a telephone. While people who find surveys to be a nuisance might welcome exclusion from participation, exclusion can also deprive segments of the population from having a voice and can lead to skewed data (Porter, 1996).

Further, BSS research also raises general issues of relationality. As noted already, BSS research may involve sensitive and potentially stigmatizing questions.

Building trusting relationships with participants may be essential to obtaining honest participation. This may require adequate community consultation and protection of confidentiality (Fisher & Wallace, 2000; Sieber, 1992).

Finally, BSS research can raise seemingly intractable concerns about "dirty hands" or sanctioning undesirable behaviors of participants. Gallant (2002) offers examples of studying clandestine militant groups or teens who use illegal drugs; in both cases, the amoral or neutral curiosity shown by "respectable" university researchers may serve to legitimate these behaviors—at least in the eyes of participants. Klockars (1979) explores scenarios—for example, field research on undercover detectives—in which researchers might need to engage in illegal or shady behaviors in order to obtain their data. He considers the effects this can have not only on society, but on researchers themselves.

The Argument Against Full IRB Review of Most BSS Research

The Milgram and the Humphreys studies highlight ways that BSS research can generate significant ethical concerns. Nevertheless, the vast majority of BSS studies are conducted using either survey or interview methods (Citro, Ilgen, & Marrett, 2003). One author recently described the bulk of BSS research as "two people talking" research; the name is meant precisely to convey the minimal nature of the risks involved (Gunsalus, 2004). Koocher and Keith-Spiegel (1990) have similarly observed that the risks in BSS "often appear trivial" (p. 125).

At least since the development of federal research regulations in the 1970s, the ethical review of BSS research has been hotly debated (Beauchamp, Faden, Wallace, & Walters, 1982; Douglas, 1979; Sieber, 2004). Our current regulatory system was developed in reaction to abuses of human subjects in biomedical research and focuses primarily on protection of participants. BSS researchers frequently blame regulations for IRBs' unreasonable demands and unnecessary delays to research. Yet, as noted in chapter 1, the federal regulations actually do not require IRB review of much BSS research. For example, some research is exempt from the regulations, such as "research involving the use of educational tests (cognitive, diagnostic, aptitude, achievement), survey procedures, interview procedures or observation of public behavior, unless data obtained is identifiable and could place subjects at risk" (101[b].ii).[2] Moreover, as noted in chapter 4, regulations allow the use of deception in social experiments under specific conditions (via a waiver or modification of informed consent); allow waivers of parental permission; and allow consent to be obtained without a signed form. However, several authors have noted that IRBs frequently do not make use of the discretion that regulations provide them (Gunsalus, 2004; Sieber, 2004; Wagener et al., 2004).

DeVries, DeBruin, and Goodgame (2004) reviewed literature indicating that approximately half of all researchers believe that the IRB system impedes research at their institutions and that the complaints of researchers have remained

2. Most IRBs subject even exempt research to some form of review; however, this is not required by federal regulations. It is rather due to guidance from the Office of Human Research Protections (OHRP) that researchers should not determine whether their own research counts as exempt and sometimes due to the content of agreements that IRBs enter into with OHRP (federal-wide assurances).

fairly constant from the mid-1970s through today. The American Psychological Association has complained that when regulators and IRB members assume that all research involves a high risk of harm and a high degree of intrusiveness, it leads to "the imposition of stipulations and requirements that unnecessarily constrain researchers and limit research, and often add little or nothing to human participants protection" (American Psychological Association, 2001, p. 2).

Sieber (1992) has argued that unreasonable IRB demands may not only harm research, but actually harm participants, for instance, when demanding use of a written consent form introduces the only threat to confidentiality or makes illiterate participants mistrustful.

Finally, inappropriate ethical review of BSS research may be harmful to the ethical oversight system itself. DuBois (2004a) has observed that when rules and IRB decisions are perceived as hindering research without contributing to the welfare of participants, then researchers question whether compliance is a professional ethical duty; evidence exists that in such cases researchers may skirt IRBs. In the end, unreasonable rules or stipulations may lead researchers to bypass IRBs wherever possible (Keith-Spiegel & Koocher, 2005; DuBois, 2004a; Gunsalus, 2004; Ilgen & Bell, 2001).

Nevertheless, it would be irresponsible simply to forego any ethical review of BSS research.

Resolving the Tension

We have seen that many, if not most, BSS researchers are dissatisfied with current ethical review and oversight practices. How can we balance the fact that BSS research may involve greater than minimal risks with the fact that it is ordinarily no riskier than two people talking? Several changes have been proposed.

Some recommend a shift toward discipline-specific or departmental review of BSS research with greater reliance upon complaint mechanisms to identify researchers who are not conducting ethical research (DuBois, 2002; Gunsalus, 2004). Others have suggested moving toward the ethical licensing of researchers in lieu of submitting minimal risk research for IRB review (Jamrozik, 2000). Still others suggest that IRBs make much greater use of their ability to exempt research from review and grant researchers limited ability to make specific design decisions during a study without submitting protocol changes to an IRB (Citro, Ilgen, & Marrett, 2003).

BSS researchers need to provide leadership in the ethical review of BSS research. For example, by serving on IRBs, BSS researchers may educate IRBs, become better educated themselves, and reduce the "us-them" mentality that hinders ethical oversight (DuBois, 2004a). A useful resource for dialogue with IRBs is found on the National Science Foundation's Web site (National Science Foundation, 2002). The National Research Council and others have also called for more research on effective methods of fostering ethical research with minimum administrative burden (Citro, Ilgen, & Marrett, 2003; De Vries et al., 2004; Stanley, Sieber, & Melton, 1987). Research ethics can only become "evidence based" if researchers are willing to engage in research in this area.

Finally, particularly in BSS research, we observe that good ethics and good science typically go hand in hand. That is, improving the ethics of a study often leads to significant improvements in the data obtained. For example, participants are more likely to honestly disclose information if they perceive that it will offer them benefits, if their confidentiality is adequately protected, and if they trust researchers. Thus, Sieber (1992) has referred to the conduct of ethical BSS research as a form of "enlightened self-interest" (p. 4).

COMMUNITY-BASED RESEARCH

Community-based or population-based research can be conducted using virtually any of the methods discussed in this chapter: experimental designs, surveys, observation, case-controlled studies using existing data, blood screening, and even vaccine trials (Glanz, Rimer, & Lerman, 1996). Although the term "community-based research" typically excludes laboratory studies and clinical trials (Glanz, Rimer, & Lerman, 1996), it has been applied to clinical trials with clearly identifiable populations, especially vulnerable populations such as people with AIDS (Melton, Levine, Koocher, Rosenthal, & Thompson, 1988; Spiers, 1991). Defining community-based research is accordingly difficult. Gostin defines it as "research and practice performed on, or which affects, groups of people or populations" (Gostin, 1991, p. 192); yet, in some sense, this is true or potentially true of all human research.

It has already been noted that communities, and not just individuals, can be stakeholders in research. Most of the harms that can accrue to individuals can also accrue to communities, and communities may benefit from research in various ways (chapter 6); communities may be left in the dark or informed and consulted for permission (chapter 4); they may be treated justly or unjustly (chapter 7); their relations and bonds can be strengthened or weakened through research participation (chapter 2). Frequently, the key to ethically conducting research that will directly impact communities is community consultation and involvement (Backlar, 1999; Fisher & Wallace, 2000; Melton, Levine, Koocher, Rosenthal, & Thompson, 1988). At least two particular scenarios—typically representing opposite extremes of consultation in community-based research— deserve special attention.

Research on Communities

Some research not only affects communities as stakeholders, but it is conducted on communities in the sense that nearly all members will be subjects; opportunities to opt out are either severely limited or nonexistent. This may be true of research involving health education campaigns that use billboards, mailers, television, and radio ads. It may be true of health outcomes research on a new, mandatory vaccine, or research on supplements to food or water, for example, folic acid, vitamin D, or fluoride. Whenever research "participation" is going to be imposed uniformly upon members of a community, there is a heightened obligation to inform people, to engage in public discussion, to seek permission from leaders who are accountable to the community, and to provide options for opting out whenever feasible (Gostin, 1991).

Community-Based Participatory Research (CBPR)

Because community-based research frequently aims at producing change in communities (e.g., their health-related beliefs, values, and behaviors) rather than knowledge or medical products, it necessarily involves a greater political dimension. Chapter 2 discussed the significance of ethical processes in addition to ethical content or conclusions. For example, when employers use processes that are perceived to be just (typically, processes described as democratic, transparent, or inclusive), employees report greater job satisfaction and greater commitment to companies (Lind & Tyler, 1988). This same dynamic can be witnessed in the world of community-based research.

Community-based participatory research—alternately known as action research (Israel, Schulz, Parker, & Becker, 2001)—is research in which community members and representatives serve as co-investigators who play a role in defining a project's goals, designing recruitment and study methods, and gathering, analyzing, and interpreting data. Participants are often viewed as co-owners of the resulting data and may have significant control over the dissemination and presentation of findings (Ahmed, Beck, Maurana, & Newton, 2004; Israel, Schulz, Parker, & Becker, 2001). This approach to research has been encouraged particularly in community-based research with vulnerable participants (Centers for Disease Control and Prevention et al., 1998; Glanz, Rimer, & Lerman, 1996; Higgins & Metzler, 2001). Data suggests that CBPR can result in richer data, enhanced trust in researchers, increased relevance of results to the needs of communities, and better translation of data into policy and practice (Felix-Aaron & Stryer, 2003; Israel, Schulz, Parker, & Becker, 2001). Nevertheless, CBPR models may generate practical concerns.

On the side of researchers, there are numerous barriers to CBPR: a history of viewing community members as "objects" of research; skepticism about the ability of community members to contribute to study design and implementation; tendencies to devalue nontraditional research models; a lack of mentors and peer reviewers with expertise in CBPR; inadequate funding and rewards for CBPR (Ahmed, Beck, Maurana, & Newton, 2004). On the side of community members, CBPR may require individuals to overcome distrust; to invest time and energy into attending meetings and self-education; to recognize expertise that researchers bring regarding scientific methodology; and willingness to accept the requirements imposed by funding agencies (*Dialogues*, DVD). Each of these barriers carries with it an ethical dimension; they pertain to behaviors and attitudes that can be changed and that impact the well-being of human communities. Overcoming these barriers typically requires a commitment to democratic ideals and fostering trusting relationship. Resulting models of collaboration tend to be as diverse as the communities that embrace CBPR (Felix-Aaron & Stryer, 2003; Higgins & Metzler, 2001).[3]

While recent publications have demonstrated that CBPR can yield valuable research (O'Toole, Aaron, Chin, Horowitz, & Tyson, 2003), proponents acknowledge that many researchers still struggle with issues of scientific rigor, cost, and

---

3. The Community-Campus Partnerships for Health Web site contains useful information and case studies on community-based participatory research: http://depts.washington.edu/ccph/index.html. Retrieved on January 13, 2007.

time, and many question the range of research questions that are suitable for CBPR methods (Felix-Aaron & Stryer, 2003; Israel, Schulz, Parker, & Becker, 2001). Ethical disagreements in CBPR are also often more complex—and more uncomfortable to resolve—precisely because CBPR gives a voice to multiple stakeholders with competing interests, views of facts, and normative commitments. Nevertheless, CBPR methods are likely to grow more common if only because many communities are refusing researchers access to their lives and data unless they are allowed to shape the design, conduct, and dissemination of research. Once again, conducting what is perceived to be ethical research may prove to be a form of "enlightened self-interest" for researchers.

RESEARCH WITH EXISTING DATA: EPIDEMIOLOGICAL AND OUTCOMES RESEARCH

Regulations provide protections for human participants in research. But what precisely constitutes human participation in research? If a nurse asks his patients to complete a quality of life survey in order to tailor their home health care to their special needs, then they have participated in treatment, not research. Equally clear, if a nurse asks patients to complete the same survey as part of his dissertation research on quality of life among local elderly persons, then they become research participants. However, what happens when the home health nurse first gathers quality of life data for therapy and later decides he would like to statistically analyze the data and use them in his dissertation?

Such activities constitute research, a systematic investigation designed to contribute to generalizable knowledge. The regulations refer to such research as research with "existing data." In the fields of medicine and public health, data from patient records are commonly used in "case controlled" studies to compare treatment outcomes, to examine factors correlated with health disorders, or to study the prevalence of disease among populations (Amdur & Speers, 2002; Speers, 2002). Health services researchers frequently examine data from satisfaction surveys, billing records, or client charts to learn how to improve client satisfaction, to provide services more economically, or to improve clinical outcomes (Amdur & Speers, 2002; Flood, 2002).

Does research with existing data involve human participants? In fact, investigators do not interact with human beings, but only with data; so in the strict sense, there are no human participants. Nevertheless, research with existing data still involves human stakeholders. That is, the people about whom data exist may still be harmed as the data is used in research. This happens primarily through breaches of confidentiality: a risk exists that individuals could be identified as having particular traits (e.g., being HIV positive, having attempted suicide, or being dissatisfied with services); this in turn can be harmful to reputation, employability, insurability, or emotional well-being, among other things. For this reason, when individuals can be identified by existing data—either directly or through identifiers linked to the individual—then regulations treat research with existing data as if it involved human participants (Department of Health and Human Services, 2001; Office of Human Research Protections, 2004). (Chapter 9 further examines threats to confidentiality and protection measures in research involving existing data.)

The exemption for research with existing data presents a possible "loophole" for researchers. It is possible that an investigator could gather research data—that is, data that they intend to publish or otherwise share as contributions to generalizable knowledge—under the guise of therapy or quality improvement and thereby bypass IRB review and regulatory oversight. As a general rule, whenever individuals intend to gather, analyze, *and publish data*, then data gathering should be treated as research, even when other legitimate motives exist for gathering the data, such as therapy or quality improvement (Amdur & Speers, 2002; DuBois, 2002). Treating data gathering as research typically means that researchers should submit a research protocol or a request for exemption to an IRB, and that consent should be obtained from participants. When data are gathered for multiple reasons, including therapeutic or service reasons, informed consent or permission may be sought only to use the data in publications rather than to gather the data (Bellin & Dubler, 2001; DuBois, 2002). Given the difficulty of determining prospective research intent, IRBs and human participants rely heavily upon investigator integrity to ensure that IRB review and consent occur as appropriate.

CLINICAL TRIALS AND BIOLOGICAL EXPERIMENTS IN MENTAL HEALTH

Clinical trials in mental health may involve testing drugs, psychotherapies, or other interventions. Early phase trials aim to test the safety of new treatments; later phases aim to test safety and efficacy, often vis-à-vis other known effective treatments. Mental health clients or patients may enroll in clinical trials for a variety of reasons, for example, to help others, to earn money, or to gain therapeutic benefits (Getz & Borfitz, 2002). Biological experiments in mental health, as the term is used here, differ from clinical trials in that they are only indirectly aimed at producing new therapies; their primary intent is to gain knowledge of the mechanisms of healthy and pathological brain and mental functioning. Both may involve greater than minimal risks, including risks of significant psychological, physical, and economic harm.

Ethical Issues Peculiar to Clinical Trials

While a significant degree of consensus exists regarding the basic principles of human subjects protections throughout the international community (Emanuel, Wendler, & Grady, 2000), clinical trials have sharply divided morally serious people across the globe.

The primary goal of research is to gain knowledge. In contrast, the primary goal of medicine is to provide individualized treatments for patients. The most acute disagreements regarding clinical research pertain to its goals, which are often unclear when key personnel in clinical research projects wear two hats, that is, when they serve as treating clinicians on the one hand and researchers on the other. In addition to the real roles played by clinical researchers, we need to consider their perceived roles, that is, the way that prospective participants perceive them. Do they view them simply as researchers, or as clinical personnel who have their best interests as patients in mind?

Few people would recommend that clinical research be discontinued. However, considerable disagreement exists on how to balance the goals of therapy and research in clinical settings. On the one hand, the World Medical Association, most European researchers, and many research ethicists embrace the view that those engaging in clinical research must embrace two, sometimes competing, goals: to gain new knowledge while offering therapeutic benefits to participants. Perhaps the clearest formulation of this position was found in the third and fourth amended versions of the Declaration of Helsinki: "In any medical study, every patient—including those of a control group, if any—should be assured of the best proven diagnostic and therapeutic method" (cited approvingly in Michels & Rothman, 2003, p. 189). A similar notion is found in the most recent version of the Declaration of Helsinki insofar as it appears to ban the use of placebo when proven effective treatments exist (World Medical Association, 2000).[4] It is also embedded in the idea of clinical equipoise (Freedman, 1987), which many IRBs use in evaluating whether a randomized, controlled clinical trial should be approved. The idea behind clinical equipoise, which the National Bioethics Advisory Commission (NBAC) recoined as "research equipoise" (National Bioethics Advisory Commission, 2001, p. 112), is that there must be genuine uncertainly about the superiority of any of the treatments administered in a clinical trial, including placebo. Thus, for example, an experimental treatment can be administered to humans only when previous research suggests that it might be at least as good as standard therapy. And placebo can be used only when there is uncertainty whether it might be preferable to standard therapy— considering not only effectiveness in abating symptoms, but also side effects or other burdens of treatment that sometimes lead patients to refuse standard therapy.

A contrasting viewpoint has been defended by the Food and Drug Administration (Food and Drug Administration, 1999) and several research ethicists (Miller & Brody, 2002; Veatch, 2002). They would agree that benefits should be offered in clinical research; however, these need not be direct, therapeutic benefits. Proponents of this view insist that the so-called therapeutic misconception must be dispelled: participants must know that they will not receive individualized medical treatment; they are rather participating in research, whose purpose is to gain new knowledge. Second, participants should not be exploited. Miller and Brody (2002) have argued that patients are not exploited if they are "not being exposed to excessive risks for the sake of scientific investigation" and they "understand that they are volunteering to participate in an experiment rather than receiving personalized medical care" (p. 5).

Ironically, IRBs in their zeal to protect participants often overlook the fact that there is some inconsistency involved in requiring researchers to dispel the

4. Despite retaining such language in its main body, the Declaration now includes a footnote stating, "However, a placebo-controlled trial may be ethically acceptable, even if proven therapy is available, under the following circumstances: Where for compelling and scientifically sound methodological reasons its use is necessary to determine the efficacy or safety of a prophylactic, diagnostic or therapeutic method; or Where a prophylactic, diagnostic or therapeutic method is being investigated for a minor condition and the patients who receive placebo will not be subject to any additional risk of serious or irreversible harm." See note on paragraph 29 at http://www.wma.net/e/policy/b3.htm#note1, retrieved on January 12, 2007.

therapeutic misconception, while at the same time insisting on clinical equipoise (that it is, ensuring that patients will receive what is known to be the best available therapy or a treatment we think might be equivalent).

As we will see, it is impossible to resolve the debates about placebo-controlled, washout, and challenge studies without first resolving this debate about the professional aims and duties of clinical researchers. Is there a duty to provide the best therapeutic treatment available or only a weaker duty to avoid exploitation through informed consent and appropriate protections from unreasonable risks? Our answer must consider feasibility and the realities of clinical research. As representatives of the National Institute of Mental Health put it, "research differs from optimized individual clinical treatment and typically contains an element of increased risk" (Hyman & Shore, 2000). Even when placebo is not administered, we know that the best proven treatment is tailored to individuals, not administered in a double-blind fashion at random according to the details of a generic protocol. This is why we are right to insist on dispelling the therapeutic misconception. However, clinical researchers still have a duty to maximize therapeutic benefits as much as possible, while ensuring that appropriate procedures for consent and risk management are in place.

Moreover, to the extent that physicians, psychologists, social workers, counselors, or nurses play the role of health care providers, they have a strict duty to put the interests of their patients above the interests of research. Accordingly, they should never enroll in a study a patient who needs treatment for a serious medical condition unless they believe that a research protocol may in fact provide the best treatment option or the patient has rejected recommended options and seeks alternatives. That is to say, the tension between therapy and research cannot be resolved by the research enterprise alone (i.e., research policies and IRB review); it must also be addressed by health care providers, who often serve as the gatekeepers of clinical research.

Ethical Issues in Nontherapeutic Biological Trials

As noted above, the tension in clinical trials arises because key personnel in studies—whether at the recruitment end or in the actual conduct of the study—play or appear to play dual professional roles: that of a health care provider and that of a researcher.

In nontherapeutic biological trials, there is no pretense of offering therapy. The only goal is to gain knowledge, even if this knowledge may eventually be used to develop therapies. Of course, conflicts of interest and confusion may arise, because sometimes patients are recruited into these studies.[5] When this occurs, extra protections may be appropriate to dispel the therapeutic misconception or to address institutional vulnerability.

Because basic research does not pose as therapy, it need not offer direct therapeutic benefits. However, in some forms of nontherapeutic biological

5. For example, Miller and Rosenstein have noted that "patients are often invited to participate in these nontherapeutic experiments either before or after receiving treatment," for example, "shortly after psychiatric hospitalization," thus raising questions of therapeutic misconception and undue influence (Miller & Rosenstein, 1997, p. 404).

research—especially in the arena of neuroendocrine research—new ethical questions arise: what counts as harm, and may researchers ever intentionally inflict harms?

These questions arise particularly with regard to challenge or symptom-exacerbation studies with participants with mental disorders. Such studies may seek to provoke symptoms in patients either simply by withdrawing patients from their medications or by administering chemical agents that are known to provoke symptoms (Ferrell, 2002). Examples of such studies include attempts to provoke panic attacks with infusions of sodium lactate, to induce temporary depressive symptoms by tryptophan depletion in patients who have responded to antidepressant medication, or to elicit obsessive-compulsive symptoms in response to administration of m-chlorophenylpiperazine (Miller & Rosenstein, 1997). Other designs have provoked psychotic symptoms in patients with schizophrenia (Sharav, 1999).

Some have flatly rejected such studies as unethical on grounds that they intentionally harm patients (Sharav, 1999). Others have argued that the so-called harms are no greater than the symptoms the participants normally encounter in daily living with their disease, and that the purpose is not to harm but to observe symptoms with the aim of gaining knowledge that will eventually lead to treatment (Carpenter, Schooler, & Kane, 1997).

Challenge studies test the limits of ethical research. However, when NBAC examined challenge studies, it voiced concern but concluded only that IRBs should exercise heightened scrutiny with such studies (National Bioethics Advisory Commission, 1998). This may be because it is difficult to praise or condemn actions in the abstract without knowing details. For example, there is a significant difference between inducing mild and temporary depressed mood and inducing a psychotic episode in a patient with schizophrenia, especially through washout, which may lead to psychotic relapse rather than a temporary hallucination. People with schizophrenia have a 10% rate of suicide, and for this reason, some commentators have insisted that it be viewed as a life-threatening illness (Shamoo & Keay, 1996). Second, provoking psychotic symptoms among schizophrenic patients sometimes has unforeseen and unintended consequences: they may not become quickly stabilized once medications resume; as a result, they may suffer prolonged psychotic episodes, which can be nightmarish and humiliating, and their social and employment arrangements can be upset. Additionally, some believe it is unknown whether psychotic episodes have lasting neurological effects, making other episodes more likely and full recovery less likely (Shamoo & Keay, 1996).

Regardless of the particular vulnerabilities that individuals with mental disorders might or might not have, challenge studies require additional safeguards. Whenever we intentionally harm another, we risk treating the other as a thing, losing sight of the other as a human being like ourselves, and special steps must be taken to prevent this from happening. Several appropriate safeguards are outlined in the case study below. Above all, community consultation, strict exclusion criteria, careful safety monitoring, and enhanced informed consent processes are needed.

Experimental Designs and Randomization

Experimental designs involve three main features: an experimental intervention group, a comparison group, and random assignment of participants to groups. Naturally, risks and benefits can arise from the experimental intervention (e.g., administering an unproven medication) or the control (e.g., providing only a placebo). Ethical issues related to placebo are discussed below. However, randomization—assigning people to comparison groups by chance—raises ethical issues of its own. Above all, it means that the intervention a participant receives is not tailored to that participant, say, using the best clinical judgment of a care provider. Additionally, double-blind assignment procedures—in which neither the participant nor the investigator is aware of group assignments—raise new issues. Double-blind is a preferred method of reducing bias in the description of the effects of interventions. However, it requires that extra steps be taken in monitoring safety and that procedures for "de-blinding" are in place (e.g., to avoid drug contraindications when treating participants who are not doing well within the study).

Randomization also places limits on the informed consent of participants and the expectations participants can have for benefits. While participants may have group assignment preferences (e.g., they may already know they do not respond well to the standard therapy, which is used as a control), they are required to agree to random assignment. Cross-over designs, in which participants are switched from a control group to the experimental group (or one arm to another) at some point during the life of a study, may provide a way for participants to be assured of receiving whatever their preferred treatment is, but only at the expense of assuring that—for a time at least—they will also receive a treatment they prefer not to receive.

Quasi-Experimental Designs

One way around some of the problems of randomization (especially randomization to placebo groups) is to use a quasi-experimental design. The main difference between experimental and quasi-experimental designs is that participants are not randomly assigned to comparator groups or that external data (e.g., historical data on placebo response) is used in the place of one or more comparison groups. The advantage is that comparisons can be made among groups who are receiving what they or their care team believes is optimal treatment or intervention. The disadvantage is that quasi-experimental designs cannot demonstrate causation because they do not control for confounding variables the same way that randomized studies do (Food and Drug Administration, 1999). That is, the comparator groups may be different in significant ways that affect outcomes (e.g., one group might be younger or receiving better general medical care). Nevertheless, some authors advocate their use when randomization poses significant risks (Rothman & Michels, 1994).

Case Study: The Ethics of Placebo Controls

The director of an advocacy group writes to you as the chair of your hospital's IRB. She writes because your teaching hospital regularly conducts behavioral health research and currently has over 10 million dollars in funding from the National Institute of Mental Health, pharmaceutical companies, and other sponsors of psychiatric research. She is requesting that you discontinue all clinical trials that involve "washout" and the use of placebo controls with patients who have severe mental health disorders such as major depression and schizophrenia. Washout studies quickly wean all participants from all symptom-controlling medications in order to better isolate the effects of an experimental drug and to avoid drug interactions. Weaning from medications is sometimes done quickly (in 5–7 days) to allow the trial to be conducted expeditiously and to reduce expenses. This practice can cause some patients to experience relapse of symptoms such as severe depression, delusions, or hallucinations. Additionally, those participants who are placed in a placebo group receive no medications throughout the entire study to enable researchers to demonstrate that the experimental medication is more effective than no medication. This practice heightens the risk that participants receiving placebo will relapse.

The letter you receive mentions two recent deaths from washout studies in which participants committed suicide. The first participant committed suicide while receiving a placebo in a study of antidepressants, the other during the washout phase of medication trial for patients with schizophrenia. The letter insists that such clinical trials should be universally discontinued because they are inhumane and clearly in violation of the Declaration of Helsinki, which also insists promising new treatments should only be tested against the best proven effective treatment, when such treatment exists.

Her organization publishes on its Web site a list of all ongoing placebo-controlled studies on severe mental illnesses and the names of their sponsoring institutions. Several studies at your institution are listed. Moreover, the advocacy group is beginning a new campaign of publishing op-ed pieces in newspapers exposing local studies that breach ethical standards. She hopes that exposing these studies will lead research institutions to heed "the voice of mental health consumers and their loved ones." She appeals to you to discontinue the use of washout and placebo controls in clinical trials both for the sake of your participants and to protect the public image of your institution.

When you bring her request to the Institutional Review Board, several psychiatric researchers strongly object. They claim that they ensure that adequate protections are in place: they exclude patients with suicidal ideations, and they allow participants who experience relapse to receive short-term treatments during the study; if their symptoms are not quickly controlled, they are excluded from further participation in order to receive optimal treatment. They argue that placebo-controlled trials with washout are the most efficient way to prove new medications are effective, and this ultimately benefits mental health consumers by requiring fewer participants and enabling new drugs to reach market quickly. Finally, one researcher points out that rejecting the use of such study designs would mean losing millions of dollars in research grants, because both pharmaceutical companies and government agencies often insist on the use of placebo controls. After this is pointed out, the chair of the department of psychiatry actually chastises you for bringing the letter to the IRB because the advocacy group making the request is known to be radical and does not speak for all consumers. He points out that the National Alliance on Mental Illness, for example, does not endorse such radical views on the use of placebo.

As Chair of the IRB, do you urge the IRB to ban all such studies? If so, why? If not, what specific actions, if any, will you take and why?

CASE COMMENTARY

While this case is unusual insofar as it addresses a matter of policy rather than a protocol, it is worthy of serious consideration insofar as a number of consumer advocates have called for a halt to washout and placebo-controlled studies (Rothman & Michels, 1994; Shamoo, 1997; Sharav, 1999) and advocates may appeal to IRB members to make policy changes (Dresser, 2001). In addition to the specific question whether studies involving placebo and washout should be generally prohibited, the case raises two interesting peripheral questions.

First, what are the characteristics of a good IRB policy? In general, a good policy will provide guidance where practices are not uniform but should be, while leaving room for legitimate variations in practice. That is, good policies need to recognize that the facts of a specific scenario may be relevant to deciding what should be done and accordingly should leave room for prudent deliberation.

Second, this case raises the question whether an IRB has a duty to take seriously the letters and allegations of advocates who contact an IRB. Given that the credibility, knowledge, and representativeness of advocates and advocacy groups vary widely, and competing groups argue to competing ends, discussing every letter at an IRB meeting might be inappropriate. However, engaging advocates who confront an IRB on an ad hoc basis can provide opportunities to educate IRB members and advocates, to review policies with fresh eyes, and to provide a healthy level of transparency.

That being said, should the IRB—in light of the reasons given in the letter or other reasons that might emerge in debate—create a policy prohibiting clinical trials that use washout and placebo?[6]

The primary stakeholders in this case are potential research participants. To the extent that the policy could affect the development of more effective or safer medications, the community of people with severe mental disorders also needs to be considered. Clearly, there are other stakeholders: pharmaceutical companies and other sponsors of research, who are interested in completing research quickly with the smallest possible number of participants; the research institution, which could lose research dollars by discontinuing placebo-controlled clinical trials, but could also be held liable should injuries occur in a study; researchers, who could lose the ability to be competitive in attracting research grants; and the IRB, which is tasked to address such issues. The interests of these latter groups should be considered secondary to those of participants and community members in evaluating the use of washout and placebo from the perspective of safety.

---

6. Note that in what follows we will only address washout as it is used prior to assignment to experimental or control groups in drug trials and not insofar as it may be used to intentionally provoke symptoms or relapse. See an earlier section of this chapter for a discussion of challenge studies.

The first question we might ask is whether washout and placebo controls are even necessary: will other research designs allow us to determine an experimental drug's safety and efficacy? The FDA has generally insisted that placebo controls are necessary in order to demonstrate that a drug is effective (Food and Drug Administration, 1999).[7] Alternative designs, for example, designs that compare an experimental treatment only to an "active control" (typically the standard therapy) can demonstrate "noninferiority"; that is, they may demonstrate that an experimental treatment is not less effective than standard treatment (Amdur & Biddle, 2002). But they cannot demonstrate effectiveness. This is especially true in psychiatric research because it is extremely difficult to use a "historical placebo control"—that is, to compare the efficacy of an experimental treatment to past rates of placebo efficacy. Studies have shown that placebo response rates (efficacy) in psychiatric studies vary widely—anywhere from 25%–50% (Miller, 2000). Partly because placebo response is sometimes very high and partly because responses to new and existing therapies are often modest (e.g., 40%), comparing new treatments to existing treatments in a given trial will only demonstrate noninferiority of the new product, not effectiveness.

Is there an acceptable balance of potential benefits and risks in placebo-controlled or washout trials? Let us begin by considering benefits. Is it the case that those participants who receive placebo in fact receive no treatment and therefore no direct benefits? Some have challenged the existence of a placebo effect (Kienle & Kiene, 1997), and others have described placebo as "nothing" or "no treatment" (Michels & Rothman, 2003; Rothman & Michels, 1994). However, a recent study by Khan and colleagues used the FDA's database to review data from 45 studies that tested the efficacy and safety of any one of seven new antidepressants that were approved from 1987 to 1997. A total of 19,639 participants were involved in these studies. All of the studies used a placebo control; almost all also used an active comparator (a form of standard therapy), thus randomizing participants into one of three groups. They found that "symptom reduction was 40.7% with investigational drugs (n = 4510), 41.7% with active comparators (n = 1416), and 30.9% with placebo (n = 2805)" (Khan, Warner, & Brown, 2000, p. 311). This is consistent with reports of placebo response in the range of 25–50%, which actually compares favorably with some FDA approved antidepressants (Miller, 2000), and presumably with fewer side effects. Thus, in reviewing benefits to participants, one might consider the benefits of placebo. However, one would need to look at data for the specific disorder and the specific proposed duration of the study, as these may vary widely. For example, one estimate of the response rate of placebo in trials involving patients with schizophrenia is 3%–26%, not negligible, but significantly lower than in depression studies (Carpenter, Schooler, & Kane, 1997).

In evaluating benefits, we need to decide whether to follow the standards set by the Belmont Report, which generally call for benefits, especially direct benefits to participants, or rather follow those who insist that research should never

7. Some have argued that the randomized controlled trial is a powerful tool but is overused (Levine, 1988). One recent article concludes, "We think that everyone might benefit if the most radical protagonists of evidence based medicine organized and participated in a double blind, randomized, placebo controlled, crossover trial of the parachute" (G. C. S. Smith & Pell, 2003).

compromise the quality of care or interfere with receiving what is known to be the best available treatment (due to clinical equipoise). Above, it was argued that the latter viewpoint is an exercise in self-deception because the methods needed to test efficacy and safety (which we have a duty to do) necessarily prevent participants from receiving the best available treatment, which would be unblinded and specially tailored to patients' changing needs. Nevertheless, in accord with the Belmont Report, IRB policy should require that benefits be maximized as much as possible, should be in proportion to the risks, and should be honestly discussed during the informed consent process.

What about the risks of using washout and placebo controls? The same study by Khan, Warner, and Brown found that rates of suicide and attempted suicide did not differ significantly among placebo- and drug-treated groups. Nevertheless, annual rates of suicide and attempted suicide were noticeably lower for the placebo groups: "0.4% and 2.7% with placebo, 0.7% and 3.4% with active comparators, and 0.8% and 2.8% with investigational antidepressants, respectively" (Khan, Warner, & Brown, 2000, p. 311). This led them to the conclusion that the "assumption that depressed patients who are assigned to placebo in antidepressant clinical trials are exposed to substantial morbidity and mortality is not based on research data" (p. 311).

Of course, IRB policy should take into account variations among patient populations. Irving and Shamoo have highlighted the risks that can attend to the use of washout and placebo in schizophrenia research, including not only relapse, but risks of worse treatment response, a more severe and prolonged course of illness, and suicide (Irving & Shamoo, 1997). Relapse rates are not negligible in schizophrenia research (Shamoo & Keay, 1996) and are consistently worse for those receiving placebo.

But even while acknowledging that risks exist, others have argued that they are not disproportionate to the benefits, especially given that there are good reasons that many patients decline the use of antipsychotic agents:

> Most patients respond only partially. Primary negative symptoms (i.e., the deficit syndrome) are largely refractory to available treatments. Many patients relapse despite continuous treatments. Available compounds are associated with adverse effects that can be subjectively distressing, can interfere with psycho-social and vocational adjustment, are associated with poor medication compliance, and in cases such as severe tardive syskinesia or tardive dystonia, can be disabling. (Carpenter, Schooler, & Kane, 1997, p. 402)

Moreover, ordinary clinical care involves numerous situations in which drug withdrawal may be indicated, including pregnancy, serious side effects, refusal of medication by stable patients, and first-episode patients who may not have a recurrent psychotic illness (Carpenter, Schooler, & Kane, 1997, p. 403).

Thus, adopting a policy that uniformly prohibits the use of placebo on grounds of a generic risk-benefit analysis is unwarranted. Clearly, risk-benefit analysis needs to be conducted on a case-by-case basis. Additionally, in accord with Belmont guidelines (and to meet requirements of least infringement discussed in chapter 4), risks to participants must be minimized to whatever extent is possible.

Finally, transparency and due process require at the least that the informed consent process be forthright and include methods of safeguarding the voluntariness of potential participants. Applebaum et al. report that 91% of patients who consented to participate in a psychopharmacological trial did not, upon later questioning, understand that their treatment might be limited in any way, and 44% did not understand that they might receive placebo (Appelbaum, Lidz, & Meisel, 1987). Michels and Rothman (2003) refer to other similarly concerning evidence that patients do not often understand or retain important information when entering into research studies. Therefore, extra safeguards should be put in place to ensure the success and validity of the informed consent process. Some of these are proposed below.

Given the considerations offered above, we should not endorse a policy that generally forbids the use of placebo controls and washout in psychiatric studies but should advocate for policy development and encourage heightened scrutiny of placebo-controlled studies. The following protections should be part of the overall policy and review plan:

- Encourage participants to consult with their clinicians before deciding whether or not to participate (Levine, 1988), and educate clinicians to put patients' needs first in considering whether or not to recommend them for a placebo-controlled or any other clinical trial
- Require a review of patients' histories prior to admitting them to the study:
  - Consider ordinarily excluding high-risk participants or adding protections such as in-patient observation (Stanley, 1988)
  - Consider ordinarily excluding patients who have done exceptionally well on existing medications
- Require that medications be withdrawn slowly to reduce the risk of relapse or symptom exacerbation (Appelbaum, 1996)
- Require that the duration of the placebo period be as short as possible to minimize the risk of relapse (Miller, 2000)
- Ensure that monitoring is adequate and the protocol clearly contains a "rescue arm" or criteria for removing participants from the study should they deteriorate and require treatment
- Improve the informed consent process throughout the span of the study (National Institutes of Health, 1999):
  - When the study offers little prospect of direct benefit and risks are high, consider the use of independent consent auditors and clinical monitors (Dresser, 1996; Fins, 1997)
  - Ask participants if they would welcome a friend, family member, or advocate to serve as a surrogate to provide ongoing consent should they lose capacity during the study or require additional assistance understanding the study (Appelbaum, Dresser, Fisher, Moreno, & Saks, 1999)
- Include a mental health consumer or advocate on the IRB (Hall & Flynn, 1999; Vogel-Scibilia, 1999), bearing in mind that consumers and advocates often disagree among themselves on the use of placebo in clinical trial.

Further EMHR Resources

- Unit two of the *Dialogues* DVD contains an interview with Joan Sieber on ethical issues in study design
- www.emhr.net contains a bibliography and case studies on study design issues

REFERENCES

Ahmed, S. M., Beck, B., Maurana, C. A., & Newton, G. (2004). Overcoming barriers to effective community-based participatory research in US medical schools. *Education for Health, 17*(2), 141–151.

Amdur, R. J., & Biddle, C. J. (2002). The placebo-controlled clinical trial. In R. J. Amdur & E. A. Bankert (Eds.), *Institutional review board: Management and function* (pp. 450–457). Sudbury, MA: Jones and Bartlett.

Amdur, R. J., & Speers, M. A. (2002). Identifying research intent. In R. J. Amdur & E. A. Bankert (Eds.), *Institutional review board: Management and function* (pp. 118–124). Sudbury, MA: Jones and Bartlett.

American Psychological Association. (2001). *Research ethics: Comments submitted by APA on the draft of the NBAC report on ethical and policy issues in research involving human participants.* Retrieved June 7, 2004, from www.apa.org/science/comment_nbac-01.html.

Appelbaum, P. S. (1996). Drug-free research in schizophrenia: An overview of the controversy. *IRB: A Review of Human Subjects Research, 18*(1), 1–5.

Appelbaum, P. S., Dresser, R., Fisher, C. B., Moreno, J. D., & Saks, E. R. (1999). *Research involving persons with mental disorders that may affect decisionmaking capacity.* Rockville, MD: National Bioethics Advisory Commission.

Appelbaum, P. S., Lidz, C. W., & Meisel, A. (1987). *Informed consent: Legal theory and clinical practice.* New York: Oxford University Press.

Backlar, P. (1999). Ethics in community mental health care: Public bioethics and research involving persons with mental disorders. *Community Mental Health Journal, 35*(5), 389–399.

Baumrind, D. (1964). Some thoughts on ethics of research: After reading Milgram's "behavioral study of obedience." *American Psychologist, 19*, 421–423.

Beauchamp, T. L., Faden, R. R., Wallace, R. J. J., & Walters, L. (Eds.). (1982). *Ethical Issues in social science research.* Baltimore: Johns Hopkins University Press.

Bellin, E., & Dubler, N. N. (2001). The quality improvement-research divide and the need for external oversight. *American Journal of Public Health, 91*, 1512–1517.

Blass, T. (1991). Understanding behavior in the Milgram obedience experiment: The role of personality, situations, and their interactions. *Journal of Personality and Social Psychology, 60*(3), 398–413.

Capron, A. M. (1982). Is consent always necessary in social science research? In T. L. Beauchamp, R. R. Faden, R. J. J. Wallace, & L. Walters (Eds.), *Ethical issues in social science research* (pp. 215–231). Baltimore: Johns Hopkins University Press.

Carpenter, W. T., Schooler, N. R., & Kane, J. M. (1997). The rationale and ethics of medication-free research in schizophrenia. *Archives of General Psychiatry, 54*, 401–407.

Centers for Disease Control and Prevention, Department of Health and Human Services, National Institutes of Health, Food and Drug Administration, Human Resources and Services Administration, Substance Abuse and Mental Health Services Administration, et al. (1998). *Building community partnerships in research: Recommendations and strategies.* Washington DC: Department of Health and Human Services.

Citro, C. F., Ilgen, D. R., & Marrett, C. B. (2003). *Protecting participants and facilitating social and behavioral sciences research.* Washington, DC: National Academies Press.

Cuellar, I., & Paniagua, F. A. (2000). *Multicultural mental health.* San Diego: Academic Press.

De Vries, R., DeBruin, D. A., & Goodgame, A. (2004). Ethics review of social, behavioral, and economic research: Where should we go from here? *Ethics & Behavior, 14*(4), 351–368.

Department of Health and Human Services. (2001). Code of federal regulations: Protection of human subjects. Title 45 public welfare, part 46. Washington, DC: Government Printing Office.

Douglas, J. D. (1979). Living morality versus bureaucratic fiat. In C. B. Klockars & F. W. O'Connor (Eds.), *SAGE annual reviews of studies in deviance: Vol. 3. Deviance and decency* (pp. 13–34). Beverly Hills, CA: SAGE Publications.

Dresser, R. (1996). Mentally disabled research subjects: The enduring policy issues. *Journal of the American Medical Association, 276*(1), 67–72.

Dresser, R. (2001). *When science offers salvation: Patient advocacy and research ethics.* New York: Oxford University Press.

DuBois, J. M. (2002). When is informed consent appropriate in educational research? *IRB: Ethics & Human Research, 24*(1), 1–8.

DuBois, J. M. (2004a). Is compliance a professional virtue of researchers? Reflections on promoting the responsible conduct of research. *Ethics & Behavior, 14*(4), 383–395.

DuBois, J. M. (2004b). Universal ethical principles in a diverse universe: A commentary on Monshi and Zieglmayer's case study. *Ethics & Behavior, 14*(4), 313–319.

Emanuel, E. J., Wendler, D., & Grady, C. (2000). What makes clinical research ethical? *JAMA, 283*(20), 2701–2711.

Felix-Aaron, K., & Stryer, D. (2003). Moving from rhetoric to evidence-based action in health care. *Journal of General Internal Medicine, 8*(7), 589–591.

Ferrell, R. B. (2002). Treatment-withholding studies in psychiatry. In R. J. Amdur & E. A. Bankert (Eds.), *Institutional review board: Management and function* (pp. 461–464). Sudbury, MA: Jones and Bartlett.

Fins, J. J. (1997). The call of the sirens: Navigating the ethics of medication-free research in schizophrenia. *Archives of General Psychiatry, 54*, 415–416.

Fisher, C. B. (2003). Participant consultation: Ethical insights into parental permission and confidentiality procedures for policy-relevant research with youth. In R. M. Lerner, F. Jacobs, & D. Wertlieb (Eds.), *Handbook of applied developmental science: Promoting positive child, adolescent, and family development through research, policies, and programs* (pp. 371–396). Thousand Oaks, CA: Sage Publications, Inc.

Fisher, C. B., Hoagwood, K., Boyce, C., Duster, T., Frank, D. A, Grisso, T., et al. (2002). Research ethics for mental health science involving ethnic minority children and youths. *American Psychologist, 57*(12), 1024–1040.

Fisher, C. B., & Wallace, S. A. (2000). Through the community looking glass: Reevaluating the ethical and policy implications of research on adolescent risk and psychopathology. *Ethics & Behavior, 10*(2), 99–118.

Flood, A. B. (2002). Health services research. In R. J. Amdur & E. A. Bankert (Eds.), *Institutional review board: Management and function* (pp. 424–427). Sudbury, MA: Jones and Bartlett.

Food and Drug Administration. (1999). *Choice of control group in clinical trials* (Draft guidance No. Docket No. 99D-3082). Rockville, MD: Food and Drug Administration.

Freedman, B. (1987). Equipoise and the ethics of clinical research. *New England Journal of Medicine, 317*(3), 141–145.

Gallant, D. R. (2002). Qualitative social science research. In R. J. Amdur & E. A. Bankert (Eds.), *Institutional review board: Management and function* (pp. 403–406). Sudbury, MA: Jones and Bartlett.

Getz, K., & Borfitz, D. (2002). *Informed consent: A guide to the risks and benefits of volunteering for clinical trials.* Boston: CenterWatch.

Glanz, K., Rimer, B., & Lerman, C. (1996). Ethical issues in the design and conduct of community-based intervention studies. In S. S. Coughlin & T. L. Beauchamp (Eds.), *Ethics and epidemiology* (pp. 156–177). New York: Oxford University Press.

Gostin, L. O. (1991). Ethical principles for the conduct of human subject research: Population-based research and ethics. *Law, Medicine & Health Care, 19*, 191–201.

Griffiths, K. M., Jorm, A. F., Christensen, H., Medway, J., & Dear, K. B. G. (2002). Research priorities in mental health, Part 2: An evaluation of the current research effort against stakeholders priorities. *Australian and New Zealand Journal of Psychiatry, 36*(3), 327–339.

Gunsalus, C. K. (2004). The nanny state meets the inner lawyer: Overregulating while underprotecting human participants in research. *Ethics & Behavior, 14*(4), 369–382.

Hadjistavropoulos, T., & Smythe, W. E. (2001). Elements of risk in qualitative research. *Ethics & Behavior, 11*(2), 163–174.

Hall, L. L., & Flynn, L. (1999). Consumer and family concerns about research involving human subjects. In H. A. Pincus, J. A. Lieberman, & S. Ferris (Eds.), *Ethics in psychiatric research* (pp. 219–235). Washington, DC: American Psychiatric Association.

Higgins, D. L., & Metzler, M. (2001). Implementing community-based participatory research centers in diverse urban settings. *Journal of Urban Health: Bulletin of the New York Academy of Medicine, 78*(3), 488–494.

Hoagwood, K. (1994). The certificate of confidentiality at the National Institute of Mental Health: Discretionary considerations in its applicability to research on child and adolescent mental disorders. *Ethics & Behavior, 4*(2), 123–131.

Hoagwood, K., Jensen, P. S., & Fisher, C. B. (1996). *Ethical issues in mental health research with children and adolescents.* Mahwah, N.J.: Lawrence Erlbaum Associates.

Humphreys, L. (1970). *Tearoom trade: Impersonal sex in public places.* Chicago: Aldine de Gruyter.

Humphreys, L. (1975). *Tearoom trade: Impersonal sex in public places* (Enlarged ed.). New York: Aldine de Gruyter.

Hyman, S. E., & Shore, D. (2000). An NIMH perspective on the use of placebos. *Biological Psychiatry, 47*, 689–691.

Ilgen, D. R., & Bell, B. S. (2001). Informed consent and dual purpose research. *American Psychologist, 56*(12), 1177.

Irving, D. N., & Shamoo, A. E. (1997). Washout/relapses in patients participating in neurobiological research studies in schizophrenia. In A. E. Shamoo (Ed.), *Ethics in neurobiological research with human subjects* (pp. 119–127). Amsterdam: Gordon and Breach.

Israel, B. A., Schulz, A. J., Parker, E. A., & Becker, A. B. (2001). Community-based participatory research: Policy recommendations for promoting a partnership approach in health research. *Education for Health, 14*(2), 182–197.

Jamrozik, K. (2000). The case for a new system for oversight of research on human subjects. *Journal of Medical Ethics, 26*, 334–339.

Johnson, D. G. (1996). Forbidden knowledge and science as professional activity. *Monist, 79*(2), 197–218.

Keith-Spiegel, P. C., & Koocher, G. P. (2005). The IRB paradox: Could the protectors also encourage deceit? *Ethics and Behavior, 15*(4), 339–349.

Khan, A., Warner, H. A., & Brown, W. A. (2000). Symptom reduction and suicide risk in patients treated with placebo in antidepressant clinical trials: An analysis of the Food and Drug Administration database. *Archives of General Psychiatry, 57*, 311–317.

Kienle, G. S., & Kiene, H. (1997). The powerful placebo effect: Fact or fiction. *Journal of Clinical Epidemiology, 50*(12), 1311–1318.

Klockars, C. B. (1979). Dirty hands and deviant subjects. In C. B. Klockars & F. W. O'Connor (Eds.), *SAGE annual reviews of studies in deviance: Vol. 3. Deviance and decency* (pp. 261–282). Beverly Hills, CA: SAGE Publications.

Koocher, G. P., & Keith-Spiegel, P. C. (1990). *Children, ethics, and the law: Professional issues and cases*. Lincoln: University of Nebraska Press.

Korn, J. H. (1997). *Illusions of reality: A history of deception in social psychology*. Albany: State University of New York Press.

Laufer, R. S., & Wolfe, M. (1977). Privacy as a concept and a social issue: A multidimensional developmental theory. *Journal of Social Issues, 33*(3), 22–42.

Levine, R. J. (1988). *Ethics and regulation of clinical research* (2nd ed.). New Haven, CT: Yale University Press.

Lind, E. A., & Tyler, T. R. (1988). *The social psychology of procedural justice*. New York: Plenum Press.

Lynch, E. W., & Hanson, M. J. (Eds.). (1992). *Developing cross-cultural competence: A guide for working with young children and their families*. Baltimore: Brookes.

Marshall, P. A. (1992). Research ethics in applied anthropology. *IRB: A Review of Human Subjects Research, 14*(6), 1–5.

Melton, G. B., Levine, R. J., Koocher, G. P., Rosenthal, R., & Thompson, W. C. (1988). Community consultation in socially sensitive research: Lessons from clinical trials on treatments for AIDS. *American Psychologist, 43*, 573–581.

Michels, K. B., & Rothman, K. J. (2003). Update on unethical use of placebos in randomised trials. *Bioethics, 17*(2), 188–204.

Milgram, S. (1974). *Obedience to authority: An experimental view*. New York: Harper & Row.

Miller, F. G. (2000). Placebo-controlled trials in psychiatric research: An ethical perspective. *Biological Psychiatry, 47*, 707–716.

Miller, F. G., & Brody, H. (2002). What makes placebo-controlled trials unethical? *The American Journal of Bioethics, 2*(2), 3–9.

Miller, F. G., & Rosenstein, D. L. (1997). Psychiatric symptom-provoking studies: An ethical appraisal. *Biological Psychiatry, 42*, 403–409.

National Bioethics Advisory Commission. (1998). *Research involving persons with mental disorders that may affect decisionmaking capacity: Vol. 1. Report and recommendations*. Rockville, MD: National Bioethics Advisory Commission.

National Bioethics Advisory Commission. (2001). *Ethical and policy issues in research involving human participants*. Bethesda, MD: National Bioethics Advisory Commission.

National Institutes of Health. (1999). Research involving individuals with questionable capacity to consent: Points to consider. *Biological Psychiatry, 46*, 1014–1016.

National Science Foundation. (2002). *Interpreting the common rule for the protection of human subjects for behavioral and social science research*. Retrieved January 12, 2007, from http://www.nsf.gov/bfa/dias/policy/hsfaqs.jsp.

Office of Human Research Protections. (2004, September 24, 2004). *Guidance: Human regulations decision charts. Chart 1: Is an activity research involving human subjects?* Retrieved January 12, 2007 from, http://www.hhs.gov/ohrp/humansubjects/guidance/decisioncharts.htm#c1.

O'Toole, T. P., Aaron, K. F., Chin, M. H., Horowitz, C., & Tyson, F. (2003). Community-based participatory research: Opportunities, challenges and the need for a common language. *Journal of General Internal Medicine, 8*(7), 592–594.

Parrot, E. S. (2002). Ethnographic research. In R. J. Amdur & E. A. Bankert (Eds.), *Institutional review board: Management and function* (pp. 407–414). Sudbury, MA: Jones and Bartlett.

Philleo, J., & Brisbane, F. L. (Eds.). (1997). *Cultural competence in substance abuse prevention*. Washington, DC: National Association of Social Workers Press.

Porter, J. P. (1996). Regulatory consideration in research involving children and adolescents with mental disorders. In K. Hoagwood, P. S. Jensen, & C. B. Fisher (Eds.), *Ethical issues in mental health research with children and adolescents* (pp. 15–28). Mahwah, NJ: Lawrence Erlbaum Associates.

Rothman, K. J., & Michels, K. B. (1994). The continuing unethical use of placebo controls. *New England Journal of Medicine, 331*(6), 394–398.

Scott, A. (1993). Challenging assumptions: Consumers/survivors reform the system, bringing a "human face" to research. *Resources, 5*(1), 3–6.

Shamoo, A. E. (Ed.). (1997). *Ethics in neurobiological research with human subjects: The Baltimore conference on ethics*. Amsterdam: Gordon and Breach.

Shamoo, A. E., & Keay, T. J. (1996). Ethical concerns about relapse studies. *Cambridge Quarterly of Healthcare Ethics, 5*, 373–386.

Sharav, V. H. (1999). The ethics of conducting psychosis-inducing experiments. *Accountability in Research, 7*, 137–167.

Shaw, I. F. (2003). Ethics in qualitative research and evaluation. *Journal of Social Work, 3*(1), 9–29.

Sieber, J. E. (1992). *Planning ethically responsible research: A guide for students and internal review boards* (Vol. 31). Newbury Park, CA: Sage Publications.

Sieber, J. E. (2004). Using our best judgment in conducting human research. *Ethics and Behavior, 14*(4), 297–304.

Singer, P. (1996). Ethics and the limits of scientific freedom. *Monist, 79*(2), 218–230.

Smith, G. C. S., & Pell, J. P. (2003). Parachute use to prevent death and major trauma related to gravitational challenge: Systematic review of randomised controlled trials. *British Medical Journal, 327*, 1461–1464.

Smith, M. W. (1995). Ethics in focus groups: A few concerns. *Qualitative Health Research, 5*(4), 478–486.

Smythe, W. E., & Murray, M. J. (2000). Owning the story: Ethical considerations in narrative research. *Ethics & Behavior, 10*(4), 311–336.

Speers, M. A. (2002). Epidemiology/public health research. In R. J. Amdur & E. A. Bankert (Eds.), *Institutional review board: Management and function* (pp. 428–433). Sudbury, MA: Jones and Bartlett.

Spiers, H. R. (1991). Community consultation and AIDS clinical trials, Part I. *IRB: A Review of Human Subjects Research, 13*(3), 7–10.

Stanley, B. (1988). An integration of ethical and clinical considerations in the use of placebos. *Psychopharmacology Bulletin, 24*(1), 18–20.

Stanley, B., Sieber, J. E., & Melton, G. B. (1987). Empirical studies of ethical issues in research: A research agenda. *American Psychologist, 42*(7), 735–741.

Veatch, R. M. (2002). Subject indifference and the justification of placebo-controlled trials. *American Journal of Bioethics, 2*(2), 12–13.

Vogel-Scibilia, S. E. (1999). The controversy over challenge and discontinuation studies: Perspective from a consumer-psychiatrist. *Biological Psychiatry, 46*, 1021–1024.

Wagener, D. K., Sporer, A. K., Simmerling, M., Flome, J. L., An, C., & Curry, S. J. (2004). Human subjects challenges in youth-focused research: Perspectives and practices of IRB administrators. *Ethics and Behavior, 14*(4), 335–349.

Warwick, D. P. (1982). Types of harm in social research. In T. L. Beauchamp, R. R. Faden, R. J. Wallace Jr., & L. Walters (Eds.), *Ethical issues in social science research* (pp. 101–124). Baltimore: Johns Hopkins University Press.

Weijer, C. (1999). Protecting communities in research: Philosophical and pragmatic challenges. *Cambridge Quarterly of Healthcare Ethics, 8*, 501–513.

Whitaker, R. (2002). *Mad in America*. Cambridge, MA: Perseus.

World Medical Association. (2000). World Medical Association declaration of Helsinki: Ethical principles for medical research involving human subjects. Edinburgh: World Medical Association.

9

Protecting Privacy and Confidentiality

Although we live in a world of noisy self-confession, privacy allows us to keep certain facts to ourselves if we so choose. The right to privacy, it seems, is what makes us civilized.

Equally important . . . whenever an invasion of privacy is claimed, there are usually competing values at stake. Privacy may seem paramount to the person who has lost it, but that right often clashes with other rights and responsibilities that we as a society deem important.

—E. Alderman and C. Kennedy, *The Right to Privacy*

In 1597, Francis Bacon wrote, "Knowledge is power" (Bacon, 2002). Whereas philosophers traditionally pursued knowledge "for its own sake" or to develop their personalities, Bacon urged his readers to consider that knowledge has the power to transform the world. While Bacon focused on knowledge of technology and the transformation of nature, we should consider that knowledge is power in many other ways. On a societal level, advances in medical knowledge have led to higher standards of health and healing; advances in knowledge of engineering have led to better tools for work, communication, travel, and entertainment; and knowledge of various languages has brought access to the literature and discoveries of diverse cultures. Knowledge is also power for individuals. For example, knowledge of a profession may increase work opportunities and income with all of the benefits that brings; knowledge of a musical instrument can bring a sense of accomplishment and pleasure; knowledge of another person may enable love or friendship to develop. Without knowledge—of language, safe foods, and basic skills—human beings could not survive, much less thrive.

On the other hand, we know all too well that knowledge can be used for evil purposes: the same knowledge of disease used to heal can be used to create biological weapons; "insider knowledge" of a publicly traded company can be used unfairly in trades that harm investors; or knowledge of another person's misdeeds can be used to blackmail them.

All research involves a pursuit of knowledge—sometimes for its own sake, but more often than not for the sake of some power it will bring: the power to heal, to develop marketable products, or to build one's career. Knowledge about research participants also brings power—power for good or evil. For example, an HIV/AIDS researcher may have a legitimate interest in knowing whether an empowerment project succeeds in reducing high-risk behaviors among women who use illegal substances. Without learning about certain behaviors—for example, intravenous drug use and sexual behaviors—the researcher cannot know what interventions might reduce rates of risky behavior and accordingly infection. Nevertheless, this same information can be harmful to i principle, it could lead to arrests, embarrassment, stigma, harm to i or loss of employment (Singer et al., 1999).

Given the stigma attached to many mental disorders and addictio and confidentiality are often of great concern to mental health consum bell (2000) discusses the worries that mental health consumers frequently have regarding both authorized and unauthorized use of their information.

> In general, medical privacy issues of a person who has bipolar disorder do not differ substantially from those of someone who is HIV positive. Not only have such people been victimized by their disease, but they also have been forced to confront attendant prejudice, discrimination, and public fear. Medical privacy, therefore, looms over their everyday lives and must be addressed within the critical context of civil liberties. (p. *l*)

Because knowledge is power, people have a vested interest in controlling the knowledge people gain of them. The concepts of privacy and confidentiality can be defined precisely with reference to these key concepts of knowledge and control. The right to *privacy* refers to *an individual's right to control others' knowledge of or access to him or her*. The right to *confidentiality* refers to *an individual's right to control the access others have to information about him or herself* (Boruch & Cecil, 1979; Sieber, 2001a).

If privacy and confidentiality refer primarily to control over others' access to us and information about us, then within the ethical framework of principlism, privacy and confidentiality are most closely related to the principle of *autonomy*, or what the Belmont Report calls respect for persons. Controlling the access of others to themselves is essentially what informed consent enables participants to do—whether this is access to one's information or access to one's body for medical treatment or research.

Protecting privacy is also related to the principle of *nonmaleficence,* our duty not to harm (which the Belmont Report subsumes under beneficence). This is because privacy violations can harm people in numerous ways, especially when the information shared is sensitive. Sieber (2001a) lists six kinds of harms that can arise from privacy violations: inconvenience, psychological, physical, social, economic, and legal. Some violations of privacy can obviously lead to several of these harms at once.

Out of respect for autonomy and nonmaleficence, we recognize rights to privacy. However, like most rights, privacy rights are limited. That is, there are times when people may breach confidentiality or invade privacy. At the level of principles, we often find that the duty to respect privacy conflicts with duties to be just and beneficent. For example, while many individuals feel that the amount of their income and their sources of income are private information, fair taxation is impossible without disclosure of this information. Similarly, while individuals may feel that their medical history is private, a clinician cannot treat patients well without knowing their history. While much of this chapter focuses on how best to respect privacy and confidentiality, it will also examine factors that limit rights to privacy and confidentiality.

IS THE RIGHT TO PRIVACY UNIVERSAL?

As we have seen, privacy can be viewed as a right or an ethical principle, but the *sense of privacy* is a developmental trait that changes with age, experience, and context (Laufer & Wolfe, 1977). It is also expressed differently across cultures—and this affects how we best respect the right to privacy. For example, Monshi and Zieglmayer (2004) describe a series of health interviews they conducted with adult patients in Sri Lanka. Out of respect for privacy, these interviews were initially conducted alone with the patients in a private room. However, this caused significant discomfort among the participants because they were accustomed to discussing their health only with family members present. Moreover, Monshi and Zieglmayer reported that persons with diseases and mental health disorders in Sri Lanka were typically viewed as innocent victims, and the family unit was viewed as afflicted rather than the individual alone. Thus, the participants seemed to risk little in making their health information known among family. In response to feedback from participants, the researchers began conducting interviews on a street-level patio next to a café; not only family but also friends who passed by sometimes joined in the interviews.

Does this case call into question the universality of the sense of privacy? DuBois (2004) has argued that it does not. First, if privacy is defined as "the interest people have in controlling the access of others to themselves," then Sri Lankans do demonstrate a concern with privacy in health care settings. They *want* others to have access to themselves during their health interviews. Moreover, Monshi and Zieglmayer (2004) observed that beginning with "the skin" Sri Lankans restrict access to themselves considerably more than do typical Westerners. Physical exams are normally conducted with clothing on, and stethoscopes are placed over clothing. Therefore, all we really observe is a difference in the ways that Sri Lankans control the access of others to themselves; the phenomenon itself, however, is hardly absent. Second, violations of a Western sense of privacy (e.g., public disclosure of health information) may be fairly innocuous in Sri Lanka; however, harms may still arise from violations of the Sri Lankan sense of privacy. When separated from friends and family, the interview process caused visible signs of distress, and there is reason to believe that health exams conducted with clothing off would cause at least social and emotional harms. Seen in this light, the norm of respecting privacy is not merely one cultural specification of the principles of autonomy and nonmaleficence, but it may have universal validity of its own. However, what it means to respect privacy clearly must be understood in local terms. Empirical research on the sense of privacy may be necessary to enabling participants to exercise control over the access researchers and others have to them in ways that fit with their personal and cultural values.

WHO DECIDES?

Particularly because individuals and cultures vary in their privacy and confidentiality needs and preferences, the question "Who decides what privacy and confidentiality protections should be afforded to participants?" has been highly controversial. In general, mental health consumers have lobbied for greater control over their health and research information, including not only greater restrictions placed on others but also greater access for themselves. Writing as a representative of the mental health consumer movement, Jean Campbell (2000) observes that

> The American Psychiatric Association has repeatedly lobbied Congress when health data access and confidentiality legislation was being considered to prevent a person's access to his or her personal psychiatric records . . . . Mental health professionals fear that giving broad access rights to mental health consumers may pose a danger to an individual's psychological health. (p. 13)

She contrasts this "paternalistic" position with a "consumerist" position that would ask, "What do customers prefer?" (p. 13). While the HIPAA privacy rule implemented in 2003 has been unpopular with many researchers and providers, largely due to the administrative burden it has created, it has granted participants greater control over what happens with their identifiable health information in both treatment and research settings.

THE HIPAA PRIVACY RULE: A REGULATORY FRAMEWORK FOR HEALTH RESEARCH

Prior to 2003, the Common Rule (45CFR46) and state laws provided the main forms of legal guidance regarding the protection of privacy and confidentiality in research conducted in the United States or using U.S. federal funding. The Common Rule requires that before approving a research study, an IRB must determine that, "when appropriate, there are adequate provisions to protect the privacy of subjects and to maintain the confidentiality of data" (45CFR46.111[a][7]). The Common Rule also addresses the connection between informed consent and confidentiality in two regards. First, the informed consent form provided to participants must include "a statement describing the extent, if any, to which confidentiality of records identifying the subject will be maintained" (45CFR46.116[a][5]). Second, if "the only record linking the subject and the research would be the consent document and the principal risk would be potential harm resulting from a breach of confidentiality," then, if the subject wishes, written informed consent may be waived (45CFR46.117[c][1]). Moreover, the Common Rule considers confidentiality in determining whether certain studies are exempt, including survey studies involving sensitive data and studies using existing data (45CFR46.101[b]). However, the Common Rule does not provide specific guidance on what constitutes "de-identified" data or when permission is explicitly required for the use of identifiable data. In these and other areas, the HIPAA privacy rule offers more specific guidance on privacy and confidentiality in research. It is important to note that while the HIPAA privacy rule pertains only to "covered entities" and their use of "protected health information" (PHI), (see box 9.1 for definitions of these and other key terms), as is often the case, when regulations provide best practice guidelines for research in one arena, research institutions frequently apply the guidelines to other arenas, whether out of fear of liability or because the regulations have served an educational role or shaped prevailing values.

Box 9.1 HIPAA Definitions

Covered Entity: A health plan, a health care clearinghouse, or a health care provider who transmits health information in electronic form in connection with a transaction for which HHS has adopted a standard.

Protected Health Information (PHI): PHI is individually identifiable health information transmitted by electronic media, maintained in electronic media, or transmitted or maintained in any other form or medium. PHI excludes education records covered by the Family Educational Rights and Privacy Act, as amended, 20 U.S.C. 1232g, records described at 20 U.S.C. 1232g(a)(4)(B)(iv), and employment records held by a covered entity in its role as employer.

Health Information: Any information, whether oral or recorded in any form or medium, that (1) is created or received by a health care provider, health plan, public health authority, employer, life insurer, school or university, or health care clearinghouse; and (2) relates to the past, present, or future physical or mental health or condition of an individual; the provision of health care to an individual; or the past, present, or future payment for the provision of health care to an individual.

Individually Identifiable Health Information: Information that is a subset of health information, including demographic information collected from an individual, and (1) is created or received by a health care provider, health plan, employer, or health care clearinghouse; and (2) relates to the past, present, or future physical or mental health or condition of an individual; the provision of health care to an individual; or the past, present, or future payment for the provision of health care to an individual; and (a) that identifies the individual; or (b) with respect to which there is a reasonable basis to believe the information can be used to identify the individual.

Reprinted from U.S. Department of Health and Human Services, 2003, p. 2.

Permissible Ways of Using Health Information in Research

While some researchers have expressed anxiety about the impact the HIPAA privacy rule might have on health research (Kulynich & Korn, 2002), HHS HIPAA guidance outlines a series of ways that health information can be used in research while complying with the privacy rule.

De-Identify Data

Researchers, including those who are part of a covered entity, may use or disclose health information that is de-identified. If health information is de-identified, then it no longer constitutes PHI, and it is not subjected to HIPAA restrictions on the use of health data. HIPAA's privacy rule allows two different methods for de-identifying data, the so-called "safe harbor" approach that removes key pieces of information, and a statistical approach. The safe harbor approach involves removing all 18 variables that are identified in box 9.2 below. The statistical approach is described as follows:

> The covered entity may obtain certification by "a person with appropriate knowledge of and experience with generally accepted statistical and scientific principles and methods for rendering information not individually identifiable" that there is a "very small" risk that the information could be used by the recipient to identify the individual who is the subject of the information, alone or in combination with other reasonably available information. The person certifying statistical de-identification must document the methods used as well as the result of the analysis that justifies the determination. (Department of Health and Human Services, 2003, p. 10)

Statistical techniques for ensuring confidentiality may include adding "noise" to data, swapping data for individual units, and limiting geographical information. The American Statistical Association's Web site provides links to training and informational resources for those who seek to use a statistical approach: http://www.amstat.org/comm/cmtepc.

Regardless of the technique used to ensure that data is de-identified, the very concept of de-identification represents an advance over the concept of "anonymous data." Data is sometimes called "anonymous" as long as it is not linked to a name; but this does not entail that the collective information gathered (e.g., sex, race, age, zip code, and profession) cannot be used to identify an individual. For this reason, the more precise concept of "de-identification" is preferable.

The remaining approaches to data use all involve the use of *individually identifiable* health information, which counts as PHI.

Authorization by Patient or Representative

While the Common Rule refers to the kind of permission individuals give to be included in a study as "informed consent," the HIPAA privacy rule refers to the permission an individual gives to use his or her PHI in a research study as an "authorization." The permission pertains only to the use or disclosure of PHI for the specific purposes stated in the written authorization. Moreover, an authorization for research purposes cannot be used as a "blank check"; it must pertain only to a specific research study, not to future, unspecified projects. The Privacy Rule "considers the creation and maintenance of a research repository or database as a specific research activity, but the subsequent use or disclosure by a covered entity of information from the database for a specific research study will require separate

Box 9.2 HIPAA "Safe Harbor" Identifiers

Data is considered "de-identified," and thus not PHI, when the following information is missing or removed:

1. Names.
2. All geographic subdivisions smaller than a state, including street address, city, county, precinct, zip code, and their equivalent geographical codes, except for the initial three digits of a zip code if, according to the current publicly available data from the Bureau of the Census: (a) the geographic unit formed by combining all zip codes with the same three initial digits contains more than 20,000 people; (b) the initial three digits of a zip code for all such geographic units containing 20,000 or fewer people are changed to 000.

[*Note*: "Limited data sets" allow use of town or city, state and zip code, but not specific postal address information.]

3. All elements of dates (except year) for dates directly related to an individual, including birth date, admission date, discharge date, date of death; and all ages over 89 and all elements of dates (including year) indicative of such age, except that such ages and elements may be aggregated into a single category of age 90 or older.

[*Note*: Restriction 3 is not placed on "limited data sets."]

4. Telephone numbers.
5. Facsimile numbers.
6. Electronic mail addresses.
7. Social Security numbers.
8. Medical record numbers.
9. Health plan beneficiary numbers.
10. Account numbers.
11. Certificate/license numbers.
12. Vehicle identifiers and serial numbers, including license plate numbers.
13. Device identifiers and serial numbers.
14. Web universal resource locators (URLs).
15. Internet protocol (IP) address numbers.
16. Biometric identifiers, including fingerprints and voiceprints.
17. Full-face photographic images and any comparable images.
18. Any other unique identifying number, characteristic, or code, unless otherwise permitted by the Privacy Rule for re-identification.

[*Note*: Restriction 18 is not placed on "limited data sets."]

Authorization unless the PHI use or disclosure is permitted without Authorization" (Department of Health and Human Services, 2003, p. 12).

An authorization form may be included as part of the informed consent form used in a research study. Box 9.3 below presents the core elements and statements that must be included in an authorization to use PHI.

Box 9.3 Essential Elements of a Privacy Rule Authorization

Authorization Core Elements

- A description of the PHI to be used or disclosed, identifying the information in a specific and meaningful manner.
- The names or other specific identification of the person or persons (or class of persons) authorized to make the requested use or disclosure.
- The names or other specific identification of the person or persons (or class of persons) to whom the covered entity may make the requested use or disclosure.
- A description of each purpose of the requested use or disclosure.
- Authorization expiration date or expiration event that relates to the individual or to the purpose of the use or disclosure ("end of the research study" or "none" are permissible for research, including for the creation and maintenance of a research database or repository).
- Signature of the individual and date. If the individual's legally authorized representative signs the Authorization, a description of the representative's authority to act for the individual must also be provided.

Authorization Required Statements

- A statement of the individual's right to revoke his/her Authorization and how to do so, and, if applicable, the exceptions to the right to revoke his/her Authorization or reference to the corresponding section of the covered entity's notice of privacy practices.
- Whether treatment, payment, enrollment, or eligibility of benefits can be conditioned on Authorization, including research-related treatment and consequences of refusing to sign the Authorization, if applicable.
- A statement of the potential risk that PHI will be re-disclosed by the recipient. This may be a general statement that the Privacy Rule may no longer protect health information disclosed to the recipient.

Reprinted from U.S. Department of Health and Human Services, 2003, p. 12.

Waiver or Alteration of Authorization

Just as the Common Rule allows for a waiver or modification of informed consent under specific conditions, so, too, the Privacy Rule allows for a waiver or alteration of authorization under specific conditions. Among other things, an IRB or Privacy Board must determine and document the following:

1. The use or disclosure of the PHI involves no more than minimal risk to the privacy of individuals based on, at least, the presence of the following elements:
   a. An adequate plan to protect health information identifiers from improper use and disclosure.
   b. An adequate plan to destroy identifiers at the earliest opportunity consistent with conduct of the research (absent a health or research justification for retaining them or a legal requirement to do so).
   c. Adequate written assurances that the PHI will not be reused or disclosed to (shared with) any other person or entity, except as required by law, for authorized oversight of the research study, or for other research for which the use or disclosure of the PHI would be permitted under the Privacy Rule;
2. The research could not practicably be conducted without the waiver or alteration; and
3. The research could not practicably be conducted without access to and use of the PHI. (Department of Health and Human Services, 2003, p. 14)

Limited Data Use Agreements

The Privacy Rule also allows the use of "limited data sets" for the purposes of research. A limited data set refers to PHI that excludes 16 categories of direct identifiers and may be used or disclosed—only for purposes of research, public health, or health care operations—without obtaining either an individual's authorization or a waiver or an alteration of authorization. The direct identifiers that must be excluded from a limited data set are the same as the "safe harbor" identifiers listed in box 9.2 above with the following exceptions: the data set may include city, state, and ZIP Code; elements of date; and it does not include the catch-all exclusion of "any other unique" identifying information. Uses of a limited data set require a data use agreement. The essential elements of a data use agreement are listed in box 9.4 below.

Preparing for Research

One of the ongoing challenges in research is the identification of individuals who are suitable for inclusion in a research study. Research would be significantly hindered if only an individual's health care providers could identify him or her as suitable for inclusion in a research study (even a study that simply uses their PHI in a way requiring authorization). HIPAA's "review preparatory to research" rule

Box 9.4 Essential Elements to a Data Use Agreement

The Privacy Rule requires that a data use agreement contain the following provisions.

- Specific permitted uses and disclosures of the limited data set by the recipient consistent with the purpose for which it was disclosed (a data use agreement cannot authorize the recipient to use or further disclose the information in a way that, if done by the covered entity, would violate the Privacy Rule).
- Identify who is permitted to use or receive the limited data set.
- Stipulations that the recipient will
  - Not use or disclose the information other than permitted by the agreement or otherwise required by law.
  - Use appropriate safeguards to prevent the use or disclosure of the information, except as provided for in the agreement, and require the recipient to report to the covered entity any uses or disclosures in violation of the agreement of which the recipient becomes aware.
  - Hold any agent of the recipient (including subcontractors) to the standards, restrictions, and conditions stated in the data use agreement with respect to the information.
  - Not identify the information or contact the individuals.

Adapted from U.S. Department of Health and Human Services, 2003, p. 16.

allows researchers to review health information to identify who may be eligible to participate in a study under the following conditions:

> For activities involved in preparing for research, covered entities may use or disclose PHI to a researcher without an individual's Authorization, a waiver or an alteration of Authorization, or a data use agreement. However, the covered entity must obtain from a researcher representations that (1) the use or disclosure is requested solely to review PHI as necessary to prepare a research protocol or for similar purposes preparatory to research, (2) the PHI will not be removed from the covered entity in the course of review, and (3) the PHI for which use or access is requested is necessary for the research. The covered entity may permit the researcher to make these representations in written or oral form. (Department of Health and Human Services, 2003, p. 16)

Interactions with participants who are identified through their PHI—for example, to recruit them into a study or to authorize use of their PHI in a study—would need to occur through the covered entity that holds the data (Muhlbaier, 2006).

Miscellaneous Privacy Rule Information

The Common Rule governs only research on living individuals. Similarly, the Privacy Rule only requires standard protections—authorizations, waivers or alterations, and data use agreements—for the use of PHI about the living. Nevertheless, before releasing PHI about decedents to a researcher, the entity must obtain from the researcher who is seeking access to decedents' PHI:

1. Oral or written representations that the use and disclosure is sought solely for research on the PHI of decedents;
2. Oral or written representations that the PHI for which use or disclosure is sought is necessary for the research purposes; and
3. Documentation, at the request of the covered entity, of the death of the individuals whose PHI is sought by the researchers.

Regardless of the specific kind of permissible use of PHI, with few exceptions, the Privacy Rule imposes a *minimum necessary* requirement: researchers should limit the information used to what is reasonably necessary to accomplish their research aims.

Finally, it is important to note that the HIPAA Privacy Rule may be changed by the Department of Health and Human Services once a year, and several changes are currently under consideration (Muhlbaier, 2006). Thus, it is important that researchers work with their IRBs, HIPAA officers, or privacy boards to establish that they are compliant with current requirements.

HIPAA and Research Ethics

Once regulations are established, there is a tendency to think about an issue only through the lens of regulatory compliance rather than ethics. But it is perhaps worthwhile to briefly examine the HIPAA Privacy Rule through the lens of ethics. The Privacy Rule embodies many ideas compatible with ethical principles. It was an attempt to respond to patient and consumer concerns about privacy, specifically about the harms that could result from breaches and patient autonomy in controlling access to private health information. At the same time, debates persist about what precisely the Privacy Rule accomplishes.[1] On the one hand, some researchers feel that it has erected yet another layer of bureaucracy that does little to assist patient-participants. Few patient-participants appear to read privacy statements that must be distributed and gaining access to data using data repositories is often expensive or cumbersome. Insofar as they may slow or thwart beneficial research (e.g., quality improvement research within hospitals), bureaucratic barriers raise ethical concerns. On the other hand, some consumers feel the Privacy Rule has not gone far enough. For example, the Privacy Rule permits a researcher to examine identifiable health information to determine who may be eligible for a study. Some participants feel this constitutes an invasion

1. The issues that are discussed here have been insufficiently researched, and the statements made are based largely on personal experience working with both researchers and mental health consumers during the NIH T15 training program, Ethical Issues in Behavioral Research Ethics.

of privacy because it is not explicitly authorized. Similarly, some feel that their health data belongs to them and should not be used when they object; however, once de-identified, researchers may have a right to use the information. Finally, while compliance with the Privacy Rule certainly minimizes the risk that de-identified data will be re-identified, the rule acknowledges that a "very small" chance may always exist. Given that these concerns are competing, it is impossible to modify the Privacy Rule in a way that would satisfy everyone. Nevertheless, the views of researchers and participants can be given further consideration on a case-by-case basis using ethical reasoning within the framework provided by the Privacy Rule.

CERTIFICATES OF CONFIDENTIALITY AND MANDATORY REPORTING

Sometimes knowledge gained through the research process is not only useful to researchers, participants, or sponsors of research, but also to public health agents, officers of the law, or the court system. In the 1970s, Congress recognized that many individuals were unwilling to participate in important research on "sensitive" issues, for example, research on the use of illegal substances, unless their confidentiality was ensured (Kaltman & Isidor, 2006).

To address these concerns, Congress empowered the Secretary of Health, Education, and Welfare to legally protect the confidentiality of research data. When initially enacted in 1970, protections were only afforded to research on illegal substances; in 1974, protections were expanded to include research related to mental health; and in 1988, they were again expanded to any research significant to the public health (Office for Protection from Research Risks, 1998). Today, these protections are provided through the issuance of Certificates of Confidentiality, which are administered by the National Institutes of Health on behalf of the Secretary of Health. The NIH provides the following brief description of a Certificate of Confidentiality:

> Certificates of Confidentiality are issued by the National Institutes of Health (NIH) to protect the privacy of research subjects by protecting investigators and institutions from being compelled to release information that could be used to identify subjects with a research project. Certificates of Confidentiality are issued to institutions or universities where the research is conducted. They allow the investigator and others who have access to research records to refuse to disclose identifying information in any civil, criminal, administrative, legislative, or other proceeding, whether at the federal, state, or local level. (National Institutes of Health, 2002)

There are a number of restrictions on who may receive a Certificate of Confidentiality. First, certificates are given only to researchers (via their institutions). Although other forms of sensitive information exist, such as health information given to a health care provider, the purpose of the Public Health Service Act (301[d], 42 U.S.C. 241[d]) was to foster research that the government considered socially important. Second, Certificates of Confidentiality can only be used for research that is "sensitive." NIH's policy states that

By sensitive, we mean that disclosure of identifying information could have adverse consequences for subjects or damage their financial standing, employability, insurability, or reputation. Examples of sensitive research activities include but are not limited to the following:

- Collecting genetic information;
- Collecting information on psychological well-being of subjects;
- Collecting information on subjects' sexual attitudes, preferences or practices;
- Collecting data on substance abuse or other illegal risk behaviors; and
- Studies where subjects may be involved in litigation related to exposures under study (e.g., breast implants, environmental or occupational exposures). (National Institutes of Health, 2004)

While the protections afforded by a Certificate of Confidentiality are robust and have been upheld by at least one court (Office for Protection from Research Risks, 1998), they are not absolute. There are three main kinds of limitations. First, participants themselves may voluntarily disclose their research data. If a participant authorizes in writing the release of information to a third party, then an investigator may not refuse disclosure. Second, the Certificate of Confidentiality protects only against involuntary disclosures by the researcher. "Researchers are not prevented from the voluntary disclosure of matters such as child abuse, reportable communicable diseases, or subject's threatened violence to self or others" (National Institutes of Health, 2004). However, if a researcher intends to make voluntary disclosures, for instance, to comply with state reporting laws, then the informed consent form must specify the conditions of disclosure. The conflict between mandatory reporting laws and the protection of confidentiality is explored in the case study found in the last section of this chapter. Finally, a researcher cannot deny data to authorized DHHS or FDA personnel when their policies require access to the data.

Information on how to apply for a Certificate of Confidentiality is available at the National Institutes of Health's "Certificate of Confidentiality Kiosk," which is currently available online at: http://grants.nih.gov/grants/policy/coc/.

PROTECTING PRIVACY ACROSS THE LIFE OF A STUDY

A research study involves several, often overlapping phases, including the identification of data sources, data collection, data management and analysis, presentation of findings, data storage and eventual destruction. At each phase, threats to privacy and confidentiality exist. People may feel an invasion of privacy if contacted by a researcher who determined they are eligible to enroll in a study by reviewing their private health information (Hull et al., 2004). Privacy may be invaded while gathering data, for example, when observing private behaviors, even those performed in public spaces (Humphreys, 1970). Data collection may threaten confidentiality when data includes direct identifiers such as names or photographs. The confidentiality of stored data may be compromised when code sheets linking names to data are stored in the same location as the data itself. Data analysis may identify individuals when independent variables (e.g., a medical diagnosis) are linked to too many demographic variables (employment institution, age, sex, race, and profession). Similarly, when such data is published, it risks identifying individuals and their information to a much larger audience. Even data destruction is not without risks related to confidentiality: voice images may not be completely erased from tapes without actually "degaussing" them, and paper documents must be shredded completely prior to disposal.

Contemporary genetic research also poses new challenges pertaining to confidentiality (Biesecker & Peay, 2003). To protect confidentiality, it is recommended that genetic material be stored separately from any links to "identifiers" (i.e., non-DNA identifiers). Genetic research additionally raises concerns when participants voluntarily request the release of their information to health care providers (e.g., as part of a medical chart, such information may be accessible to life and health insurance providers). Further, genetic information may also pertain to nonparticipating family members. When a genetic trait poses a potentially preventable health threat, is there a duty to warn, and if so, what would its implementation look like? Despite these challenges and risks, without permitting research on at least some identifiable health information—including genetic material that is linked to health information—it will be impossible to identify the full effects of psychotropic medications, to determine the genetic correlates to diseases and disorders, or to identify how drug reactions are affected by genetic make up (Simon et al., 2000).

Table 9.1 presents various protections to confidentiality that are appropriate to the various stages of research with references to literature that provides further details. However, it is worth noting that the best practices for protecting privacy are typically related to very specific kinds of research (e.g., genetic research, research with medical records, or survey research) and that best practices are constantly evolving; for example, new HIPAA Security Standards for the Protection of Electronic Protected Health Information were issued in 2003 (see http://www. hhs.gov/ocr/combinedregtext.pdf), which specify requirements such as protection from malicious software, log-in monitoring, and data back-up plans. Local IRBs, research mentors, and professional associations may provide excellent information about the protection of confidentiality that is tailored to specific kinds of projects, such as those involving the use of electronic PHI.

ETHICS AS AN INSTITUTIONAL RESPONSIBILITY

This book focuses on identifying ways of conducting research in an ethical manner. Frequently it is assumed that researchers alone have ethical duties pertaining to the conduct of research. This idea was strongly challenged by the Institute of Medicine (IOM) and the National Research Council (NRC) as they issued a joint report on *Integrity in Scientific Research*. The subtitle of the report conveyed one of their core messages: *Creating an Environment that Promotes Responsible Conduct*. Some of the specific responsibilities institutions have in promoting research integrity, which were identified by IOM/NRC, are summarized below in box 9.5.

Table 9.1 Privacy and Confidentiality Protection at Different Phases of Research

Research Phase	Confidentiality Protection	Useful Literature
Prior to beginning research	• Consider whether a Certificate of Confidentiality is needed to prevent the subpoena of research data • Consider whether data will include PHI; if so, comply with HIPAA privacy rule • Obtain consent as appropriate • Identify a complaint mechanism for participants • Educate subcontractors, e.g., call centers, about confidentiality requirements	Department of Health and Human Services, 2003; Easter, Davis, & Henderson, 2004; Hoagwood, 1994; Kelsey, 1981; Wolf, Zandecki, & Lo, 2004
Conducting interviews	• Provide a private setting • Train interpreters, facilitators, and other participants to respect confidentiality • Discourage use of names when referring to self and third parties	Sieber, 2001b; Smith, 1995; Tangney, 2000
Obtaining existing data from a database	• Remove identifiers using "safe harbor" or statistical criteria • Use as few identifying variables as possible; remove when no longer needed	Barnes & Gallin, 2003; Kelsey, 1981; Simon, Unutzer, Young, & Pincus, 2000; Steinberg, 1983; Wallace, 1982
Surveys or research requiring recontacting or data linking	• Link data to codes or aliases • Eliminate need to store code sheet by allowing participants to memorize or store code in sealed envelope • Explore alternative linking systems • Payments to participants should not identify the study or sponsoring department, e.g., on checks or envelopes	Black & Hodge, 1987; Boruch, 1982; Boruch & Cecil, 1979; Sieber, 2001a
Data management and storage	• Data stored using codes if reidentification or linking is needed • Code sheets kept separately with restricted access • Restrict paper access using two locks (office, file cabinet) • Restrict electronic access using firewalls, unique passwords, audit trails, and other technology as appropriate given risks and resources • Use statistical techniques deidentify data • Biological specimens including genetic material should not be stored with identifying data	Fisher, 2003; Freedland & Carney, 1992; Health Privacy Working Group, 1999; National Research Council, 1997; Rada, 2003
Data analysis and presentation	• Use only as many variables as needed • Use only aggregated data or else remove identifiers in narratives • Use statistical analysis or safe harbor techniques to ensure deidentification	Boruch, 1982; Boruch & Cecil, 1979; National Library of Medicine, 1996; Rada, 2003
Data destruction	• Finely shred paper and properly dispose • Degauss (demagnetize) tapes • Consult with information technology personnel to permanently delete electronic data and destroy removable data storage systems	Rada, 2003

Adapted from DuBois (2005).

Box 9.5 Institute of Medicine / National Research Council Description of Integrity in Research at the Institutional Level

Institutions seeking to create an environment that promotes responsible conduct by individual scientists and that fosters integrity must establish and continuously monitor structures, processes, policies, and procedures that:

- provide leadership in support of responsible conduct of research;
- encourage respect for everyone involved in the research enterprise;
- promote productive interactions between trainees and mentors;
- advocate adherence to the rules regarding all aspects of the conduct of research, especially research involving human participants and animals;
- anticipate, reveal, and manage individual and institutional conflicts of interest;
- arrange timely and thorough inquiries and investigations of allegations of scientific misconduct and apply appropriate administrative sanctions;
- offer educational opportunities pertaining to integrity in the conduct of research; and
- monitor and evaluate the institutional environment supporting integrity in the conduct of research and use this knowledge for continuous quality improvement.

Reprinted from Institute of Medicine & National Research Council, 2002, p. 5.

Some specific institutional responsibilities related to human subjects research deserve discussion.

Training

Complying with HIPAA regulations is no easy task. First and foremost, it presupposes that one is adequately informed, for example, about what constitutes PHI, how data can be de-identified, and when authorization is required. Even with HIPAA training, researchers may need access to privacy officers or experts to receive answers to specific questions. Equally important, in chapter 1, it was argued that training should aim beyond compliance and should engage ethical issues in an effort to assist researchers in understanding the rationale behind ethical best practices and to foster the internalization of professional ethical norms.

Creating an Ethical Culture

Even with the best knowledge and processes available to protect confidentiality, breaches may occur simply from carelessness. Campbell (2000) recounts working at a state department of mental health in the 1990s where confidential patient information was regularly faxed to a machine in a public area, where documents might lie for hours before being picked up. A few years later, while working at a research institution, she found that surveys of mental health consumers "with respondent names on the cover sheets were routinely left in plain sight in an un-locked room. Again, I was the only one who seemed to notice or to care" (p. 12). Institutions need to provide leadership in creating a culture that cares about ethical issues, monitors behavior, and provides further training or even sanctions when violations are detected.

Identifying and Promoting Best Practices

Institutions should encourage research on the ethics of human research (Sieber, 2004). Moreover, institutions should collaborate with professional associations and other research institutions in identifying and disseminating best practices. Even an IRB application form can be educational to researchers and IRB reviewers. For example, an application form may define the concepts of privacy and confidentiality, distinguish between de-identified and confidential data, and between ordinary and sensitive data. It may also list best practices for protecting privacy and confidential data, asking researchers to identify which approaches they intend to use.

Providing Necessary Technology and Resources

Some of the best practices for protecting the confidentiality of data require resources that may or may not be within a researcher's control. For example, hard copies of files should be "double" locked, for example, placed in a locked file cabinet within a locked office. This may require institutions to provide researchers with appropriate space and furniture. While electronic data does not require "locks," it does require storage in an appropriately secure manner. Data stored on servers should be behind firewalls, should be password protected, log-ins should be monitored, and servers should scan for malicious software. Researchers frequently lack control over these matters. Institutions should provide not only adequately secured server space, but access to information technology professionals who may answer researchers' questions regarding confidentiality issues, such as who other than they may have access to data stored on an institutional server.

Case Study: Confidentiality and Mandatory Reporting

The Powers Institute, based in a large metropolitan area, is conducting a study with women who suffer from sexual addiction and compulsivity. Women who sexually act out frequently experience difficulty sustaining meaningful relationships, feelings of guilt and depression, higher than normal rates of alcohol abuse, and higher rates of STDs and unwanted pregnancy. This type of addiction is less common in women than in men, and few studies have been done involving women. The current study combines a modified 12-step program with professionally facilitated group counseling based on a cognitive-behavioral model. This approach has been used with modest success among men with sexual addictions, but no literature has been published demonstrating its effectiveness with women.

Potential harms to participants would be significant if their research data or even participation in the study were disclosed. Due to the sensitive nature of this study, the consent form promises strict confidentiality. Dr. Jane Smith, the principal investigator on the project, has obtained a Certificate of Confidentiality from the National Institutes of Health to protect her from involuntarily disclosing data in response to a court order or subpoena. Women who participate in the study must also sign an agreement indicating that they will not discuss information about other participants that is learned through the group counseling sessions. At the beginning of each counseling session, participants are reminded of their agreement and the investigator's strict guarantee of confidentiality.

During one group therapy session, Amanda, a high school math teacher, discloses that she is having sex with an unnamed 16-year-old student. Sexual relations with an individual under 17 by an individual over 21 years old constitutes statutory rape 2 in the state where the Powers Institute is located and is reportable by law.

A co-investigator was present during Amanda's disclosure and later asks Dr. Smith whether she intends to report it. Dr. Smith is aware of the law but argues against reporting. She says it would break their promise of confidentiality to the women and destroy their trust in the researchers. This would ruin both the study and the therapeutic alliance they have established. She notes that many of the participants are minority members who were very mistrustful of researchers, and their participation and the trust they have shown mean a lot to her. Moreover, she says that reporting the offense would be devastating to Amanda; she would lose her job and her relationship with her two daughters would be damaged. She says that the situation might be different if the boy were younger, say 12, or did not consent.

Is Dr. Smith right, or should she report Amanda's sexual relationship? Why? Why not?[2]

CASE COMMENTARY

This case involves multiple stakeholders who are subject or subjected to harm, ambiguous legal facts and norms, conflicting professional norms, and no clear option that avoids all harms to all stakeholders. In discussing over two dozen ethics cases with participants in training programs over a four-year period, the author found that this case generated strong disagreement more consistently than any other case.

Rarely do so many stakeholders have so much at stake. As the narrative states, Amanda, the woman who is having sex with her student, could lose her job, be imprisoned, lose custody of her two children, and experience severe social harms. Although Amanda alleges that her student has consented to their sexual relations, the law criminalizes sex with children below "the age of consent." The law's choice of terminology offers the rationale: below a certain age, it should not be assumed that an individual is capable of granting more than assent. Often teenagers appear able to grant consent, but their ability to appreciate the long-range consequences of their actions (e.g., risks of STDs, pregnancy, and emotional harm) is often not fully developed. Moreover, our

2. This book does not aim to provide legal advice to researchers. Researchers are encouraged to work with legal counsel at their institutions while navigating complex legal issues such as those presented in this case.

society generally frowns upon or explicitly prohibits sexual relations with "subordinates" precisely because power dynamics might interfere with their freedom to refuse the relationship. The National Education Association's code of ethics approaches this issue quite generally, stating that a teacher "shall not use professional relationships with students for private advantage" (National Education Association, 1975). There should be no question that what Amanda is doing is wrong, that her student's ability to consent is compromised, and he could be harmed in significant ways. Thus, little weight should be given to Dr. Smith's statement that "the situation might be different if the boy were younger, say 12, or did not consent."

Dr. Smith could be harmed by this situation in a variety of ways. On the one hand, if she reports Amanda, her ability to maintain a trusting and therapeutic relationship with her current participants and her ability to recruit future clients and participants could be jeopardized. Further, she has made a strict promise of confidentiality and appears to feel her personal integrity is at stake. On the other hand, if she does not report, she could be accused of failing to execute legal and ethical responsibilities and could suffer legal, professional, and social harm. The other participants in Dr. Smith's study are deeply affected by this situation. The study, which is intended to be a therapeutic study, could be discontinued; if confidentiality is breached, some may leave the group feeling vulnerable or betrayed. Others may feel they have a duty to report and experience distress. If the study is in fact capable of yielding important knowledge about the treatment of sexual addictions in women, then other women with addictions would be deprived of potential benefits. The student's parents are also stakeholders because they are still responsible for their son and will need to deal with the possible fall-out from this relationship. They would likely be very upset if they knew a psychologist was aware of the sexual abuse and did not report it. Finally, Dr. Smith's co-investigator must decide how to respond. If she chooses to become a whistle blower, she may deal with the negative consequences that frequently accompany whistle blowing.

Whether Dr. Smith can properly discharge all of her current legal duties is unclear. On the one hand, her state law requires the reporting of child or elderly abuse. While not all laws require every citizen to serve as a reporter, health care professionals are always designated as reporters. Moreover, the federal Certificate of Confidentiality guidelines provided by NIH state that a researcher may voluntarily report such matters. Sieber (2001a) writes that IRBs would not permit researchers to ignore reportable evidence even after obtaining a Certificate of Confidentiality. IRBs typically recommend that the matter be addressed through the informed consent process by adding a statement such as the following:

> What is discussed during our session will be kept confidential with two exceptions: I am compelled by law to inform an appropriate other person if I hear and believe that you are in danger of hurting yourself or someone else, or if there is reasonable suspicion that a child, elder or dependent adult has been abused. (Sieber, 2001a)[3]

3. This statement was adapted from a statement developed by David H. Ruja and is discussed in Gil (1982).

All this speaks to the legal obligation to report. On the other hand, guidance on Certificates of Confidentiality states that researchers *may voluntarily* report. Can one read this as stating that federal law protects a researcher who refuses to breach confidentiality in the presence of a Certificate of Confidentiality? One legal textbook presents the argument that "if researchers promise subjects that they will not disclose confidential information to third parties, they 'will be bound by that promise, as a matter of the research contract between subject and researcher' Mark Barnes & Sara Kraus, *The Effect of HIPAA on Human Subjects Research,* 10 Health L. Rep (BNA) 1026, 1032 (2001)" (Coleman et al., 2005, p. 454).

To fully appreciate the ethical complexity of this case, one needs to consider the ways that socially defined professional relationships affect ethical duties. Compare Dr. Smith's role to two other professional roles, those of a detective and those of a defense attorney. A detective's job is to defend citizens in a specific geographic area from criminals by investigating crimes and cooperating in their prosecution. While detectives may not violate the rights of criminals, they are not meant primarily to serve criminals. They may even bait criminals—that is, present scenarios that might tempt a criminal to engage in illegal activity. For example, a detective might pose as a minor in an online chat room to bait child molesters or might leave a car unlocked on a street overnight to bait a car thief. In contrast, a defense attorney's job is to serve those who are accused of a crime. Society has deemed the defense attorney's job to be so essential to due process and due process to be so important to a civilized society that communication between a client and attorney is privileged: it is confidential and disclosure cannot be compelled (Sagarin & Moneymaker, 1979, p. 176). Dr. Smith's job, as a researcher and therapist, establishes competing duties. Her primary responsibilities are to her clients and participants. Unlike the detective, her job is not to bait or investigate crimes such as sexual abuse of minors. In fact, it would be unethical for her to set up a study to bait confessions of crimes because her primary professional obligation is to serve her clients. Nevertheless, unlike the attorney, her job is not considered so fundamental to a human right that communication with her is privileged (though some interpret a Certificate of Confidentiality in this fashion).

Given the complexity of this situation, no matter what Dr. Smith does, she will violate some legal and ethical norms. For example, if she reports out of a legal duty to report or to protect the student, she will have violated a promise made in the consent form and in discussions and will harm individuals. If she does not report, she will fail in her statutory duty to report, will permit harm to the student to continue, and possibly enable Amanda to harm other minors. Some might argue that some of the relevant ethical norms—such as maintaining confidentiality—are "only" prima facie or are limited, but this is less reassuring when important stakeholders are unaware of this and act on contrary ethical assumptions. That is, if Amanda disclosed her actions out of a desire to get help and to change her behavior, based solely on the assumption that she was guaranteed the kind of confidentiality a priest or defense attorney could provide—an assumption that was reasonable given Dr. Smith's statements—then stating that confidentiality is merely a prima facie or limited norm is not terribly helpful. Given the complexity of the ethical situation, it should come as no surprise that the ethics literature on this subject is somewhat divided. For example, while warning that confidentiality should not be breached when there is reasonable doubt that abuse is occurring or that the abuse will be substantiated, Scott-Jones (1994) asserts that "child abuse should certainly not go unreported" (p. 102). In contrast, others argue that researchers cannot appeal only to state and local laws but must rely on their own ethics in determining when confidentiality should be broken, considering, for example, whether the mother of a child abused by his father would consider an intervention from Child Protective Services beneficial or harmful (Sullivan & Cain, 2004).

There is an old adage that "hard cases make bad law." Given the ethical complexities of this case, readers should be leery of any advice given on this case for it will involve an imperfect solution. Nevertheless, whatever solution is chosen, it should involve the principle of least infringement: that is, it should seek to optimize the situation by diminishing harms to the least necessary. Because Dr. Smith has a Certificate of Confidentiality and made a promise of strict confidentiality, and because Amanda presumably would never have disclosed to Dr. Smith except for her participation in this study and her understanding of strict confidentiality, one might recommend trying to "start all over." Dr. Smith should work with her IRB to modify her consent form to disclose when she might be obliged to breach confidentiality. One such circumstance would be to report abuse of a minor or the elderly. Participants should be reminded of these conditions at the start of each counseling session. While counseling requires open disclosure, she might encourage participants to avoid disclosing any details that could put them at risk (Cowburn, 2005). Clients who begin to make such disclosures might be interrupted and reminded; if they continue with such disclosure, the researcher might interpret such a statement as an intent to "confess." If they seek advice on a specific scenario, they might be encouraged to speak hypothetically, "Let's imagine I have a friend who . . . ." While all this might seem to skirt the spirit of mandatory reporting, it is crucial to bear in mind that the purpose of this therapeutic study is to assist women with sexual addictions; it is not meant to be a creative criminal baiting program.

Common wisdom maintains, "an ounce of prevention is worth a pound of cure." This is true not only in matters of health, but also in matters of research ethics. The approach sketched above basically seeks to start over and prevent a similar situation from occurring again. In addition to modifying the protocol to avoid the problematic situation, we also need to ask whether society should work harder to diminish such dilemmas for researchers. After reviewing possible legal duties to report, Appelbaum and Rosenbaum (1989) write:

> Research on sensitive topics, such as violence, child maltreatment, substance abuse, AIDS, and sexuality, might seriously be compromised by such obligations [to report]. If we value research, the validity of data must be protected to the extent possible by assuring subjects' confidentiality. Countervailing obligations, such as the duty to protect potential victims, should be imposed only after careful consideration of their probable impact and in as circumscribed a manner as possible. (p. 893)

Further EMHR Resources

- Unit seven of the *Dialogues* DVD contains an interview with Dorothy Webman and a focus group with mental health consumers on privacy and confidentiality in research
- www.emhr.net contains a bibliography and further case studies on the topics of privacy and confidentiality in research

REFERENCES

Alderman, E., & Kennedy, C. (1997). *The right to privacy.* New York: Vintage Books.

Appelbaum, P. S., & Rosenbaum, A. (1989). Tarasoff and the researcher: Does the duty to protect apply in the research setting? *American Psychologist, 44*(6), 885–894.

Bacon, F. (2002). *The major works.* New York: Oxford University Press.

Barnes, M., & Gallin, K. E. (2003). "Exempt" research after the privacy rule. *IRB: Ethics & Human Research, 25*(4), 5–6.

Biesecker, B., & Peay, H. (2003). Ethical issues in psychiatric genetics research: Points to consider. *Psychopharmacology, 171*(1), 27–35.

Black, K. J., & Hodge, M. H. (1987). Protecting subjects' identity in test-retest experiments. *IRB: A Review of Human Subjects Research, 9*(2), 10–11.

Boruch, R. F. (1982). Methods for resolving privacy problems in social research. In T. L. Beauchamp, R. R. Faden, R. J. J. Wallace, & L. Walters (Eds.), *Ethical issues in social science research* (pp. 292–314). Baltimore: Johns Hopkins University Press.

Boruch, R. F., & Cecil, J. S. (1979). *Assuring the confidentiality of social research data.* Philadelphia: University of Pennsylvania Press.

Campbell, J. (2000). Consumers' perspectives of confidentiality and health records. In J. J. Gates & B. S. Arons (Eds.), *Privacy and confidentiality in mental health care* (pp. 5–32). Baltimore: Paul H. Brookes.

Coleman, C. H., Menikoff, J. A., Goldner, J. A., & Dubler, N. N. (2005). *The ethics and regulation of research with human subjects.* Newark, NJ: LexisNexis.

Cowburn, M. (2005). Confidentiality and public protection: Ethical dilemmas in qualitative research with adult male sex offenders. *Journal of Sexual Aggression, 11*(1), 49–63.

Department of Health and Human Services. (2003). Protecting personal health information in research: Understanding the HIPAA privacy rule. Retrieved November 22, 2006, from http://privacyruleandresearch.nih.gov/pdf/HIPAA_Booklet_4–14–2003.pdf.

DuBois, J. M. (2004). Universal ethical principles in a diverse universe: A commentary on Monshi and Zieglmayer's case study. *Ethics & Behavior, 14*(4), 313–319.

DuBois, J. M. (2005). Ethics in behavioral and social science research. In Ana Smith (Ed.), *Research ethics* (pp. 102–120). New York: Routledge.

Easter, M. M., Davis, A. M., & Henderson, G. E. (2004). Confidentiality: More than a linkage file and a locked drawer. *IRB: A Review of Human Subjects Research, 26*(2), 13–17.

Fisher, C. B. (2003). *Decoding the ethics code: A practical guide for psychologists.* Thousand Oaks, CA: Sage Publications.

Freedland, K. E., & Carney, R. M. (1992). Data management and accountability in behavioral and biomedical research. *American Psychologist, 47*(5), 640–645.

Health Privacy Working Group. (1999). *Best principles for health privacy: A report of the health privacy working group.* Washington, DC: Health Privacy Project. Retrieved January, 12, 2007 from: http://www.healthprivacy.org/usr_doc/33807.pdf.

Hoagwood, K. (1994). The certificate of confidentiality at the National Institute of Mental Health: Discretionary considerations in its applicability to research on child and adolescent mental disorders. *Ethics & Behavior, 4*(2), 123–131.

Hull, S., Glanz, K., Steffen, A., & Wilfond, B. (2004). Recruitment approaches for family studies: Attitudes of index patients and their relatives. *IRB: A Review of Human Subjects Research, 26*(4), 12–17.

Humphreys, L. (1970). *Tearoom trade: Impersonal sex in public places.* Chicago: Aldine.

Iltis, A. S. (2005). Timing invitations to participate in clinical research: Preliminary versus informed consent. *Journal of Medicine and Philosophy, 30*(1), 89–106.

Institute of Medicine, & National Research Council. (2002). *Integrity in scientific research: Creating an environment that promotes responsible conduct.* Washington, DC: National Academies Press.

Kaltman, S. P., & Isidor, J. M. (2006). Certificates of confidentiality. In E. A. Bankert & R. J. Amdur (Eds.), *Institutional review board: Management and function* (2nd ed., pp. 311–312). Sudbury, MA: Jones and Bartlett.

Kelsey, J. L. (1981). Privacy and confidentiality in epidemiological research involving patients. *IRB: A Review of Human Subjects Research, 3*(2), 1–4.

Kulynich, J., & Korn, D. (2002). The effect of the new federal medical-privacy rule on research. *New England Journal of Medicine, 346*(3), 201–204.

Laufer, R. S., & Wolfe, M. (1977). Privacy as a concept and a social issue: A multidimensional developmental theory. *Journal of Social Issues, 33*(3), 22–42.

Monshi, B., & Zieglmayer, V. (2004). The problem of privacy in trans-cultural research: Reflections on an ethnographic study in Sri Lanka. *Ethics & Behavior, 14*(3), 305–312.

Muhlbaier, L. H. (2006). Health insurance portability and accountability act and research. In E. A. Bankert & R. J. Amdur (Eds.), *Institutional review board: Management and function* (2nd ed., pp. 272–277). Sudbury, MA: Jones and Bartlett.

National Education Association. (1975). Code of ethics of the education profession. Retrieved December 24, 2006, from http://www.nea.org/aboutnea/code.html.

National Institutes of Health. (2004). Certificates of confidentiality kiosk. Retrieved November 25, 2006, from http://grants.nih.gov/grants/policy/coc/.

National Institutes of Health, Office of Extramural Research. (2002). Certificates of confidentiality: Background information. Retrieved January 13, 2007, from http://grants1.nih.gov/grants/policy/coc/background.htm.

National Library of Medicine. (1996). *Current bibliographies in medicine: Confidentiality of electronic health data. No. 95-10.* Rockville, MD: National Library of Medicine. Retrieved January, 12, 2007 from: http://www.nlm.nih.gov/archive/20040829/pubs/cbm/confiden.html.

National Research Council. (1997). *For the record: Protecting electronic health information.* Washington, DC: National Academy Press.

Office for Protection from Research Risks. (1998). Privacy protection for research subjects: "Certificates of confidentiality." Retrieved November 25, 2006, from http://www.hhs.gov/ohrp/humansubjects/guidance/certconpriv.htm.

Rada, R. (2003). *HIPAA@IT essentials: Health information transactions, privacy and security.* (2nd ed.). Baltimore: HIPAA-IT.

Sagarin, E., & Moneymaker, J. (1979). The dilemma of research immunity. In C. B. Klockars & F. O'Connor (Eds.), *Deviance and decency* (pp. 175–196). Beverly Hills, CA: Sage.

Scott-Jones, D. (1994). Ethical issues in reporting and referring in research with low-income minority children. *Ethics & Behavior, 4*(2), 97–108.

Sieber, J. E. (2001a). Privacy and confidentiality as related to human research in social and behavioral science. In National Bioethics Advisory Commission (Ed.), *Ethical and policy issues in research involving human participants: Vol. 2. Commissioned papers and staff analysis* (pp. N1-N50). Bethesda, MD: National Bioethics Advisory Committee. Retrieved January 12, 2007 from, http://www.georgetown.edu/research/nrcbl/nbac/human/overvol2.pdf.

Sieber, J. E. (2001b). *Summary of human subjects protection issues related to large sample surveys.* (No. NCJ 187692). Washington, DC; U.S. Department of Justice.

Sieber, J. E. (2004). Empirical research on research ethics. *Ethics & Behavior, 4*(4), 397–412.

Simon, G. E., Unutzer, J., Young, B. E., & Pincus, H. A. (2000). Large medical databases, population-based research, and patient confidentiality. *American Journal of Psychiatry, 157*(11), 1731–1737.

Singer, M., Marshall, P. L., Trotter, R. T. I., Schensul, J. J., Weeks, M. R., Simmons, J. E., et al. (1999). Ethics, ethnography, drug use, and AIDS: Dilemmas and standards in federally funded research. In P. L. Marshall, M. Singer, & M. C. Clatts (Eds.), *Integrating cultural, observational, and epidemiological approaches to the prevention of drug abuse and HIV/AIDS.* Bethesda, MD: U.S. Department of Health and Human Services; National Institutes of Health; National Institute of Drug Abuse.

Smith, M. W. (1995). Ethics in focus groups: A few concerns. *Qualitative Health Research, 5*(4), 478–486.

Steinberg, J. (1983). Social research use of archival data: Procedural solutions to privacy problems. In R. F. Boruch & J. S. Cecil (Eds.), *Solutions to ethical and legal problems in social research* (pp. 249–261). New York: Academic Press.

Sullivan, C., & Cain, D. (2004). Ethical and safety considerations when obtaining information from or about battered women for research purposes. *Journal of Interpersonal Violence, 19*(5), 603–618.

Tangney, J. (2000). Training. In B. D. Sales & S. Folkman (Eds.), *Ethics in research with human participants.* Washington, DC: American Psychological Association.

Wallace Jr., R. J. (1982). Privacy and the use of data in epidemiology. In T. L. Beauchamp, R. R. Faden, R. J. J. Wallace, & L. Walters (Eds.), *Ethical issues in social science research* (pp. 274–291). Baltimore: Johns Hopkins University Press.

Wolf, L. E., Zandecki, J., & Lo, B. (2004). The certificate of confidentiality application. *IRB: Ethics & Human Research, 26*(1), 14–18.

10

Identifying and Managing Conflicts of Interest

Careers, money and fame are at stake.
—J. Willwerth, "How to Tell If the Men in White Coats
Are Lying to You"

Sometimes ordinary people do very bad things. There are many reasons. Stanley Milgram investigated one of them.

Milgram's Study of Obedience to Authority

In the early 1960s, 40 men aged 20–50 and representing various occupations came to the psychological laboratory of Yale University to take part in what they believed would be a study of memory and learning. They were paid $4.50 for their participation. When they arrived, each was met by two other men—one pretending to be the experimenter and another pretending to be a research subject. The subject was played by a 47-year-old accountant, whom most observers found mild mannered and likable. Stanley Milgram, the actual principal investigator, was positioned behind a one-way mirror observing events.

As a pretext for administering shock, the actual subjects were told that the research concerned the effect of punishment on learning. A rigged drawing of slips of paper from a hat always resulted in the naïve subject being the teacher and the accomplice (the pretend subject) being the learner or victim. The learner was then led to an adjacent room where the experimenter strapped the learner into an apparatus that looked like an electric chair. The wires attached to the learner were said to be attached to a shock generator in the next room, and the experimenter said "although the shocks can be painful, they cause no permanent tissue damage." The false experiment involved learning a list of pairs of words. False answers by the learner were to be punished by administering a shock. The shock generator was a realistic-looking panel with 30 switches labeled with voltages ranging from 15–450, with sets of switches labeled as "slight shock, moderate shock, . . . extreme shock, . . . danger–severe shock, and XXX." The "teachers" were told to punish incorrect responses starting with mild shock, but increasing the voltage with each wrong response. The 45-volt switch was used to give a mild shock to the teacher to convince him that the machine really did work. As the experiment proceeded, the learner gave about three wrong answers for every correct one. No sound was heard from the learner in the other room until the 300-volt level. Then the learner pounded on the wall, but his answer did not appear on the response panel. The experimenter told the teacher to treat "no response" as an incorrect response and to increase the voltage. At this point, many teacher-subjects were unwilling to continue, but the experimenter urged them to do so using a series of prods: (1) "please continue" for the first refusal to administer a shock; then (2) "the experiment requires that you continue," for the next refusal; then (3) "it is absolutely essential that you continue"; and finally, (4) "you have no other choice, you must go on." If the teacher refused to continue after all four prods, the experiment was ended. The measure of obedience to authority was the level of the last shock given by the teacher.

The major finding of the study was that, of the 40 subjects, 26 obeyed the orders of the experimenter to the end, proceeding to punish the victim until they reached the most potent shock available on the shock generator. Only 5 subjects stopped when the learner began pounding the wall at the 300-volt mark.

Within the field of research ethics, Stanley Milgram's obedience to authority study is frequently cited as the classic example of an experimental design involving the use of deception, and accordingly it has generated significant debate (Baumrind, 1964; Milgram, 1964, 1974). While it is appropriate to consider the ethics of the study's design, the study itself has an important moral message: *do not blindly assume that you will do what is right*.[1] Milgram's study was largely inspired by the phrase "I was only following orders," which was frequently heard during the Nuremberg trials of Nazi war criminals. He hypothesized that ordinary individuals would sometimes behave immorally toward others under the right circumstances, for instance, when instructed to do so by a person perceived as being in authority. An important dimension to research ethics training is training investigators to identify circumstances that might lead them to engage in misconduct. Might a research assistant or coordinator do something wrong because a principal investigator requested it? Are there other relationships—to clients, funding agencies, or employers—that can lead people to do wrong?

INHERENT AND INDUCED CONFLICTS OF INTEREST

In his essay on nonfinancial conflicts of interest in research, Dr. Norman Levinsky writes:

> In 1963, before the advent of institutional review boards (IRBs), I was a young academic physician studying the regulation of sodium excretion by the kidneys. I paid medical students approximately $50 to serve as subjects for experiments involving only saline infusions and the collection of blood and spontaneously voided urine samples. I do not remember exactly what I told the students about the risks of the experiments but am quite certain that

---

1. Michael Mumford's course in the Responsible Conduct of Research at the University of Oklahoma, funded by the National Institutes of Health, uses Milgram's case precisely to teach participants not to trust themselves blindly. See "Block 3: Personal Biases Influencing Ethical Decision-Making."

I characterized them as nominal. In one subject, severe phlebitis developed at the site of an intravenous infusion and required extensive therapy. The research project was funded by the National Institutes of Health. I had no possibility of financial gain from it. My primary motive was academic—the desire to advance knowledge about an important physiological mechanism with a bearing on clinical conditions such as edema. A potent secondary motive was to advance my career by publishing the results of the research and maintaining grant support—academic currency that buys prestige and promotion. (Levinsky, 2002, p. 359)

Writing nearly 40 years after the experiment he describes, Levinsky observes that the dual motives of advancing medical science and obtaining personal benefits from publications and the acquisition of grants have not changed; they are, presumably, universal among researchers.

Black's Law Dictionary defines a *conflict of interest* as a "real or seeming incompatibility between one's private interests and one's public or fiduciary duties" (Garner, 1999). Fiduciary duties exist when the public may reasonably trust a professional to do certain things such as obtain informed consent or reduce research risks to the minimum necessary. In the narrow definition that *Black's Law Dictionary* provides, the term "conflict of interest" refers only to a "real or seeming incompatibility" between one's private interests and one's public duties; but in common usage, it also refers to *potential* incompatibilities. In either case, the term does *not* imply that a professional intends to put his or her personal interests first; it does not in itself imply wrongdoing (Johnson, 2004). It simply implies that a motive exists—regardless of whether one intends to act on the motive—to neglect one's professional duties (Friedman, 1992). However, one reason that conflicts of interest can be so insidious is that individuals are often unaware of their biases and the ways their biases influence their behavior, often in self-serving manners (Dana & Loewenstein, 2003).

Levinsky's recollection of his earliest research experience is at once troubling and insightful: some conflicts of interest—such as the desire for new knowledge, for career advancement, or for recognition—may be inherent to the research enterprise. Perhaps the most basic, inherent conflict in research is a conflict of attitudes, one described by Hans Jonas in the 1960s when the merits of research regulations were being debated. Jonas described the risk of "reification." While ethics requires us to relate to human participants as "subjects" or persons, science tends to view its matter as objects or things (*res* in Latin): the gaze of science is an "objectivizing" gaze. This deeply concerned Jonas. Although he sought ways to minimize this risk of reification and the attending risk that a human being might be treated merely as a means to an end, it is the most basic conflict, and one that can hardly be eliminated. Thus, investigators must be reminded in a variety of ways that their human subjects are firstly human and secondly subjects (chapter 2).

In contrast to conflicts that are inherent in the research enterprise, other conflicts are "induced" (Hansen & Hansen, 1993). They may be temporary and generally involve financial matters, including funds to support research. In a guidance document intended for IRBs, researchers, and research institutions, the Department of Health and Human Services (HHS) identifies some financial interests that could negatively affect the best interests of research participants. HHS identifies these interests through a series of questions:

Do individuals or institutions involved in the research:

- Have any proprietary interests in the product, including patents, trademarks, copyrights, or licensing agreements?
- Have an equity interest in the research sponsor and, if so, is the sponsor a publicly held company or non-publicly held company?
- Receive significant payments of other sorts? (e.g., grants, compensation in the form of equipment, retainers for ongoing consultation, or honoraria)
- Receive payment per participant or incentive payments, and are those payments reasonable? (Department of Health and Human Services, 2004, p. 6)

Financial conflicts of interest are pervasive in clinical research, including psychiatric research. For example,

- "almost 90% of authors published in the *Journal of the American Medical Association* have received research funding from, or acted as a consultant for, a drug company" (Healy & Thase, 2003, p. 388);
- 100% of the expert panelists responsible for overseeing the development of the fourth edition of the American Psychiatric Association's *Diagnostic and Statistical Manual of Mental Disorders'* (DSM-IV) sections on mood disorders and schizophrenia/psychotic disorders had some type of financial tie to the drug industry, which sold $34 billion of drugs to treat these disorders in 2004 (Cosgrove et al., 2006);
- From 2001 to 2003, 60% of the clinical trials identified in the four most widely cited general psychiatry journals were funded by a pharmaceutical company or other interested party. (Perlis et al., 2005)

How might such financial interests negatively affect either human participants or the integrity of science? First, consider that in a review of placebo-controlled psychiatric clinical trials, studies that reported financial conflicts of interest were 4.9 times more likely to report positive results (Perlis et al., 2005). Whatever legitimate reasons might exist for a portion of this difference, there are ethically suspect ways of increasing the odds of publishing a successful study. These include: refusing to publish negative findings from trials (Gilbody & Song, 2000; Healy & Cattell, 2003); failing to mention serious adverse events, including suicide (Healy & Cattell, 2003), that might lead readers to question whether a new drug is clinically superior overall; comparing an experimental medication to lower than usually prescribed doses of a competitor medication (Bero & Rennie, 1996); and testing a drug with a population that is healthier than its intended market population (Bero & Rennie, 1996; Rochon et al., 1998). Mental health consumers are at risk when studies that involve questionable scientific and publication practices are translated to therapeutic practice.

Second, "for each day's delay in gaining FDA approval of a drug, the manufacturer loses, on average, $1.3 million. Speed is paramount for pharmaceutical firms" (Bodenheimer, 2000, p. 1540). Thus, when sponsors pay investigators per participant enrolled or when investigators own significant stock in a sponsoring company, a motive exists to enroll participants as quickly as possible. This could lead to compromises in informed consent (e.g., down playing the risks of foregoing individualized treatment) or compromises in inclusion criteria (e.g., enrolling high-risk patients who would ordinarily be excluded). While it is difficult to cite rigorous evidence that this actually occurs, 73% of faculty investigators participating in a recent survey expressed fears that financial conflicts of interest could bias research design (Lipton et al., 2004); a report of HHS's Office of the Inspector General on the recruitment of human subjects explicitly expressed concerns that financial conflicts of interest may decrease the quality of informed consent and lead to compromises in inclusion criteria (Office of the Inspector General, 2000a); and financial conflicts of interest have been involved in several high profile cases that involved inadequate informed consent and eventual harms to patient-participants (Coleman et al., 2005; Elliot & Lemmens, 2005; Wilson & Heath, 2001).

Some authors have reasonably argued that financial conflicts of interest must be managed or reduced in order to preserve public trust in researchers (Goldner, 2000; Shamoo & Khin-Maung-Gyi, 2002). While the public's loss of trust in researchers would surely interfere with the progress of science and technologies, misplaced or naïve public trust would interfere with participants' ability to protect their own best interests. A recent survey indicated that "more than 90% of patients expressed little or no worry about financial ties that researchers or institutions might have with drug companies" (Hampson et al., 2006). While this study was conducted with patients in cancer trials and other populations might be less trusting, it appears that investigators, IRBs, and funding agencies may need to do some of the worrying for participants if their interests are to be protected.

ROLE CONFLICTS

Thus far we have only examined cases in which personal interests—whether inherent or induced—potentially conflict or compete with professional or public obligations. But conflicts may also exist among professional or social obligations, particularly when individuals play multiple roles. These are called *role conflicts* (Sales & Lavin, 2000). The term "conflicts of commitment," while very fitting as a description of role conflicts, is often reserved to describe competing demands on one's time or "percent effort" (Porter, 1992). Currently, federal regulations require researchers to monitor and report the percentage of their full-time effort dedicated to funded research versus other job responsibilities (e.g., teaching and administrative), and academic centers typically restrict the percent effort one may dedicate to consulting for outside entities (Association of American Medical Colleges, 1989). Nevertheless, conflicts of time commitment (frequently with attending financial conflicts of interest) represent just one kind of conflict that can arise when one plays multiple roles. The following vignettes serve to illustrate a small subset of role conflicts that can arise in the context of human research; the heading for each vignette identifies basic risks that such cases raise.

Researcher-Clinician Roles

The Risk of Therapeutic Misconception or Inappropriate Deference

Dr. Miller has proposed a placebo-controlled study with a new drug used to treat schizophrenia. She decides to offer the protocol to patients in her practice. She explains to the patients that there may be a chance of medication-free intervals during which they would be given placebos instead of antipsychotic meds. She also indicates that recent studies have shown that during short periods of medication-free intervals, rational decision-making did not seem to be affected. She does acknowledge that there could be increased risk of suicidality, but studies have had mixed results. Most of Dr. Miller's patients listened to her explanation and replied with, "Whatever you think is best."[2]

The Risk of Altered Prescribing Habits Due to a Research Protocol

Dr. Bentham is participating in a study of a new drug, Seifromax, which has been proven to effectively reduce the symptoms of clinical depression in adults with far fewer side effects than its competitors. The current study is aimed to test effectiveness and safety among people aged 10–17, because original tests were only done on those 18 and older. Physicians often prescribe the drug "off-label" to children, but the manufacturer hopes that through this study the FDA will approve its use with children; this might increase sales and the number of insurance companies that include the drug in its formulary.

The manufacturer of Seifromax pays Dr. Bentham a fee of $5,000 for every patient he enrolls in the study, which covers all costs of the study and also helps to underwrite the general operating expenses of his psychiatric practice.

Dr. Bentham has enrolled many patients in the study because parents were excited their child could receive this drug or the current "gold-standard" at no cost. However, after hearing about how promising Seifromax was from Dr. Bentham, several parents told him they would prefer to take their child out of the study so they can have Seifromax prescribed off-label. Dr. Bentham insists that the drug is still experimental, and he refuses to prescribe it to those outside of the study. Also, he does not mention the possibility of receiving Seifromax off-label on his consent form as an alternative to participation in the study.

The Risk of Leveraging a Professional Relationship

Mark, a case manager, is very well liked at the large group home for high functioning developmentally disabled persons where he works. He is currently writing his

2. This case was written by Sarah Hill based on Dunn et al. 2006.

dissertation proposal in a psychology Ph.D. program. He proposes to study the tendency toward violent/aggressive behavior in high functioning developmentally disabled individuals as a function of their spatial brain activity and abuse history. He bases his study on previous research involving persons with schizophrenia. His study includes a closed MRI and record review of physical, mental, and/or sexual abuse. He knows this is quite a lot to ask of the population he would like to study, but he believes his clients at the group home would be willing to participate. Because he knows the clients would probably not say "no" to him, he agrees to meet with their next-of-kin or surrogate decision makers to explain the study to them as well. Most of them are parents of the clients and trust and like Mark.[3]

The Risk of Prioritizing Clinical Research
Data Above Patient Best Interests

A psychiatric trial conducted at a major academic medical center involved long-term withdrawal—6 months or more—from all psychotropic medication. The standards for emergency re-medication were set unusually high. Participants needed to reach level 6 or 7 on the Brief Psychiatric Rating Scale in order to be pulled out of the blinded study. Level 6 involves being frequently delusional, prone to violence, and thinking about committing suicide; level 7 involves being constantly violent, always delusional, and actively planning suicide. During the trial, one patient, Greg Aller, committed suicide while off his medications. The Office for Protection from Research Risks (now OHRP) eventually investigated the study and ruled that its consent forms had not sufficiently informed participants of study-related risks. In an article entitled, "How to tell if the men in white coats are lying to you," Willwerth (1997) describes the conflict of roles that may have contributed to the insufficient patient care that Greg Aller received:

> Careers, money and fame are at stake, and there is a lot of pressure to do dramatic research as fast as possible. The most vulnerable person in all this, of course, is the research subject, who in medical research is often called the patient-subject. His researcher is also his doctor, exactly the conflict occurring [...in this case]. If the "patient" is becoming dangerously ill, but in his role as a "subject," his illness provides data for the ongoing research project, how does his "physician-researcher" respond? As a physician who wants to help his patient? Or as a researcher who needs to preserve the data? Clearly, Greg Aller ... had been treated as a research subject far more than a patient. (Willwerth, 1997, p. 55)

Researcher-Service Provider

The Risk That Quality Improvement Research
Might Be Prioritized Above Patient Best Interests

The staff of an HMO decided to enroll babies who had febrile convulsions into a quality improvement research project aimed at finding out if brain damage had

---

3. Written with Angela Dunn.

occurred. Staff told parents that their children would be given EEGs to test for brain damage. One parent requested that the EEG be performed but did not want her child to be a part of the study. The staff told her this would not be possible. (Based on Koocher & Keith-Spiegel, 1990)

The Risk of an Advocate Prioritizing Research Data
Over the Welfare of Vulnerable Participants

The purpose of a new study was to examine psychological stressors and disorders including depression and anxiety in 14- to 17-year-old gay and lesbian adolescents. Access to the adolescents was gained through a gay and lesbian community center. Many of the teens had not told their parents about their sexual preference and feared negative repercussions if this information was released. Because of this, a waiver of parental/guardian consent was granted. However, the researchers felt that a participant advocate was needed to make sure each teen was fully informed and gave assent based on information they could understand. The researchers and those who worked at the community center had a hard time finding someone appropriate because they both had an interest in the study's being successful. (Based on Hoagwood, Jensen, and Fisher, 1996, p. 192)

Researcher-Teacher / Student-Researcher

The Risk of Unfair Treatment When Recruiting One's
Own Students

Dr. Smith wants to conduct a pilot study she feels will be significant in securing a grant for her research on the role of race and ethnicity in personal identity development. Dr. Smith teaches two 100-student sections of Introduction to Psychology. She explains to her students the importance of this pilot research in obtaining research funding and asks them to stay after class for 30 minutes at some point during the semester to complete two surveys. She explains that extra credit will not be given to those who enroll, but some students believe that those who do enroll will be favored.

Decreasing Benefits to Student-Participants Because One's
Own Professors Insist

Sherry needs to complete research for her master's thesis in a counseling program.   •
While completing her studies, she takes a job as an academic counselor at a technical college. She works with students who are at risk of dismissal if their grades do not improve. Because she is the only one in this position, and because of the large number of students requiring help, she is only able to see each student for 45 minutes per semester. She feels this is not enough. She develops a 10-week course on study skills that she will offer to these students, allowing her to spend time with them for 10 hours per semester. She realizes this could be an interesting topic for her thesis. She writes her proposal and design, which includes pre-test/intervention/post-test, where the "pre" will be students' GPA prior to the study

course and the "post" will be their GPA at the end of the course. She decides not to use a control group because she feels this would be unfair to the students who do not get to take the course. Her thesis committee feels otherwise. They will not approve her study without a control group. (Based on Schrag, 2000)

Additional role conflicts in psychological research are discussed in Sales and Lavin (2000) and Fisher (2003). While role conflicts do not necessarily pit personal interests against the public good, as the above vignettes illustrate, they may nevertheless provide powerful motives for putting the interests of research participants second to other professional interests.

THE POSITIVE SIDE OF CONFLICTS, OR, WHY THEY POSE GENUINE DILEMMAS

If conflicts of interest can cause ethical problems in research, then why are they tolerated to the extent that they are? There are several reasons. First, researchers must be motivated to engage in research. In addition to altruistic motives and intellectual curiosity, recognition, job security, promotions, and financial reimbursement all provide significant motivation (Hansen & Hansen, 1993). Second, rewards are often considered proportionate to certain research contributions. In other sectors of society, people are often rewarded for success using very similar mechanisms. Third, sources of conflicts—for example, collaboration with industry by academic researchers—frequently enrich the research enterprise in a variety of ways. For example, some argue that it is useful for IRBs to have members who are familiar with how industry-sponsored research works (Healy & Cattell, 2003). Papers that are sponsored by industry frequently get published in a more timely manner and have greater impact on the literature than papers published by principal investigators without industry funding (Healy & Cattell, 2003). Similarly, despite the problems associated with industry research funding, researchers are often quick to point out that there is little academic-based or departmental funding available to underwrite large research studies, and the pharmaceutical industry has been a consistent source of funding (Healy & Thase, 2003). This is why the HHS guidance document on financial conflicts of interest states that

> HHS recognizes the complexity of the relationships between government, academia, industry and others, and recognizes that these relationships often legitimately include financial relationships . . . . Financial interests are not prohibited, and not all financial interests cause conflicts of interest or affect the welfare of human subjects. (Department of Health and Human Services, 2004, p. 3)

Similarly, conflicting roles sometimes cannot be eliminated without causing significant problems. For example, given the privacy of medical records, clinicians are often the only people who know when a patient is suitable for a given study; so prohibiting clinicians from enrolling or referring patients to clinical trials would be problematic. Likewise, because service providers frequently obtain data to assess or improve the quality of services, it is difficult to separate their roles as service providers from their roles as researchers, particularly when they count as researchers only when they consider their quality improvement data to merit publication (thereby contributing to generalizable knowledge) (45CFR46.102[d]).

Nevertheless, as we have seen, conflicts of interest and conflicting roles establish motives for researchers to compromise the well-being or informed consent of participants. While conflicts do not, of course, determine that researchers will act on these motives, the very existence of the motives typically requires some self-awareness and some form of disclosure or management.

MANAGING CONFLICTING INTERESTS AND ROLES

Debate Over Inherent Conflicts of Interest

Recall from chapter 2 that while some researchers advocated for education and self-regulation alone, following the Tuskegee syphilis study, the U.S. government established an ethical framework (the Belmont Report), research regulations (the "Common Rule"), and oversight processes (first, the existence of IRBs, then the existence of data and safety monitoring boards). All this was largely an acknowledgement of the conflicts of interest that might lead researchers to fail in self-regulation despite the best training. That is to say that our human research protections system as a whole is a form of managing the conflicts of interest inherent in research.

Accordingly, some have argued that *inherent* conflicts of interest need little additional management. Additionally, Hansen and Hansen (1993) write that

it is reasonable and prudent to simply assume the presence of such natural biases, and to rely upon further replication and validation to provide confidence in research findings . . . . [Further,] the time-honored practice of identifying the scientists involved in a publication [or protocol] by reference to their institution or employer and the sources of support for the research should serve to place the public on notice of potential biases . . . . such inherent conflicts generally need no specific mitigation, as they are readily apparent and their impact can be assessed by an observer. (p. 128)

Hansen and Hansen (1993) are clearly focused primarily on the issue of bias and scientific integrity, and they assume that the public is generally aware of such conflicts.

In contrast, Sollitto et al. (2003) are far more concerned about the impact inherent conflicts of interest might have on participant risks, autonomy, and self-protection. They advocate for routine disclosure of intrinsic conflicts of interest to participants.

One of our IRBs has approved the following wording: "All investigators and institutions have an "intrinsic" conflict of interest, since professional advancement for physicians and scientists (such as promotion and reputation) depends in part on successfully enrolling patients like you into studies like this one." Additionally, some physicians may choose to discuss their secondary interests with patients directly. (Sollitto et al., 2003, p. 89)

Their main interest is to enhance the quality of informed consent. However, a statement like the one above could have unintended consequences: (1) patients who like their physicians may be unduly influenced to enroll in a study if they believe their physician's career will suffer if they do not enroll; and (2) patients who are mistrustful of the medical establishment may mistakenly assume that the physician has offered the opportunity to enroll simply for self-gain and decline enrollment into a potentially beneficial study out of ill-founded mistrust.

In considering whether or not to require disclosure of nonfinancial or "inherent" conflicts of interest, IRBs need to consider whether such conflicts are readily apparent to participants and, if not, whether disclosure will in fact enhance informed consent, including voluntariness. Other recommendations to address inherent conflicts of interest involve the composition of IRBs:

> The National Bioethics Advisory Commission [(2001)] has recommended that persons who represent the perspectives of subjects, who are not researchers, and who are not affiliated with the institution should collectively make up at least one quarter of IRB membership. I believe that this would be an important step in dealing with non-financial conflicts of interest. (Levinsky, 2002, p. 760)

Induced Conflicts of Interest

While one might argue that inherent conflicts of interest require little management in addition to compliance with existing protections of human participants, there is widespread agreement that induced conflicts, especially financial conflicts of interest, require some form of management.

Complete Elimination

One of the approaches to conflicts of interest that HHS asks institutions and investigators to consider is the complete elimination of the conflict (Department of Health and Human Services, 2004). In general, this approach is advocated only for certain kinds of conflicts, those commonly viewed as posing the greatest threat. Given that for-profit industry now funds most clinical trials, few will suggest a complete cessation of industry funding for research. Nevertheless, several major associations, including the American Medical Association and the American College of Physicians, have recommended that the use of some recruitment incentives—so-called "finder's fees" and enrollment bonuses—be prohibited, and some IRBs refuse to approve research involving recruitment incentives (Nelson, 2006b; Office of the Inspector General, 2000b).

Disclosure

Sometimes disclosure is proposed as a first step in addressing a conflict of interest. For example, both PHS (42CFR50.604) and the FDA (21CFR54) require disclosure of significant financial interests to these agencies; federal funding requires investigators to disclose significant conflicts of interest to their institutions (Nelson, 2006c); and HHS guidance recommends routine disclosure of conflicts of interest to IRBs, whether directly or through a separate institutional conflict of interest committee (Department of Health and Human Services, 2004). Moreover, in a recent survey of bioethicists, research administrators, investigators, editors, and agency administrators, the vast majority of participants strongly support disclosure of conflicts of interest to IRBs and funding agencies (Brody et al., 2003). In these cases, the disclosure is meant to enable an oversight body to decide whether to ignore the conflict, to require that the conflict be eliminated, or to require management of the conflict.

In other cases, disclosure is considered to be the solution or at least a significant part of the management plan. Ordinarily, this includes disclosure to participants (thereby enabling them to decide whether to ask further questions or to decline participation) and/or disclosure to readers of a publication (thereby enabling them to consider whether the results are in any way biased). Recent surveys indicate that the vast majority of bioethicists, research administrators, and investigators (Brody et al., 2003) as well as the vast majority of potential participants in clinical trials (Kim et al., 2004) support routine disclosure of conflicts of interests during the informed consent process. Additionally, some professional associations have supported disclosure of financial conflicts of interest during the consent process (Nelson, 2006a). Such disclosures are meant to inform participants of a potential factor that might influence risks (Sollitto et al., 2003) as well as to empower them to ask further questions.

Nevertheless, social science data suggests that disclosure is often not sufficient and may actually make matters worse if it leads investigators and potential participants to perceive the investigator as highly ethical through their disclosure of information or if investigators feel penalized by requirements to disclose (Miller, 2005). Further, some evidence exists that advisors may provide more biased advice after disclosure than they otherwise would have (Cain et al., 2005).

Role Reduction

When a complete elimination of a conflict of interest is deemed unfeasible or undesirable and disclosure alone is not considered sufficient, then investigators may be asked to delegate certain roles to others. For example, if an investigator receives any sort of financial incentive on a per participant enrolled basis, then an IRB might reasonably require that a neutral third party obtain informed consent from prospective participants. Such consent facilitators ordinarily should not be subordinates of the principal investigator (Nelson, 2006c).

Additional Oversight

HHS asks institutions and investigators to consider whether additional oversight or monitoring of research is appropriate in the face of some conflicts of interest (Department of Health and Human Services, 2004). This could include additional monitoring and reporting of adverse events by a third party (Nelson, 2006c).

Managing Role Conflicts

Chapter 3 of the OHRP "IRB guidebook" states that IRBs should examine role conflicts:

IRBs should determine whether the investigators ... serve dual roles (*e.g.*, treating physician, teacher, or employer in addition to researcher) that might complicate their interactions with subjects. For example, an investigator's eagerness for a subject to continue in a research project (to obtain as much data as possible) may conflict with the responsibility, as a treating physician, to discontinue a therapy that is not helpful or that results in significant adverse effects without countervailing benefit. Likewise, teachers or supervisors who conduct research could (wittingly or unwittingly) coerce student- or employee-subjects into participating. Thus any potential conflicts of interest must be identified and resolved before IRB approval is granted. (Office of Human Research Protections, 1993)

As discussed, some role conflicts may be considered analogous to inherent conflicts of interest, insofar as they are virtually impossible to eliminate completely. Nevertheless, it is often possible to achieve some level of role separation. Even if a treatment provider is in the best position to identify potential participants for a study, others can play the role of a consent facilitator (Iltis, 2005). Similarly, in research conducted by faculty in psychology departments, recruitment can occur via Web sites that list and describe research volunteering opportunities, and alternatives to research participation may be provided to reduce risks of coercion (Tickle & Heatherton, 2002).

CONFLICTS WITH NONPARTICIPANTS' INTERESTS AND VALUES

Above, we saw that industry sponsors of research are criticized when they require investigators to change scientific designs to maximize the likelihood of outcomes that they might find acceptable, when they require veto power over publications, or censure the reporting of findings. Yet investigators often allow sponsors compromises to scientific freedom because sponsors control access to essential research funding.

While such compromises are often frowned upon when the "funding gatekeepers" are motivated to avoid financial losses, similar compromises also occur when research interests conflict with other nonparticipant groups that may be affected by research.

Employer-Gatekeepers

The Risk of Modifying Study Design and the Reporting of Results Due to Employer Demands

Researchers decided to study nurses during a strike at a large public teaching hospital. They wanted to describe and contrast the motives of striking and nonstriking nurses. Their survey examined ethical, political, economic, and social motives. They quickly discovered that they would need the cooperation of the hospital administrators to obtain a list of nurses and to distribute the surveys. On the one hand, this cooperation led to improvements in the study. Administrators suggested that the study be anonymous, rather than confidential, given the level of paranoia among employees; and they pointed out that some nurses were represented by a different union, leading to a revision in the inclusion criteria. On the other hand, administrators insisted on removal of items they found inflammatory or offensive (e.g., an item on threats of reprisal); they would not mail surveys to homes or employees who left the institution after the strike; and they insisted on reviewing any manuscripts prior to publication (but without reserving veto power). (Kravitz, 1990)

This study led the researchers to ask whether they were bound to inform the employers about their research plans; whether interested parties should have been given the power to veto or revise manuscripts; whether methodology should have been compromised to obtain cooperation; and whether such compromises needed to be disclosed in any publication of results. While some might consider such compromises to be illegitimate, it is important to bear in mind that the stakeholders who could influence access to participants—the hospital and the union—did not consider themselves likely to gain directly from the research, and they considered themselves potentially vulnerable to harm. In such cases, both to ensure an ethical balance of benefits and burdens to participants and the groups to which they belong and to ensure feasibility, researchers may need to compromise their methodologies and reporting of results. This may be legitimate as long as the results remain valid and accurately reported.

Similar issues arise as researchers attempt to work with communities that are socially vulnerable, that have been overstudied, or that perceive researchers to contribute to their stigmatization.

Communities as Stakeholders

The Risk That Communities Might Insist on Study Modifications to Protect Their Interests

Dr. Sam decides to conduct a community-based participatory action research project on employment, health, and patterns of alcohol use with a tribe of Native Americans near her university. In her study, nearly a dozen individuals she will study will also be on the project's steering committee, helping to define goals for the study, the methodology, and the analysis of data. Because many Native Americans are mistrustful of researchers, feel overstudied, and believe that some published studies represent them in a bad light, Dr. Sam believes a robust participatory design is necessary and ethically appropriate, but she fears that problems may arise in honestly and completely describing the results of the study.[4]

Increasingly, it is considered both necessary and ethically appropriate to work with community representatives to develop and revise study questions, to recruit participants, to interpret results, and to review manuscripts prior to publication (Centers for Disease Control and Prevention et al., 1998; Norton & Manson, 1996). As noted in chapter 6, within participatory models of research, participants may be viewed as co-investigators with expertise of their own and a right to shape methodologies. As the cases presented above indicate, methodologies may be strengthened in some regards through such collaborative processes. Nevertheless,

---

4. This case was written with Sarah Hill.

it is important to note that many of the powers that communities may insist upon (e.g., the right to modify a study's design or to approve published data) are precisely those powers that industry often insists upon, due to a similar dynamic of scientific interests competing with the interests of stakeholders.

Peer Reviewers

The Risk of Compromising Methodology to Satisfy a Peer Reviewer

Jack submitted a grant proposal that involves assessing mental health status in an HIV prevention study involving people with substance abuse disorders. He is dissatisfied with existing assessment instruments and plans to use an instrument that he developed in a pilot study, which was specifically designed for administration by a nonclinician and for use with individuals with a history of addictions and substance abuse. He submitted his proposal for funding from the National Institutes of Health. When he receives his scientific review, he finds his score was insufficient to be funded primarily because one peer-reviewer was concerned that he is not using a standard assessment. He resubmits providing a clearer rationale for developing a new instrument and provides additional pilot data on the instrument's validity and reliability. However, the peer-reviewer again scores him poorly for the same reason. Jack can only resubmit one more time and must now decide whether to use what he believes is an inferior assessment instrument in order to obtain a fundable scientific review score.

In dealing with peer-reviewers, investigators naturally have their own biases and may be reluctant to receive legitimate criticism that could lead to improvements in a study's design. Particularly when research funding uses public money, it is appropriate for research designs to be peer-reviewed. Nevertheless, there may be times when researchers have evidence that their peer-reviewer is mistaken or is advocating for a weaker design. Researchers may respond to reviewers, request new reviewers, or choose new funding agencies. In deciding what compromises to make—as in all of the cases presented above—researchers need to consider whether changes will affect the overall trustworthiness of the data.

CONFLICTED OVERSIGHT

Federal regulations state that "no IRB may have a member participate in the IRB's initial or continuing review of any project in which the member has a conflict of interest, except to provide information requested by the IRB" (45CFR46.107[e]).

"Will Everyone Please Leave the Room So We Can Vote?"

The following builds upon Nelson's (2006a) identification of seven sources of conflicting interests that institutional or academic IRB members may have.

Individual Sources

1. Research by Members. Sometimes IRB members conduct research themselves. It is easy and standard to require that such members recuse themselves from the review of their protocols.

2. Members' Financial Interests. In a random survey of 893 IRB members at 100 institutions, Campbell et al. (2006) found that 36% of IRB members "had at least one relationship with industry in the past year" (p. 2321). Only 57% reported that they always disclose these relationships to an IRB official; and only 64% always abstained from voting on protocols involving personal conflicts of interest. As noted above, federal regulations prohibit IRB members from participating in the review of a protocol when they have a conflict of interest; presumably, such induced conflicts of interest are the focal cases of conflicting interests the regulations have in mind.

3. Loyalty to Colleagues. Most IRB members work at the institution whose research is reviewed, and thus they review work of their colleagues. Some IRBs prohibit members from reviewing protocols of department members. However, frequently the need for expertise requires that members of departments review each other's work. Moreover, as interdisciplinarity increases, the significance of departmental borders decreases.

4. The Impact of One's Field or Expertise. Expertise in a field may lead a reviewer to be unusually severe to competitor protocols; or it may lead one to be overly accustomed to risky or controversial designs (e.g., in social psychology, the use of deception was routine for decades [Korn, 1997]). Additionally, IRB members may become privy to proprietary information or novel information relevant to their own work.

5. Impact of Precedent Setting Decisions. To the extent that decisions may set precedence or establish policy that could adverse affect one's own work or that of colleagues, one is conflicted in evaluating them.

6. Personal Agendas. While many of the sources of conflicts of interest only pertain to institutional members (especially scientific institutional members), even non-scientist, non-affiliated members may have personal agendas. For example, members of an advocacy group may be overly keen to see research conducted in a given area, or may be overly protective of members of certain groups.

7. Non-IRB roles. Certain administrative roles or the role of legal counsel for an institution may create conflicts insofar as institutional well-being may lead to overly loose or overly defensive reviews of protocols.

Institutional Sources

Institutions may be conflicted in the review of research. Such conflicts may derive from an institution's interest in protecting itself from liability or harm to reputation; seeking to enhance its reputation; promoting research and increasing external funding; and institutional financial holdings or interests (Bekelman et al., 2003; Nelson, 2006a). Additionally, institutions affect the quality of review by how they value service on IRBs (e.g., do they count IRB service as equivalent to teaching or other administrative service?); the educational resources provided to IRB members; and the extent to which they unduly pressure IRBs for speed in reviews.

The above lists make it clear that every or nearly every member of an IRB has some kind of conflict of interest in reviewing protocols. This makes it profoundly difficult to interpret the Common Rule's requirement that no conflicted member participate in the review of a protocol.

One way around several of the inherent conflicts of interest that IRBs have would involve the use of a central IRB—a neutral IRB that would provide sole review—of all multisite research proposals. If liability protection were given to local institutions, then this approach would save time and IRB resources and provide review by a nonconflicted body (Emanuel et al., 2004). In the meantime, apart from recusal of conflicted members, IRBs can minimize the effects of conflicts of interest by expanding the number of institutionally nonaffiliated members on the IRB (Levinsky, 2002; Nelson, 2006a) and by educating and reminding IRB members about conflict of interest policies (Department of Health and Human Services, 2004).

Independent IRBs

It was noted above that pharmaceutical companies may lose more than $1 million per day while drugs are in development. At the same time, academic IRBs are often slow, overworked, understaffed, and heavily dependent on the voluntary participation of unpaid members who may lack expertise in human subjects protection (Office of the Inspector General, 1998b). In a report that documented some concerns with independent IRBs, HHS's Office of the Inspector General observed several advantages independent IRBs typically had over many institutional IRBs:

- They Are Geared to Quick Decisions on Research Plans. Independent IRBs are organized to respond to commercial sponsors' expectations for timely reviews. On average, those we interviewed reported that they could provide initial research protocol decisions in about 11 days. For the academic health centers we reviewed, the average was about 37 days
- They Provide a Detached Source of Expertise. Independent IRBs are not affiliated with the institutions whose research they review and are unlikely to have collegial relationships with the investigators. This detachment facilitates research plan review without institutional or collegial biases
- They Can Provide Unified Reviews for Multi-Site Trials. For such trials, an independent IRB can serve as a single entity reviewing the applicability of a specific research plan to various sites. This eliminates the complications that result from multiple, local IRB reviews. It also facilitates analysis of adverse-event reports from various sites. (Office of the Inspector General, 1998a, p. ii)

These advantages have led to tremendous growth in the number of researchers, companies, and agencies relying on independent IRBs. One independent IRB now reviews more than 50% of all new drug submissions to the FDA (Emanuel, Elliott, & Lemmens, 2006). Given their growing popularity, it is worth considering the three primary concerns that the Office of the Inspector General identified with independent IRBs:

- They Are Not Local Review Bodies. Local review is a long-established principle of human subject protection. Familiarity with the conditions of the institution, the investigators, and the local community have been viewed as vital to effective human-subject protection. Concerns about independent IRBs' ability to provide local review have inhibited their participation in federally sponsored research. The independent IRBs have sought to ease such concerns by keeping abreast of the research site's circumstances through site visits, local contacts, newspaper clipping services, and other means
- They May Be Subject to Conflicts of Interest. Some IRB officials are concerned that independent IRBs, almost all of which are for-profit enterprises, may compromise the review process to please their sponsors/ customers and to advance their financial well-being. Yet, these officials also express concern that in an increasingly competitive environment, all IRBs are subject to conflicting pressures that could compromise their core mission
- They Heighten Concerns about IRB Shopping. Sponsors who are unhappy with the reviews of one independent IRB may seek out another that they expect to be more accommodating. The independent IRBs themselves may not know if a sponsor's research plan has been turned down, or found lacking, by another IRB. (Office of the Inspector General, 1998a, pp. ii–iii)

At the same time, a significant percentage of academic IRBs are now charging industry sponsors a protocol review fee ranging from a few hundred to a few thousand dollars per protocol (Nelson, 2006a); where this is the case, academic IRBs may experience some of the same conflicts that for-profit or independent IRBs face, in addition to those observed above.

Whether these conflicts actually interfere with the proper review of research protocols has been the subject of some debate. Shamoo and Khin-Maung-Gyi (2002) offer an *a priori* argument based on the self-interests of independent IRBs and their contractors:

> This role of private IRBs is similar to the public accounting firms that insure financial institutions comply with federal requirements. It is not in the interest of either party to by-pass the federal regulations . . . . The sponsor's and investigator's entire clinical program can be at risk. (Shamoo & Khin-Maung-Gyi, 2002, p. 68)

Emanuel has argued that "the crucial question is whether an IRB, regardless of its tax status, is performing at a high level of quality" (Emanuel, Elliott, & Lemmens, 2006, p. 0941). He goes on to observe that many independent IRBs have attained full accreditation from the Association for the Accreditation of Human Research Protection Programs (AAHRP) and that the FDA has issued "only one warning letter to a for-profit IRB compared to hundreds to IRBs at not-for-profit institutions" (Emanuel, Elliott, & Lemmens, 2006, p. 0942).

IRBs, whether institutional or independent, face conflicts of interest—often greater conflicts than do researchers themselves. Many of these are inherent to the context of a specific IRB (i.e., inherent to its academic or for-profit corporate setting). Thus, solutions are not easy to come by. Nevertheless, the effects of these conflicts may be minimized to the extent that IRB best practices are identified and widely embraced. The absence of widely recognized best practices actually creates space in which conflicts of interest may operate, that is, they leave ample room for biased deliberation.

CONCLUSION: COMPLETING THE CIRCLE

This book, like most applied ethics books, makes two assumptions about its readers. First, it assumes they want to know what is the right thing to do. For example, it assumes that they want to know how best to protect confidentiality and when it might be right to breach confidentiality. Second, it assumes that they generally intend to do what is right, and thus the effort to examine what is right is not wholly academic or futile.

This chapter, which explores conflicts of interest, conflicting roles, and conflicts with stakeholders' priorities, in fact makes precisely the opposite assumption. Namely, it assumes that sometimes we fool ourselves about what is right and sometimes we have powerful motives for doing what is wrong. Often we are unaware of the effect of situational factors on our judgments and behaviors. This chapter thus brings us full circle. In conclusion, we find that it is necessary to consider the roles of regulations, institutional policies, and oversight in promoting good behavior (chapter 1), as well as the roles of virtue and procedural ethics (chapter 2) in promoting morally good actions. If it is naïve to think that one can regulate morally good action (and it is), it is equally naïve to think that we will always do what is right if only we know it. As unhappy as the marriage is at times, the field of research ethics will likely remain wedded to the field of compliance until researchers develop vaccines against temptation, undue self-interest, and self-deception.

Further EMHR Resources

- Unit eight of the *Dialogues* DVD contains an interview with Gerald Koocher and a focus group with mental health consumers on conflicts of interest in research
- www.emhr.net contains a bibliography and further case studies on conflicts of interest

REFERENCES

Association of American Medical Colleges. (1989). *Report of the ad hoc committee on misconduct and conflict of interest in research.* Washington, DC: Association of American Medical Colleges.

Baumrind, D. (1964). Some thoughts on ethics of research: After reading Milgram's "behavioral study of obedience." *American Psychologist, 19*, 421–423.

Bekelman, J. E., Li, Y., & Gross, C. P. (2003). Scope and impact of financial conflicts of interest in biomedical research. *Journal of the American Medical Association, 289*(4), 454–465.

Bero, L. A., & Rennie, D. (1996). Influences on the quality of published drug studies. *International Journal of Technology Assessment in Health Care, 12*(2), 209–237.

Bodenheimer, T. (2000). Uneasy alliance: Clinical investigators and the pharmaceutical industry. *New England Journal of Medicine, 342*(20), 1539–1544.

Brody, B., Anderson, C., Van McCrary, S., McCullough, L., Morgan, R., & Wray, N. (2003). Expanding disclosure of conflicts of interest: The view of stakeholders. *IRB: A Review of Human Subjects Research, 25*(1), 1–8.

Cain, D. M., Loewenstein, G., & Moore, D. A. (2005). Coming clean but playing dirtier. In D. A. Moore, D. M. Cain, G. Loewenstein, & M. Bazerman (Eds.), *Conflicts of interest: Challenges and solutions in business, law, medicine, and public policy* (pp. 104–125). New York: Cambridge University Press.

Campbell, E. G., Weissman, J. S., Vogeli, C., Clarridge, B. R., Abraham, M., Marder, J. E., et al. (2006). Financial relationships between institutional review board members and industry. *New England Journal of Medicine, 355*(22), 2321–2329.

Centers for Disease Control and Prevention, Department of Health and Human Services, National Institutes of Health, Food and Drug Administration, Human Resources and Services Administration, Substance Abuse and Mental Health Services Administration, et al. (1998). *Building community partnerships in research: Recommendations and strategies.* Washington, DC: Department of Health and Human Services.

Coleman, C. H., Menikoff, J. A., Goldner, J. A., & Dubler, N. N. (2005). *The ethics and regulation of research with human subjects.* Newark, NJ: LexisNexis.

Cosgrove, L., Krimsky, S., Vijayaraghavan, M., & Schneider, L. (2006). Financial ties between DSM-IV panel members and the pharmaceutical industry. *Psychotherapy and Psychosomatics, 75*(3), 154–160.

Dana, J., & Loewenstein, G. (2003). A social science perspective on gifts to physicians from industry. *Journal of the American Medical Association, 290*(2), 252 255.

Department of Health and Human Services. (2004). *Financial relationships and interests in research involving human subjects: Guidance for human subject protection.* Washington, DC: Department of Health and Human Services.

Dunn, L. B., Candilis, P. J., & Roberts, L. W. (2006). Emerging empirical evidence on the ethics of schizophrenia research. *Schizophrenia Bulletin, 32*(1), 47–68.

Elliot, C., & Lemmens, T. (2005). Ethics for sale: For-profit ethical review, coming to a clinical trial near you. *Slate,* posted December 13. Unpaginated. Accessed May 6, 2007, at http://www.slate.com/id/2132187/

Emanuel, E., Elliott, C., & Lemmens, T. (2006). Should society allow research ethics boards to be run as for-profit enterprises? *PLoS Medicine, 3*(7), e309.

Emanuel, E., Wood, A., Fleischman, A., Bowen, A., Getz, K. A., Grady, C., et al. (2004). Oversight of human participant research: Identifying problems to evaluate reform proposals. *Annals of Internal Medicine, 141*(4), 282–291.

Fisher, C. B. (2003). *Decoding the ethics code: A practical guide for psychologists.* Thousand Oaks, CA: Sage Publications, Inc.

Friedman, P. J. (1992). The troublesome semantics of conflict of interest. *Ethics and Behavior, 2*(4), 245–251.

Garner, B. (Ed.). (1999). *Black's law dictionary* (7th ed.). St. Paul, MN: West Group.

Gilbody, S. M., & Song, F. (2000). Publication bias and the integrity of psychiatry research. *Psychological Medicine, 30,* 253–258.

Goldner, J. A. (2000). Dealing with conflicts of interest in biomedical research: IRB oversight as the next best solution to the abolitionist approach. *Journal of Law, Medicine & Ethics, 28*(4), 379–404.

Hampson, L. A., Agrawal, M., Joffe, S., Gross, C. P., Verter, J., & Emanuel, E. (2006). Patients' views on financial conflicts of interest in cancer research trials. *New England Journal of Medicine, 355*(22), 2330–2337.

Hansen, B. C., & Hansen, K. D. (1993). Managing conflict of interest in faculty, federal government, and industrial relations. In D. Cheney (Ed.), *Ethical issues in research* (pp. 127–137). Frederick, MD: University Publishing Group.

Healy, D., & Cattell, D. (2003). Interface between authorship, industry and science in the domain of therapeutics. *British Journal of Psychiatry, 183*, 22–27.

Healy, D., & Thase, M. E. (2003). Is academic psychiatry for sale? *British Journal of Psychiatry, 182*, 388–390.

Hoagwood, K., Jensen, P. S., & Fisher, C. B. (1996). *Ethical issues in mental health research with children and adolescents.* Mahwah, N.J.: Lawrence Erlbaum Associates.

Iltis, A. S. (2005). Timing invitations to participate in clinical research: Preliminary versus informed consent. *Journal of Medicine and Philosophy, 30*(1), 89–106.

Johnson, S. H. (2004). Five easy pieces: Motifs of health law. *Health Matrix: Journal of Law-Medicine, 14*(1), 131–140.

Kim, S., Millard, R., Nisbet, P., Cox, C., & Caine, E. (2004). Potential research participants' views regarding researcher and institutional financial conflicts of interest. *Journal of Medical Ethics, 30*, 73–79.

Koocher, G. P., & Keith-Spiegel, P. C. (1990). *Children, ethics, and the law: Professional issues and cases.* Lincoln: University of Nebraska Press.

Korn, J. H. (1997). *Illusions of reality: A history of deception in social psychology.* Albany: State University of New York Press.

Kravitz, R. (1990). Serving several masters: Conflicting responsibilities in health services research. *Journal of General Internal Medicine, 5*(2), 170–174.

Levinsky, N. G. (2002). Nonfinancial conflicts of interest in research. *New England Journal of Medicine, 347*(10), 759–761.

Lipton, S., Boyd, E., & Bero, L. A. (2004). Conflicts of interest in academic research: Policies, processes, and attitudes. *Accountability in Research, 11*(2), 83–102.

Milgram, S. (1964). Issues in the study of obedience: A reply to Baumrind. *American Psychologist, 19*, 848–852.

Milgram, S. (1974). *Obedience to authority: An experimental view.* New York: Harper & Row.

Miller, D. (2005). Commentary: Psychologically naïve assumptions about the perils of conflicts of interest. In D. A. Moore, D. M. Cain, G. Loewenstein, & M. Bazerman (Eds.), *Conflicts of interest: Challenges and solutions in business, law, medicine, and public policy, psychological ethics* (pp. 126–129). New York: Cambridge University Press.

National Bioethics Advisory Commission. (2001). *Ethical and policy issues in research involving human participants.* Bethesda, MD: National Bioethics Advisory Commission.

Nelson, D. K. (2006a). Conflict of interest: Institutional review boards. In E. Bankert & R. Amdur (Eds.), *Institutional review board management and function* (2nd ed., pp. 177–181). Sudsbury, MA: Jones and Bartlett.

Nelson, D. K. (2006b). Conflict of interest: Recruitment incentives. In E. Bankert & R. Amdur (Eds.), *Institutional review board management and function* (2nd ed., pp. 173–176). Sudsbury, MA: Jones and Bartlett.

Nelson, D. K. (2006c). Conflict of interest: Researchers. In E. Bankert & R. Amdur (Eds.), *Institutional review board management and function* (2nd ed., pp. 166–172). Sudbury, MA: Jones and Bartlett.

Norton, I. M., & Manson, S. M. (1996). Research in American Indian and Alaska Native communities: Navigating the cultural universe of values and process. *Journal of Consulting and Clinical Psychology, 64*(5), 856–860.

Office of Human Research Protections. (1993). Protecting human research subjects: Institutional review board guidebook. Retrieved January 12, 2007, from http://www.hhs.gov/ohrp/irb/irb_guidebook.htm.

Office of the Inspector General. (1998a). *Institutional review boards: The emergence of independent boards* (No. OIE-01-97-00192). Washington, DC: Department of Health and Human Services.

Office of the Inspector General. (1998b). *Institutional review boards: Their role in reviewing approved research* (No. OIE-01-97-0090). Washington, DC: Department of Health and Human Services.

Office of the Inspector General. (2000a). *Recruiting human subjects: Pressures in industry-sponsored clinical research* (No. OEI-01-97-00195). Washington, DC: Department of Health and Human Services.

Office of the Inspector General. (2000b). *Recruiting human subjects: Sample guidelines for practice* (No. OEI-01-97-00196). Washington, DC: Department of Health and Human Services.

Perlis, R., Perlis, C., Wu, Y., Hwang, C., Joseph, M., & Nierenberg, A. (2005). Industry sponsorship and financial conflict of interest in the reporting of clinical trials in psychiatry. *American Journal of Psychiatry, 162*(10), 1957–1960.

Porter, R. J. (1992). Conflicts of interest in research: The fundamentals. In R. J. Porter & T. E. Malone (Eds.), *Biomedical research: Collaboration and conflict of interest* (pp. 121–134). Baltimore: Johns Hopkins University Press.

Rochon, P., Berger, P., & Gordon, M. (1998). The evolution of clinical trials: Inclusion and representation. *Canadian Medical Association Journal, 159,* 1373–1374.

Sales, B. D., & Lavin, M. (2000). Identifying conflicts of interest and resolving ethical dilemmas. In B. D. Sales & S. Folkman (Eds.), *Ethics in research with human participants* (pp. 109–128). Washington, DC: American Psychological Association.

Schrag, B. (Ed.). (2000). *Research ethics: Cases and commentaries* (Rev. ed., Vol. 4). Bloomington, IN: National Science Foundation.

Shamoo, A. E., & Khin-Maung-Gyi, F. A. (2002). *Ethics of the use of human subjects in research.* New York: Garland Science.

Sollitto, S., Hoffman, S., Mehlman, M., Lederman, R., Youngner, S. J., & Lederman, M. (2003). Intrinsic conflicts of interest in clinical research: A need for disclosure. *Kennedy Institute of Ethics Journal, 13*(2), 83–91.

Tickle, J. J., & Heatherton, T. F. (2002). Research involving college students. In R. J. Amdur & E. A. Bankert (Eds.), *Institutional review board: Management and function* (pp. 399–400). Boston: Jones and Bartlett.

Willwerth, J. (1997). How to tell if the men in white coats are lying to you [investigative journalism and research abuse]. *Accountability in Research, 5,* 51–58.

Wilson, D., & Heath, D. (2001, March 12). The whistleblower: He saw the tests as a violation of "trusting, desperate" patients. *Seattle Times,* A1.

Index